Praise for *The Software Architect Elevator*

"This book is a treasure chest full of tips and techniques for becoming an effective software architect. If you are serious about your career, then read this book."

—*Mark Richards, Author of* Fundamentals of Software Architecture

"This outstanding book is a must-read for software architects. In a witty style, Gregor Hohpe covers a lot of ground in this field; from Software Engineering to Organization science, all packed in an entertaining journey every software architect will benefit from understanding clearly and deeply."

—*Schahram Dustdar, Professor of Computer Science, Head of Research Division of Distributed Systems, TU Wien, Austria*

"*The Software Architect Elevator* has probably been the best book on IT Architecture (as a function) I have read. It describes how I see the architect role; as a leader, an advisor, an enabler, and an agent of change. It repeatedly provides brilliant analogies as introductions to the subjects; it has many references and does describe many of the struggles architects face while performing their roles. Any person outside of the architecture practice, especially the ones dealing with architects, will benefit from reading this book as well."

—*Nuno Abrantes, Head of Enterprise Architecture, Unicre*

T0261722

The Software Architect Elevator

Redefining the Architect's Role
in the Digital Enterprise

Gregor Hohpe

Beijing · Boston · Farnham · Sebastopol · Tokyo

The Software Architect Elevator

by Gregor Hohpe

Published by O'Reilly Media, Inc., 1005 Gravenstein Highway North, Sebastopol, CA 95472.

O'Reilly books may be purchased for educational, business, or sales promotional use. Online editions are also available for most titles (*http://oreilly.com*). For more information, contact our corporate/institutional sales department: 800-998-9938 or *corporate@oreilly.com*.

Acquisitions Editors: Ryan Shaw, Melissa Duffield	**Proofreaders:** Kim Wimpsett, Justin Billing
	Indexer: Judith McConville
Development Editor: Melissa Potter	**Cover Design:** Randy Comer
Production Editor: Deborah Baker	**Interior Designer:** Monica Kamsvaag
Copyeditor: Octal Publishing, LLC	**Illustrators:** Rebecca Demarest, Jose Marzan Jr.

April 2020:   First Edition

Revision History for the First Edition

2020-04-07:   First Release
2020-11-20:   Second Release

See *http://oreilly.com/catalog/errata.csp?isbn=9781492077541* for release details.

978-1-492-07754-1

[LSI]

Contents

Foreword by
Simon Brown

My aspiration to become a software architect stemmed from my interest in the technical side of software design. I really enjoy discussions about how we can best use technology to solve a problem, and how to create codebases that are highly modular, well-structured, and easy to work with.

What nobody tells you though, is that these technical aspects are just one part of the architecture puzzle. It's not just about technology and designing software. It's about designing software and solving problems within a specific organizational context, and being aware of what's happening around you, so that you can successfully navigate and influence that context where necessary. It's crucial, therefore, that architects realize they need to communicate and influence at different levels, with different audiences, both inside and outside of their immediate team environment.

As an industry, however, we do a relatively poor job teaching software developers how to move into software architecture roles, let alone providing help for those who are currently in such a role. This is especially true for the nontechnical aspects. A quick browse of your favorite bookstore will reveal a plethora of books about software architecture, architectural styles, architectural patterns, DevOps, automation, enterprise architecture, Lean, Agile, and so on. You'll find far fewer books related to people and communication. And it's even rarer to find a single book that covers all of these topics.

The Software Architect Elevator fills this gap by discussing an architect's role from a broader set of perspectives than usual. It will teach you how to avoid the traditional, somewhat dysfunctional "business versus IT" mindset, how to see the bigger picture to map and influence the organizational landscape, how to make effective decisions, how to deal with vendors, and how to communicate across all levels of an organization. All of this is essential for those who want to be successful in their role as an architect.

References to additional reading complement the practical tips and techniques presented in the book. Many of the relatable stories will, unfortunately, sound far too familiar! Although Gregor's stories will relate more to people working in larger organizations with a traditional IT function, many of them are equally applicable to the newer wave of "digital companies." I've been surprised to see some of these situations play out in such organizations, too!

In summary, this is a fabulous book for current and aspiring architects, going beyond what you will find in other books on the subject. It's a great way to fast-track the collection of tools in your architecture toolbox. I thoroughly recommend this book to aspiring software architects and CTOs alike. Whether you're looking to broaden your skills and get a feel for what architecture is all about, or you've been tasked with improving organizational productivity and performance, there's something here for everybody.

—Simon Brown, Author of
Software Architecture
for Developers

Foreword by David Knott

I remember the first time I was asked to form an architecture team within an IT function. I didn't know what it meant, but thought it sounded cool, and was confident that I could figure it out. That confidence lasted about five minutes, until a team member asked whether we were going to be technology architects or enterprise architects, and I realized that I didn't know the difference!

Twenty years later, I am privileged to be chief architect of a global organization, and although I still haven't found a perfect job description for architects, I have learned that being comfortable with ambiguity is one of the most important attributes of a good architect—asking awkward questions, as my team member illustrated, being another!

This book will help you understand what being an architect is like by painting a vivid picture of an architect's life and mission in the current phase of the information technology revolution. Riding the architecture elevator is how my team and I spend our time: racing from one part of our organization to another, connecting, explaining, questioning, and trying to make good decisions about complex systems with imperfect information. The elevator takes us from code to business strategy and back again, all within the same day.

Architecture has been intermittently in and out of fashion within enterprise technology, and architects are sometimes accused of "not making anything." I believe that architects make two things that are of vital importance and in short supply: they make sense and they make decisions. Whenever architects help their organizations understand a world that is increasingly difficult to grasp, figure out what decisions need to be taken, and help take those decisions in a rational way at the right time, then they have had a good day at the office. And, as this book explains, if you're not taking meaningful decisions (see Chapter 6), making them explicit, and helping people understand them, you're not doing architecture.

However, these are difficult skills to master. Humans have been shown to be notoriously bad at understanding complexity and at making good decisions with limited information. Architects can help themselves and their companies by adopting techniques and ways of thinking which have been won through years of experience. They can create understanding by making sure that they turn learning curves into ramps rather than cliffs and can make better decisions by adopting the language of the market (see Chapter 18), as well as by selling options to the business (see Chapter 9).

One of the reasons that architecture has been in and out of fashion is that what organizations need from architects has changed. At many points in my career, the organizations I worked for believed that they wanted me to define their current state and future state, and to figure out the path between them. This was an understandable belief: it seems reasonable to want to know where we are, where we want to go, and how we are going to get there. But it was also based on a static view of the world, in which all change was deviation from a steady state.

In today's world, the technology running any organization must be dynamic, and the organization must be able to change that technology to adapt to economies of speed (see Chapter 35). The job of architects now is to create the conditions for speed and dynamism within their organizations: to satisfy the design goals of change velocity and service quality at the same time (and to help people understand that these goals are not in conflict; see Chapter 40). If you still believe that the job is to define future state architectures delivered through a multiyear plan, you would do well to read Part V of this book.

The image of the architecture elevator is apt because it is one of continuous motion running through the center of an organization. Elevators are also a transformational technology: they are one of the inventions which made skyscrapers possible, and changed our skylines forever. If you want to be an architect then you are signing up for a life of movement and transformation. If you are curious and have a need to explain, a desire to connect, and the drive to make decisions, then it might be the job for you. You still won't get a job description that describes everything you need to do, but this book will help you figure it out.

—*Dr. David Knott,*
Chief Architect, HSBC

About This Book

As the digital economy changes the rules of the game for traditional enterprises, the role of architects also fundamentally changes. Rather than focus on technical implementations alone, they must connect the organization's penthouse, where the business strategy is set, with the technical engine room, where the enabling technologies are implemented. Only if both parts are connected can IT change its role from a cost center to a competitive digital advantage. Making this connection by walking from one organizational floor to the next won't work. Instead, modern architects bypass existing structures by taking the fast track: the *Architect Elevator*.

This book helps (aspiring) architects embrace a new view of what it means to be an architect and equips them to ride the architect elevator across many levels, aligning organization and technology and effecting lasting change.

A Chief Architect's Life: It's Not That Lonely at the Top

A lot is expected from IT leaders and chief architects: they must maneuver in an organization in which IT is often still seen as a cost center, operations means "run" as opposed to "change," and middle management has become cozy neither understanding the business strategy nor the underlying technology. All the while they are expected to stay up to date with the latest technology, manage vendors, translate buzzwords into a solid strategy, and recruit top talent. It's no surprise, then, that senior software and IT architects have become some of the most sought-after IT professionals around the globe.

With such high expectations, though, what does it take to become a successful chief architect? And after you get there, how do you keep up? When I became a chief IT architect, I wasn't expecting any magic answers, but I was looking for a book that would at least spare me from having to reinvent the wheel all the time.

I attended many CIO/CTO events, which proved useful but focused mainly on high-level direction instead of on how to actually accomplish the mission on a technical level. Having been unable to find such a book, I decided to collect my experience of over two decades as software engineer, consultant, startup cofounder, and chief architect into a book of my own.

What Will I Learn?

This book is organized into major sections that correspond to an architect's journey of supporting a large-scale IT transformation. The journey begins close to the IT engine room and slowly inches up to the organizational penthouse:

Part I, Architects
> Understanding the qualities of an architect in the enterprise context

Part II, Architecture
> Redefining architecture's value proposition as a change driver

Part III, Communication
> Conveying technical topics effectively to a variety of stakeholders

Part IV, Organizations
> Using an architectural mindset to understand organizational structures and systems

Part V, Transformation
> Effecting lasting change in an organization

Part VI, Epilogue: Architecting IT Transformation
> Living the life of a change agent

You are invited to read this book from beginning to end, following the progression from technical to organizational topics. However, you are just as welcome to peruse the book and start reading whichever chapter piques your interest, using the extensive cross-references I've provided to aid your nonlinear navigation. After all, that's how the internet works, so I figured it would probably also work for my book.

This isn't a technical book. It's a book about how to grow your horizon as an architect to effectively apply your technical skill in large organizations. This book won't teach you how to configure a Hadoop cluster or how to set up container orchestration with Docker and Kubernetes. Instead, it teaches you how to reason about large-scale architectures; how to ensure your architecture benefits the business strategy; how to leverage vendors' expertise; and how to communicate critical decisions to upper management.

Is It Proven to Work?

If you're looking for a scientifically proven, repeatable "method" of transforming a technical organization, you might be disappointed (but if you find one, please let me know). This book's structure is rather loose, and you might even be annoyed at having to read through little anecdotes when all you want is the one bit of advice you need in order to be successful. However, that's what the life of an architect is like. You won't be able to copy-paste other people's decisions, but you can learn from their experience to make better decisions of your own.

This book is based on my daily experiences of two decades in IT, which led me through being a startup cofounder (lots of fun, not lots of money), system integrator (made tax audits more efficient), consultant (lots of PowerPoint), author (collecting and documenting insights), internet software engineer (building the future), chief architect of a large multinational organization (tough, but rewarding), and CTO advisor (lots of insights and sharing). I felt that taking a personal account of IT transformation might be appropriate because architecture is by nature a somewhat personal business. When looking at a famous building, you can easily identify the architect from afar. White box: Richard Meier; all crooked: Frank Gehry; looks like made from fabric: Zaha Hadid. Although not quite as dramatic, every (chief) IT architect also has their personal emphasis and style that's reflected in their works.

The collection of insights that make up this book reflect my personal point of view but are written such that the "nuggets" can be easily extracted and put to broader use. Sidebars show you experiences from both traditional and digital companies.

Architects are busy people. I therefore tried to package my insights into anecdotes that are easy to consume and hopefully even a bit fun to read. I hope you'll experience a mix of "I'm not the only person facing this problem" and "that's a new way of looking at things" along the way.

There's a lot more to say about architecture and transformation than would ever fit into a book. You'll therefore find many references to other books and articles that help you dive deeper into any particular topic.

Tell Me a Story

I chose to structure the book as a collection of stories because in our complex world, telling stories is a great way to teach. Studies have shown that people remember stories much better than sheer facts, and there appears to be evidence that listening to a story activates additional parts of our brain that help with understanding and retention. Aristotle already knew that a good speech contains not only *logos*, the facts and structure, but also *ethos*, a credible character, and *pathos*, emotions, usually triggered by a good story.

To transform an organization, you don't need to solve mathematical equations. You need to move people, and that's why you need to be able to tell a good story and paint a compelling vision. It's fine to start out by using some of the attention-catching slogans from this book ("Zombies will eat your brain!") and later supplement them with your own stories. Have you seen people cry and laugh when watching movies, even though they know that the story is fictitious and all acting is fake? That's the power of storytelling in action.

Conventions Used in This Book

This book contains many real-life stories that highlight the contrast between traditional and digital companies. The respective examples are indicated by the following icons:

 The "manager" icon indicates examples describing how traditional IT organizations think and work.

 The "digital native" icon indicates examples describing how modern, "digital" organizations operate.

 This icon signifies a general note or comment.

 This icon indicates a warning or caution.

Staying Up-to-Date

My brain doesn't stop generating new ideas with the publication date. To see what's on my mind and to chime in:

- Follow me on Twitter: *https://twitter.com/ghohpe*
- Find me on Linkedin: *http://www.linkedin.com/in/ghohpe*
- And find bigger ideas and articles on my blog: *https://architectelevator.com/blog*

O'Reilly Online Learning

 For more than 40 years, *O'Reilly Media* has provided technology and business training, knowledge, and insight to help companies succeed.

Our unique network of experts and innovators share their knowledge and expertise through books, articles, and our online learning platform. O'Reilly's online learning platform gives you on-demand access to live training courses, in-depth learning paths, interactive coding environments, and a vast collection of text and video from O'Reilly and 200+ other publishers. For more information, please visit *http://oreilly.com*.

How to Contact Us

Please address comments and questions concerning this book to the publisher:

O'Reilly Media, Inc.

1005 Gravenstein Highway North

Sebastopol, CA 95472

800-998-9938 (in the United States or Canada)

707-829-0515 (international or local)

707-829-0104 (fax)

You can access the web page for this book, where we list errata and any additional information, at *https://oreil.ly/Software_Architect_Elevator*.

Email *bookquestions@oreilly.com* to comment or ask technical questions about this book.

For news and more information about our books and courses, see our website at *http://www.oreilly.com*.

Find us on Facebook: *http://facebook.com/oreilly*

Follow us on Twitter: *http://twitter.com/oreillymedia*

Watch us on YouTube: *http://www.youtube.com/oreillymedia*

Acknowledgments

Many people have knowingly or unknowingly contributed to this book through hallway conversations, meeting discussions, manuscript reviews, Twitter dialogues, or casual chats over a beer. It's challenging to give due credit to all of the people I learned from, but I'd like to highlight a few whose input has significantly shaped this book. Michael Plöd, Simon Brown, Jean-Francois Landreau, and Michele Danieli have been a substantial source of suggestions and feedback. Matthias "Maze" Reik has been an enormously thorough proofreader, while Andrew Lee spotted a few more typos. My former boss, Barbara Karuth, reviewed and approved many stories that emerged from insightful conversations with current and former colleagues. And, last but certainly not least, *Kleines Genius* provided untiring moral support.

PART I

Architects

Architects have an exciting but sometimes challenging life in corporate IT. Some managers and technical staff might consider them to be overpaid ivory tower residents who, detached from reality, bestow their thoughts upon the rest of the company with slides and wall-sized posters, while their quest for irrelevant ideals causes missed project timelines.

On the upside, IT architects have become some of the most sought-after IT professionals as traditional enterprises are looking to transform their IT landscape to compete with digital disruptors. Ironically, though, many of the most successful digital companies have a world-class software and systems architecture, but don't have architects at all.

So, what makes a person an architect, besides that it's printed on their business card?

What Architects Are Not

Sometimes, it's easier to describe what something *isn't* rather than trying to come up with an exact definition of what it is. In the case of architects, exaggerated expectations can paint a picture of someone who solves intermittent performance problems in the morning and then transforms the enterprise culture in the afternoon. This leads to a scenario in which architects are pulled into several roles that clearly miss the purpose of being an architect:

Senior developer
> Developers often feel they need to become an architect as the next step in their career (and their pay grade). However, becoming an architect and a superstar engineer are two different career paths, with neither being superior to the other. Architects tend to have a broader scope, including organizational and strategic aspects, whereas engineers tend to specialize and

deliver running software. Mature IT organizations understand this and offer parallel career paths.

Firefighter

Many managers expect architects to be able to troubleshoot and solve any crisis based on their broad understanding of the current system landscape. Architects shouldn't ignore production issues, because they provide valuable feedback into possible architectural weaknesses. But an architect that runs from one fire drill to the next won't have time to think about architecture. Architecture isn't operations.

Project manager

Architects must be able to juggle many distinct, but interrelated topics. Their decisions also take into account—and affect—project time lines, staffing, and required skill sets. As a result, upper management often comes to rely on architects for project information, especially if the project manager is busy *filling out status report templates* (Chapter 30). This is a slippery slope for an architect because it's valuable work, but it distracts from the architect's main responsibility.

Scientist

Architects need to sport a sharp intellect and must be able to think in *models and systems* (Chapter 10), but the decisions they make impact real business projects. Hence, many organizations separate the role of the *chief architect* from that of a *chief scientist*. Personally, I prefer the title *chief engineer* to highlight that architects produce more than paper. Lastly, although scientists may get their papers published by making things sound complex and difficult to understand, an architect's job is the inverse: *making complex topics easy to digest* (Chapter 18).

Many Kinds of Architects

Architects operate at different levels of abstraction. Just like real-life architecture has city planners, building, landscape, and interior architects, IT architects can have many specializations: you'll have network architects, security architects, software architects, solution architects, enterprise architects, and many more. Just like in the real world, no one architect is more important than the other. For example, living in a house with great architecture in a poorly planned city with endless traffic jams but few public facilities is going to be equally frustrating as living in a house with poor architecture in a well-functioning city. The same is true in IT—your beautifully designed and perfectly modularized application isn't any good if it solves the wrong problem or is duplicating an existing application. Likewise, if the application is unable to connect to the corporate network, few users will be able to appreciate it. Therefore, it's not about which type of architect is more important; it's about getting all types of architects to work together.

Architects Deal with Nonrequirements

It's commonly assumed that developers deal with functional requirements, whereas architects deal with nonfunctional requirements, often referred to as the "ilities": scalability, maintainability, availability, interoperability, and so on. The reality isn't as simple, though. I find that more often, architects deal with *nonrequirements*. This term doesn't indicate things that aren't required; rather, it refers to requirements that aren't stated anywhere. This includes context, tacit assumptions, hidden dependencies, and other things that were never spelled out. Unearthing these implicit requirements and making them explicit is one of an architect's most valuable contributions. Again, this work can take place at any level from enterprise architect to software architect—it's the connection that counts.

Measuring an Architect's Value

Articulating an architect's value isn't always easy. I often explain to people that if an IT system can still absorb high rates of change after many years, the project team probably included a good architect. Now, waiting several years to assess an architect's value is slightly impractical. Instead, we can see architects bringing value in several dimensions:

Architects "connect the dots"
> Often, each individual element of an IT architecture is well thought out and well run, but the sum of all these fine systems still isn't delivering what the business needs. Architects look between the boxes to make sure interdependencies are well understood.

Architects see trade-offs
> System design and development involves innumerable decisions. Most meaningful decisions don't just have upsides, but also downsides. Architects see both sides of the coin and balance trade-offs in line with overarching goals and principles.

Architects look beyond products
> Too much of IT decision-making is driven by *product selection* (Chapter 16). Architects look beyond the product names and feature lists to distill decision options and trade-offs.

Architects articulate strategy
> IT's purpose is to support the business strategy. Architects establish this linkage by translating business needs into technical drivers.

Architects fight complexity
> IT is complex. Architects harmonize to reduce complexity, for example, through governance in the form of architecture review boards and *inception* (see Chapter 32). It also includes "retiring" systems (in the *Blade Runner* sense of the word), lest you want to *live among zombies* (Chapter 12).

Architects deliver
> Staying grounded in reality and receiving feedback on decisions from real project implementations is vital for architects. Otherwise, *control remains an illusion* (Chapter 27).

So, architects do a lot more than draw pretty architecture diagrams!

Architects as Change Agents

Today's successful architects aren't just IT specialists, they're also major change agents. Architects must therefore possess a special set of skills beyond just technology.

The chapters in this part prepare you for this role by teaching you how to:

Chapter 1, The Architect Elevator
> Transcend organizational levels by riding the architect elevator.

Chapter 2, Movie-Star Architects
> Adopt multiple personas that might resemble movie characters.

Chapter 3, Architects Live in the First Derivative
> Live in the first derivative.

Chapter 4, Enterprise Architect or Architect in the Enterprise?
> Connect business and IT.

Chapter 5, An Architect Stands on Three Legs

> Bring more than skill because that's just one of the three legs architects stand on.

Chapter 6, Making Decisions

> Exercise good decision-making discipline in the face of uncertainty.

Chapter 7, Question Everything

> Get to the root of problems by questioning everything.

I

The Architect Elevator

From the Penthouse to the Engine Room and Back

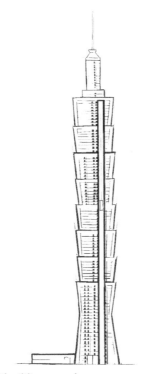

Tall buildings need someone to ride the elevator

Architects play a critical role as a connecting and translating element, especially in large organizations where departments speak different languages, have different viewpoints, and drive toward conflicting objectives. Many layers of management only exacerbate the problem as communicating up and down the corporate ladder resembles the telephone game.[1] The worst-case scenario materializes when people holding relevant information or expertise aren't empowered to make decisions, whereas the decision makers lack relevant information. Not a good state to be in for a corporate IT department, especially in the days when technology has become a driving factor for most businesses.

The Architect Elevator

Architects can fill an important void in large enterprises: they work and communicate closely with technical staff on projects, but are also able to convey technical topics to upper management *without losing the essence of the message* (Chapter 18). Conversely, they understand the company's business strategy and can translate it into technical decisions that support it.

If you picture the levels of an organization as the floors in a building, architects can ride what I call the *architect elevator*: they ride the elevator up and down to move between a large enterprise's board room and the *engine room* where software is being built. Such a direct linkage between the levels has become more important than ever in times of rapid IT evolution and digital disruption.

Stretching the analogy to that of a large ship, if the bridge officers spot an obstacle and need to turn the proverbial tanker, they will set the engines to reverse and the rudder to hard starboard. But if in reality the engines are running full speed ahead, a major disaster is preprogrammed. This is why even old steamboats had a pipe to echo commands directly from the captain to the boiler room and back. In large enterprises architects need to play exactly that role!

Some Organizations Have More Floors Than Others

Coming back to the building metaphor, the number of floors an architect has to ride in the elevator depends on the type of organization. Flat organizations might not need the elevator at all—a few flights of stairs are sufficient. This also means that the up-and-down role of an architect might be less critical: if management is keenly aware of the technical reality at the necessary level of detail and technical staff have direct access to senior management, fewer "enterprise" architects are needed. We could say that digital companies live in a bungalow and hence don't need the elevator.

---

1 In the telephone game, children form a circle and relay a message from one child to the next. By the time the message returns to the originator, it typically has completely changed along the way.

However, classic IT shops in large organizations tend to have many, many floors above them. They work in a sky-scraper so tall that a single architect ele-vator might not be able to span all levels. In this case, it's OK if a technical archi-tect and an enterprise architect meet in

The value of the architects in the elevator metaphor shouldn't be measured by how "high" they travel but by how many floors they span.

the middle and cover their respective "halves" of the building. The value of the architects in this scenario shouldn't be measured by how "high" they travel but by how many floors they span. In large organizations, the folks in the penthouse might make the mistake of seeing and valuing only the architects in the upper half of the building. Conversely, many developers or technical architects consider such "enterprise" architects less useful because they don't code. This can be true in some cases—such architects often enjoy life in the upper floors so much that they aren't keen to take the elevator down ever again. But an "enterprise" archi-tect who travels halfway down the building to share the strategic vision with tech-nical architects can have a significant value.

Not a One-Way Street

Invariably you will meet folks who ride the elevator, but only once to the top and never back down. They enjoy the good view from the penthouse too much and feel that they didn't work so hard to still be visiting the grimy engine room. Fre-quently you can identify these folks by statements like: "I used to be technical." I can't help but retort: "I used to be a manager" (it's true) or "Why did you stop? Were you no good at it?" If you want to be more diplomatic (and philosophical) about it, cite Fritz Lang's movie *Metropolis* in which the separation between pent-house and engine room almost led to the city's complete destruction before peo-ple realized that "the head and the hands need a mediator." In any case, the elevator is meant to be ridden up and down. Eating caviar in the penthouse while the basement is flooded isn't the way to transform corporate IT.

Riding the elevator up and down the organization is also an important mech-anism for the architect to obtain feedback on decisions and to understand their ramifications at the implementation level. Long project implementation cycles don't provide a good *learning loop* (Chapter 36) and can lead to an "Architect's Dream, Developer's Nightmare" scenario, in which the architects have achieved their abstract ideals, but the actual implementation is impractical. Allowing architects to only enjoy the view from high up invariably leads to the dreaded authority without responsibility antipattern.[2] This pattern can be broken only if architects have to live with, or at least observe, the consequences of their decisions. To do so, they must keep riding the elevator.

High-Speed Elevators

In the past, IT decisions were fairly far removed from the business strategy: IT was pretty "vanilla," and the main parameter, or key performance indicator (KPI), was *cost*. Therefore, riding the elevator wasn't as critical as new information was rare. Nowadays, though, the linkage between business goals and technology choices has become much more direct, even for "traditional" businesses. For example, the desire for faster time-to-market to meet competitive pressures translates into the need for an elastic cloud approach to computing, which in turn requires applications that scale horizontally and thus should be designed to be stateless. Targeted content on customer channels necessitates analytical models, which are tuned by churning through large amounts of data via a Hadoop cluster, which in turn favors local hard-drive storage over shared-network storage. The fact that in one or two sentences a business need has turned into application or infrastructure design highlights the need for architects to ride the elevator. Increasingly they need to take the express elevator, though, to keep up with the pace at which business and IT are intertwined.

In traditional IT shops, the lower floors of the building can be exclusively occupied by *external consultants* (Chapter 38), which allows enterprise architects to avoid getting their hands dirty. However, because it focuses solely on efficiency and ignores *economies of speed* (Chapter 35), such a setup doesn't perform well in times of rapid technology evolution. Architects who are used to such an environment must stretch their role from being pure consumers of vendors' technology roadmaps to actively defining it. To do so, they need to develop their own *IT worldview* (Chapter 16).

Other Passengers

If you are riding the elevator up and down as a successful architect, you might encounter other folks riding with you. You might, for example, meet business or nontechnical folks who learned that a deeper understanding of IT is critical to the business. Be kind to those folks, take them with you, and show them around.

---

2 "Authority Without Responsibility," Wikiwikiweb, 2004, *https://oreil.ly/WhXg-*.

Engage them in a dialogue—it will allow you to better understand business needs and goals. They might even take you to the higher floors you haven't been to.

You might also encounter folks who ride the elevator down merely to pick up buzzwords to sell as their own ideas in the penthouse. We don't call these people architects. People who ride the elevator but don't get out are commonly called *lift boys*. They benefit from the ignorance in the penthouse to pursue a "technical" career without touching actual technology. You might be able to convert some of these folks by getting them genuinely interested in what's going on in the engine room. If you don't succeed, it's best to maintain the proverbial elevator silence, avoiding eye contact by examining every ceiling tile in detail. Keep your "elevator pitch" for those moments when you share the cabin with a senior executive, not a mere messenger.

The Dangers of Riding the Elevator

You would think that architects riding the elevator up and down are highly appreciated by their employer. After all, they provide significant value to businesses transforming their IT to better compete in a digital world. Surprisingly, such architects can encounter resistance. Both the penthouse and the engine room might actually have grown quite content with being disconnected: the company leadership is under the false impression that the digital transformation is proceeding nicely, whereas the folks in the engine room enjoy the freedom to try out new technologies without much supervision. Such a disconnect between penthouse and engine room resembles a cruise ship heading for an iceberg with the engines running at full speed ahead: by the time the leadership realizes what's going on, it's likely too late.

I was once criticized by the engine room for pushing corporate agenda against the will of the developers while at the same time corporate leadership chastised me for wanting to try new solutions just for fun. Ironically, this likely meant I found a good balance.

One can liken such organizations to the Leaning Tower of Pisa where the foundation and the penthouse aren't vertically aligned. Riding the elevator in such a building is certainly more challenging. When stepping into such an environment, the elevator architect must be prepared to face resistance from both sides. No one ever said being a disruptor is easy, especially as *systems resist change* (Chapter 10).

The best strategy in these situations is to start linking the levels carefully, waiting for the right moment to share information. For example, you could begin by helping the folks in the engine room convey to management what great work they are doing. It will give them more visibility and recognition while you gain access to detailed technical information.

Other corporate denizens not content with you riding the elevator can be found on the middle floors: seeing you whiz by to connect leadership and the engine room makes them feel bypassed. Thus, the organization has an "hourglass" shape of appreciation for your work: top management sees you as a critical transformation enabler, whereas the folks in the engine room are happy to have someone to talk to who actually understands and appreciates their work. The folks in the middle, though, see you as a threat to their livelihood, including their children's education and their vacation home in the mountains. This is a delicate affair. Some might even actively block you on your way: being stopped at every floor to give an explanation—aka *aligning* (Chapter 30)—makes riding the elevator not really faster than taking the stairs.

Lastly, because folks riding the elevator are rare, being good at one thing often leads others to conclude that you aren't good at anything else. For example, architects giving meaningful and inspiring presentations to management are often assumed to not be great technologists, even though that's the very reason their presentations are meaningful. So, every once in a while, you're going to want to let the upper floors know that you can hold your own down in the engine room.

Flattening the Building

Instead of tirelessly riding the elevator up and down, why not get rid of all those unnecessary floors? After all, the digital companies your business is trying to compete with have much fewer floors. Unfortunately, you can't simply pull some floors out of a building. And blowing the whole thing up just leaves you with a pile of rubble, not a lower building. The guys on the middle floors are often critical knowledge holders about the organization and IT landscape, especially if there's a large *black market* (Chapter 29), so the organization can't function without them in the near term.

Flattening the building little by little can be a sound long-term strategy, but it would take too long because it requires fundamental changes to the company culture. It also changes or eliminates the role played by the folks inhabiting the middle floors, who will put up a fierce resistance. This isn't a fight an architect can win. However, an architect can start to loosen things up a little bit; for example, by getting the penthouse interested in information from the engine room or by providing faster feedback loops.

2

Movie-Star Architects

Most Architects Carry Multiple Personas

The architect walk of fame

What should an architect be doing besides riding the elevator? Let's try another analogy: movie characters.

Before the movie starts, you get to watch advertisements or short films. In our case, it's a short film about the origin of the word *architect*: it derives from the Greek ἀρχιτέκτων (*architekton*), which roughly translates into "master builder." Keeping in mind that this word was meant for people who built houses and structures, not IT systems, we should note that the word implies "builder," not "designer"—an architect should be someone who actually builds, not someone who only draws pretty pictures. An architect is also expected to be accomplished in their profession as to deserve the attribute of being a "master." Now to the main feature…

The Matrix: The Master Planner

If you ask tech folk to name a prototypical architect in the movies, they'll likely mention the *The Matrix* trilogy. The Architect of the *Matrix* is (per Wikipedia (*https://oreil.ly/xuDWC*)) a "cold, humorless, white-haired man in a light-gray suit," qualities he largely owes to the fact that he is a computer program himself. Wikipedia also notes that the Architect "speaks in long logical chains of reasoning," something that many IT architects are known to do. So perhaps the analogy holds?

 Fun fact: Vint Cerf, one of the key architects of the internet, bears a remarkable resemblance to the Matrix Architect. Considering Vint designed much of the Matrix we live in, this might not be pure coincidence.

The Matrix Architect is also the ultimate authority: he designed the "Matrix" (the computer program that simulates reality to humans who are being farmed by machines as an energy source) and knows and controls everything. The enterprise architect is sometimes seen as such a person—the all-knowing decision maker. Some even wish themselves into such a role, partly because it is neat to be all-knowing and partly because it gets you a lot of respect.

Naturally, this role model has some issues: all-knowingness turns out to be a little too ambitious for humans, leading to poor decision-making and all sorts of other problems. Even if the architect is a super-smart person, they can base decisions on only those facts that are known to them. In large companies with a complex IT, it would be impossible to stay in touch with all technology that is in place, no matter how often they *ride the elevator* (Chapter 1) down to the engine room. They'll therefore inevitably need to rely on presentations, documents, or statements from management on the middle floors. Such an information channel to the supreme decision maker has severe challenges: every floor through which such a document passes understands its value as an influencing vehicle. This means that the middle floors are tempted to inject their favorite messages and project proposals, often irrespective of any technical merit. Further up, any real technical content or potentially controversial topics are sure to be removed. As a result, the top architect is being fed indirect, distorted, and often biased information. Making decisions based on such information is dangerous.

I have observed senior management briefings in which the proposed solutions were rather a list of people's favorite projects than actual solutions. Interestingly, and fortunately, despite having less IT experience, top management sensed that there was a missing link between the two.

In summary: corporate IT is no movie, and its role isn't to provide an illusion for humans being farmed as power sources. We should be cautious with this architect model.

Edward Scissorhands: The Gardener

A slightly more fitting analogy for enterprise architects is that of a gardener. I tend to depict this metaphor with a character from one of my favorite movies, *Edward Scissorhands*. Large-scale IT is much like a garden: things evolve and grow on their own, with weeds growing the fastest. The role of the gardener is to trim and prune what doesn't fit and to establish an overall balance and harmony in the garden, keeping in mind the plants' needs. For example, shade-loving plants should be planted near large trees or bushes, just like automated testing and continuous integration (CI)/continuous development (CD) will be happier in the neighborhood of rapidly evolving systems.

A good gardener, just like a good architect, is no dictatorial master planner and certainly doesn't make all the detailed decisions about which direction a strain of grass should grow—Japanese gardens being a possible exception. Rather, gardeners see themselves as the caretaker of a living ecosystem. Some gardeners, like Edward, are true artists!

I like this analogy because it has a soft touch to it. Complex enterprise IT does feel organic, and good architecture has a sense of balance, which we can often find in a nice garden. Top-down governance with weed killer is unlikely to have a lasting effect and usually does more harm than good. Whether this thinking leads to a new application for *The Nature of Order*,[1] I am not sure yet. I should go read it.

Vanishing Point: The Guide

Erik Dörnenburg, ThoughtWorks' head of technology, Europe, introduced me to another very apt metaphor. Erik closely works with many software projects, which tend to loathe the ostensibly all-knowing, all-decision-making architect

---

1 Christopher Alexander, *The Nature of Order* (Berkeley, CA: Center for Environmental Structure, 2002).

who is disconnected from reality. Erik even coined the term *architecture without architects*, which might cause some architects to worry about their career.

Erik likens an architect to a tour guide, someone who has been to a certain place many times, can tell a good story about it, and can gently guide you to pay attention to important aspects and avoid unnecessary risks. This is a guiding role: tour guides cannot force their guests to follow their advice, except maybe those who drop off a bus load of tourists at a tourist-trap restaurant in the middle of nowhere.

This type of architect needs to "lead by influence" and must be hands-on enough to earn the respect of those whom they're leading. The tour guide also stays along for the ride and doesn't just hand a map to the tourists like some consultant architects are known to do. An architect who acts as a guide often depends on strong management support because evidence that good things happened due to their guidance can be subtle. In purely "business case–driven" environments, this could be limiting the "tour guide" architect's impact or career.

An unconventional guide out of another one of my favorite movies is the blind DJ Super Soul from the 1971 road movie *Vanishing Point*. Like so many IT projects, the movie's protagonist, Kowalski, is on a death march to meet an impossible deadline and overcome numerous obstacles along the way. He isn't delivering code, but a 1970 Dodge Challenger R/T 440 Magnum from Denver to San Francisco—in 15 hours. Kowalski is being guided by Super Soul who has tapped the police network, just like architects plugging into the management network, to get access to crucial information. The guide tracks Kowalski's progress and keeps the hero clear of all sorts of traps that police (i.e., management) have set up. After Super Soul is compromised by "management," the "project" goes adrift and ends like too many IT projects: in a fiery crash.

The Wizard of Oz

Architects can sometimes be seen as wizards who can solve just about any technical challenge. Although that can be a short-term ego boost, it's not a good job description and expectation to live up to. Hence, by the "wizard" architect analogy, I don't mean an actual wizard waving the magic wand but the "Mighty Oz": a video projection that appears large and powerful but is in fact controlled by a mere human "wizard," who turns out to be an ordinary man using the big machinery to garner respect.

A gentle dose of such engineered deception can be of use in large organizations in which "normal" developers are rarely involved in management discussions or major decisions. This is where the "architect" title can be used to make oneself a bit more "great and mighty." The projection can garner the respect of the general population and can even be a precondition to taking the elevator to the top floors. Is this cheating? I would say "no" as long as you don't get enamored in so much wizardry that you forget about your technical roots.

Superhero? Superglue!

Similar to the wizard, a common expectation of an architect is that of the super-hero: if you believe some job postings, enterprise architects can single-handedly catapult companies into the digital age, solve just about any technical problem, and are always up to date on the latest technology. These are tough expectations to fulfill, so I'd caution any architect against taking advantage of this common misconception.

Amir Shenhav from Intel appropriately pointed out that instead of the super-hero we need "super glue" architects—the guys who hold architecture, technical details, business needs, and people together across a large organization or complex projects. I like this metaphor because it resembles the analogy of an architect being a catalyst. We just need to be a little careful: being the glue (or catalyst) means understanding a good bit about the things you glue together. It's like being a good matchmaker: you need to find matching parts, and to do that you need to understand what your parts are made from.

Making the Call

Which type of architect should you be? First, there are likely many more types and movie analogies. You could play *Inception* and create architectural dream worlds with a (dangerous) twist. Or be one of the two impostors debating Chilean architecture in *There's Something about Mary* or (more creepily) Anthony Royal in the utopian drama *High-Rise*—the opportunities are manifold.

In the end, most architects exhibit a combination of these prototypical stereotypes. Periodic gluing, gardening, guiding, impressing, and a little bit of all-knowing every now and then can make for a pretty good architect.

3

Architects Live in the First Derivative

In a Constantly Moving World, Your Current Position Isn't Very Meaningful

Deriving the need for architecture

Defining a system's architecture is a balancing act between many, often-conflicting goals: flexible systems can be complex; high-performing systems can be difficult to understand; easy-to-maintain systems can take more effort to construct initially. Although this is what makes an architect's work so interesting, it also makes it difficult to pin down what exactly drives architectural decisions.

Rate of Change Defines Architecture

If I had to name one primary factor that influences architecture, I'd put *rate of change* at the top of my list, based on reasoning about the inverse question: when does a system not need any architecture at all? Although as an architect this isn't a natural question to ask (nor to answer), it can reveal what system property makes architecture valuable. In my mind, the only system that wouldn't benefit from architecture is one that doesn't change at all. If everything about a system is 100% fixed, just getting it working somehow seems good enough.

Now, reverting the logic back to the original proposition, it appears natural that the rate of change is a major driver of architecture's value and architectural decisions. It's easy to see that a system that doesn't need to change much will have a substantially different architecture than one that needs to absorb frequent changes over long periods of time. Good architects, therefore, deal with change. This means that they live in the system's *first derivative*: the mathematical expression for how quickly a function's value changes.[1]

Once we understand the influence change has on architecture, it's useful to consider the various forms of change affecting an IT system. The first change that comes to mind is a change in functional requirements, but there's a lot more: changes in the volume of traffic or data to be processed, changing the runtime environment to the cloud, or changes to the business context such as using the system in different languages or by different people.

Change = Business as Unusual?

Despite the popular saying that "the only constant is change," traditional IT organizations tend to have a somewhat uneasy relationship with change. This mindset is often revealed by a popular engine room slogan: *"never touch a running system"* (Chapter 12). When change can't be avoided, IT departments neatly package it into a project. The most celebrated part of an IT project is the end, or launch, which ironically is often the first time real users actually get to use the system. The reason for celebration is that things can return to "business as usual," that is, stable operations without any change.

---

1 The derivative of a function measures the sensitivity to change of the function's output value with respect to a change in its input value.

Packaging change into projects reflects an organization's belief that "no change" is the normal, desired state and "change" is the intermittent, unusual state.

Thus, many organizational systems are designed to control and prevent change: budgeting processes limit spending on change; quality gates limit changes going to production; project planning and requirements documents limit scope changes. Transforming a software delivery organization such that it embraces constant change requires adjusting these processes to support rather than prevent change without ignoring the (generally useful) motivation for setting them up in the first place. That's not an easy task and is the reason why this book devotes an entire part to *transformation* (Part V).

Varying Rates of Change

Technology is a fast-moving field: we don't think much of IT products carrying a three-part version number: "well, if you're still on 2.4.14, I can't help you much; it's really time to upgrade to .15."

Luckily, not everything in IT moves fast: the most common processor architecture, the base for Intel's x86 processors, originates from 1978. The ARM chips that dominate today's mobile devices are based on a design from around 1985. Both Linux and Windows operating systems are well past their teenage years, and even Java passed the 20-year mark at version 9 some years ago, closely followed by the Java Spring Framework, which has surpassed a respectable 15 years.

Naturally, such low rates of change can largely be observed in lower layers of the so-called IT stack: hardware and operating systems have such a vast installed base and so many dependencies that the cost of an all-out replacement would be huge. Hence, we tend to see more evolution than revolution here. These technologies form the *base of the pyramid* (Chapter 28), giving us a stable foundation to build on.

On top, things move a lot faster. For example, the popular AngularJS framework was essentially replaced by the very different Angular framework just five years after its inception. Google's Fabric framework also lived just five years before being subsumed by Firebase. And Google Mashup Editor, one of my favorites of the day, survived a mere two years.

Things are moving fast and are only getting faster. If rate of change is a driver for architecture, it looks like we'll need more of it!

Although we're surely sad to witness products' early demise, the rate at which new products and tools arrive paints an even more dramatic picture. For example, a look at the Cloud Native Interactive Landscape (*https://oreil.ly/bnk5E*) offered by the Cloud Native Computing Foundation (CNCF) will quickly convince you that building modern applications requires a fast-growing list of ingredients.

A Software System's First Derivative

If the first derivative is an architect's primary concern, how does this somewhat abstract concept translate into the reality of systems architecture? We can get a hint by thinking about which part of a software system determines its rate of change. For a custom-built system, the critical element for change is the build toolchain, the part that converts source code into an executable format that is subsequently deployed onto the runtime infrastructure.

A software system's first derivative is its build and deployment toolchain.

All changes to the software (better) go through this build and deployment toolchain. Knowing that the software toolchain is the first derivative, increasing a software system's rate of change requires a *well-tuned toolchain* (Chapter 13).

It's no surprise, then, that in recent years the industry has put much attention and effort into reducing friction in software delivery: Continuous Integration (CI), Continuous Deployment (CD), and configuration automation are all aspects of increasing the first derivative of software systems and thus speeding up software delivery. Without such innovations, daily or hourly software deployments wouldn't be possible, and companies wouldn't be able to compete in digital markets, which thrive on constant improvement and frequent updates.

Whereas build systems previously were the proverbial *shoemaker's children*, meaning they didn't get a lot of attention, they now run on the same type of infrastructure as the production systems. Containerized, fully automated, elastic, cloud-based, on-demand build systems are quickly becoming the norm. Teams building and maintaining such sophisticated build systems clearly live in the first derivative!

Designing for the First Derivative

When designing a system for change, it's again helpful to think about the opposite—the aspects that impede change:

Dependencies
> Too many interdependencies between a system's components will result in small changes needing adjustments in many places, increasing both effort and risk. Systems with fewer interdependencies—for example, because they are modular and cleanly separate responsibilities—localize changes and can therefore generally absorb a higher rate of change. The research conducted by the authors of the book *Accelerate*[2] shows that decoupling system components is the biggest contributor to sustained software delivery.

Friction
> Both cost and risk of change increase with friction, generated, for example, by long lead times for infrastructure provisioning or numerous manual deployment steps. Teams that live in the first derivative therefore ensure that their software build chain is fully automated.

Poor quality
> There's a common misbelief that good quality requires extra time and effort. The inverse is actually true: poor quality *slows down* software delivery. Changes to a poorly tested or poorly built system take more time and are more likely to break things.

Fear
> Often ignored, a programmer's attitude has a major impact on the rate of change. Poor quality and low levels of automation make change a risky proposition. Developers will thus be afraid of making changes. This leads to code rot, which in turn increases the risk of change—a nasty spiral.

The list shows that an architect has several levers with which they can increase velocity, some technical in nature and others that relate to team attitude. It's another example of how technical and organizational architecture go hand in hand.

---

2 Nicole Fosgren, Jez Humble, and Gene Kim, *Accelerate: Building and Scaling High Performing Technology Organizations* (Portland, Oregon: IT Revolution, 2018).

Confidence Brings Speed

If fear slows you down, confidence should speed you up. Automated tests do just that: they give teams confidence and thus increase the rate of change. That's why determining whether a system has sufficient test coverage shouldn't be measured in the percentage of lines of code covered. Rather, it should be measured by whether teams can make changes confidently.

 Propose to a development team that they let you delete 20 arbitrary lines from their source code. Then, they'll run their tests—if they pass, they'll push the code straight into production. From their reaction, you'll know immediately whether their source code has sufficient test coverage.

Despite an abundance of tools that are supposed to speed up software delivery, the determining factor remains decidedly human. The change that's never made out of fear cannot be accelerated by the world's best toolchain.

Rate of Change Trade-Offs

Increasing an organization's rate of change is not an all-or-nothing affair and involves balancing trade-offs. Borrowing one more time from the routinely overstretched analogy between IT architecture and building architecture yields useful advice on the multiple facets of designing for change. If either a large software project or housing project is undertaken without a conscious decision about its architecture, the "default" architecture converges toward the "Big Ball of Mud," also referred to by its real-world incarnation of a *shantytown* (Chapter 8).

A shantytown, or slum, is generally constructed using cheap materials and unskilled labor. Low cost and a broad labor pool are actually desirable properties. Additionally, local changes, such as adding a wall or even another floor, are often quick and inexpensive—in contrast to fancier high-rise buildings. However, besides not providing a very comfortable living environment, slums also lack common infrastructure, such as a well-built electrical or sewer system. The lack of such infrastructure ultimately limits their rate of growth. This is a good reminder that optimizing for local or short-term change can inhibit global or long-term change.

Multispeed Architectures

If a system's rate of change influences its architecture, it would seem natural to construct a system such that components are separated by rate of change. This approach forms the basis for the popular concepts of *two-speed architecture* or *bimodal IT*, which suggest that traditional companies looking to become competitive in a digital world should initially increase the rate of change in the interaction layer ("Systems of Engagement") while keeping legacy systems ("Systems of Record") stable. In doing so, rapid changes can supposedly be applied to the customer-facing systems, whereas the record-keeping systems are kept stable and reliable.

Although dividing systems by rate of change is a fair idea, this particular approach has significant shortcomings. First, it's based on the flawed assumption that one can *move faster by compromising quality* (Chapter 40). Otherwise we wouldn't need to keep a low rate of change in systems of record to maintain their reliability. Second, a company will be hard pressed to localize change into the interaction layer. For example, the addition of a simple field to the system of engagement typically also requires a change to the system of record, coupling the two systems' rates of change: if the system of record follows a six-month release cycle, there won't be much speed inside this two-speed architecture.

It turns out that the separation between systems of engagement and systems of record is artificial and doesn't line up well with the overall rate of change from a business or end-user perspective. This insight is underlined by the fact that hardly any digital business follows such a setup.

 Digital companies only know one speed: fast.

Separating rate of change along a different dimension might well be beneficial, though. For example, a company's accounting or payroll system will likely have a lower rate of change and can utilize a different architecture from the core business systems, which form a competitive differentiator for the organization, and hence should support a higher rate of change.

The Second Derivative

If the first derivative describes a software system's rate of change, following our mathematical analogy, increasing the rate of change is dependent on a positive second derivative. Using the speed of a car as an analogy, a car's speed is the first derivative of its position: it defines how much distance it can cover over a given time interval. Accelerating—that is, increasing the speed—is the second derivative.

Back in IT, the second derivative is the essence of most transformation programs: they aim to increase the rate of change in an organization or its IT systems. Thus, for an organization to appreciate and successfully conduct a transformation program, it first needs to appreciate the importance of the first derivative; that is, it must understand *economies of speed* (Chapter 35). It's hard to sell a stronger engine and a shorter gear ratio for faster acceleration to someone who prefers to coast along on cruise control.

Rate of Change for Architects

Lastly, technical systems and organizations aren't the only systems that need to increase their rate of change. Architects also do because new technologies arrive at an ever-faster pace, leaving architects with an enormous challenge of staying up to date. If they don't, they might be relegated to life in the *ivory tower* (Chapter 1), far away from the engine room.

How can architects expect to keep up in today's world of rapid innovation? Trying to do so by yourself appears futile—no one can stay current on everything. Instead, architects should be part of a trusted but diverse network of experts, which can provide unbiased information.

When you sit near a large IT budget that's being vied for by vendors, you'll have many folks wanting to update you on new technologies, or rather *products* (Chapter 16). However, neutrality is an architect's major asset, so they're expected to cut through the buzzword fog to discern what's really new and what's just clever repackaging of old concepts.

Even though living in a world that's moving ever faster can be tiring, it's also what keeps architects' jobs interesting and makes architecture more valuable. So, embrace life in the first derivative!

4

Enterprise Architect or Architect in the Enterprise?

The Upper and Lower Floors of the Ivory Tower

Architecture from the ivory tower

When I was hired as an enterprise architect, the *head of enterprise architecture* to be more precise, I had little idea what *enterprise architecture* really entailed. I also wondered whether my team should be called the "Feet of Enterprise Architecture," but that contemplation didn't find much love. The driver behind the tendency to prefix titles with "head of" was aptly described in an online forum I stumbled upon:[1]

> This title typically implies that the candidate wanted a director/VP/executive title but the organization refused to extend the title. By using this obfuscation, the candidate appears senior to external parties but without offending internal constituencies.

I am not particularly fond of the "head of xyz" title because it focuses on the person heading (no pun intended) a team rather than accomplishing a specific function. I'd rather name the person by what they need to achieve, assuming that they don't do this alone but have a team supporting them.

All title prefixes aside, when IT folks meet an *enterprise architect*, their initial reaction is to place this person high up *into the penthouse* (Chapter 1), where they draw pretty pictures that bear little resemblance to reality. To receive a warmer welcome from IT staff, one should therefore be careful with the label *enterprise architect*. However, what is an architect who works at enterprise scale supposed to be called, then?

Enterprise Architecture

The recurring challenge with the title *enterprise architect* tends to be that it could describe a person who architects the enterprise as a whole (including the business strategy level) or someone doing IT architecture at the enterprise level (as opposed to a departmental architect, for example).

To help resolve this ambiguity, let's defer to the defining book on the topic, *Enterprise Architecture as Strategy* by Jeanne Ross, Peter Weill, and David Robertson.[2] Here, we learn the following:

> Enterprise architecture is the organizing logic for business processes and IT infrastructure reflecting the integration and standardization requirements of the company's operating model.

Following this definition, *enterprise architecture* (EA) isn't a pure IT function but also considers business processes, which are part of a company's operating

1 Keith Rabois, Quora, May 11, 2010, "What does "Head" usually mean in job titles like "Head of Social," "Head of Product," "Head of Sales," etc.?", *https://oreil.ly/5LmbY*.

2 Jeanne W. Ross, Peter Weill, and David C. Robertson, *Enterprise Architecture as Strategy: Creating a Foundation for Business Execution* (Boston, MA: Harvard Business Review Press, 2006).

model. In fact, the book's most widely publicized diagram (*https://oreil.ly/D8ehD*) shows four quadrants depicting business operating models with higher or lower levels of process standardization (uniformity across lines of business) and process integration (sharing of data and interconnection of processes). Giving industry examples for all quadrants, Weill and Robertson map each model to a suitable high-level IT architecture strategy. For example, a data and process integration program might yield little value if the business operating model is one of highly diversified business units with few shared customers. For such enterprises, IT should instead provide a common infrastructure, on top of which each division can implement its diverse processes. Conversely, a business that's composed of largely identical units, such as a franchise, benefits from a highly standardized application landscape. The matrix demonstrates perfectly how EA forges the connection between the business and IT. Only if the two are well aligned does IT provide value to the business.

Connecting Business and IT

Connecting business and IT is easier if the business side of the organization also has a well-defined architecture. Luckily, as business environments become more complex and digital disruptors force traditional enterprises to evolve their business models more rapidly, the notion of *business architecture* has gained significant attention in recent years. Business architecture translates the *structured, architectural way of thinking* (Chapter 8) that's guided by a formalized view of components and interrelationships into the business domain. Rather than connecting technical system components and reasoning about technical system properties such as security and scalability, business architecture describes the "the structure of the enterprise in terms of its governance structure, business processes and business information."[3]

The business architecture essentially defines the company operating model, including how business areas are structured and integrated, derived from the business strategy. Meanwhile, the IT architecture builds the corresponding IT capabilities. If the two work seamlessly side by side, you don't need much else. In the more likely case that the two aren't well connected, you need something to pull them together. Therefore, here's my proposed definition of enterprise architecture:

---

3 Object Management Group website. *http://www.omg.org/bawg*.

Enterprise architecture is the glue between business and IT architecture.

This definition clarifies that EA, unlike IT architecture at enterprise level, isn't an IT function. Accordingly, the EA team should be positioned close to the company leadership and not be buried deep within the IT organization, so that it can balance business, technical, and organizational considerations.

The definition also implies that after business and IT are tightly interlinked, you won't need much EA, which is one reason why you don't find much EA within so-called digital giants.

Most digital giants don't have EA departments because their business and IT are tightly interlinked.

Alas, don't panic! The translation between business needs and IT architecture remains a domain that's perennially short of talent. It appears that most folks find comfort on one or the other side of the fence, but only a few can, and choose to, credibly play in both worlds. It's a good time to be an enterprise architect.

IT Is from Mars, Business Is from Venus

The strict separation between IT and business that is commonly found in enterprises seems troublesome to me. I tend to jest that in the old days, when everything was running on paper instead of computers, companies also didn't have a separate "paper" department and a CPO—the chief paper officer. In digital companies business and IT are inseparable; IT is the business, and the business is IT.

Connecting business and IT gives EA a whole new relevance but also new challenges. It's like adding a mid-floor elevator that connects the business folks in the penthouse with the IT folks in the engine room because the respective elevators don't quite reach each other. Although highly valuable, in the long run such an enterprise architecture department's objective must be to make itself obsolete, or at least smaller, by extending the respective elevators. But no worries, rapid changes in both the business and technical environments make it unlikely that the need for enterprise architecture disappears altogether.

Building a fruitful, bidirectional connection between business and IT architecture becomes easier if the business architecture is at a comparable level of maturity as IT architecture. More often than not, though, business architecture is even less mature as a domain than IT architecture. That's not because businesses had no architecture; rather, it's because the folks doing business architecture were not identified as such but were the business leaders, division heads, or COOs. Also, designing the business was rather attributed to business acumen than structured thinking. Where the business produced architecture-like arti-facts, they often ended up being "functional capability maps" that don't include any *lines* (Chapter 23).

Supporting the business is the ultimate goal and *raison d'être* of all enterprise functions. Positioning IT architecture on par with business architecture high-lights, though, that the days when IT was a simple order-taker that provides a commodity resource at the lowest possible cost are (luckily) over. In the digital age, IT is a competitive differentiator and opportunity driver, not a commodity like electricity.

 Digital giants like Google or Amazon aren't technology companies; they are advertising or fulfillment companies that understand how to use technology for competitive advantage.

Therefore, the common excuse that "Google and Amazon are technology companies while we are an insurance company/bank/manufacturing business" no longer holds. These companies will compete with you, and if you want to be competitive, you also need to change your view of IT. It's not an easy thing to do, but the digital giants have demonstrated how powerful that insight is.

Value-Driven Architecture

The scale and complexity of doing architecture at enterprise scale makes large-scale IT architecture exciting, but it also presents one of the biggest dangers. It's far too easy to become lost in this complexity and have an interesting time explor-ing it without ever producing tangible results. Such instances are the source of the stereotype that EA resides in the ivory tower and delivers little value. EA teams therefore need to have a clearly articulated path to value: any effort that is made needs to be paid back by providing value to the organization.

Another danger lies in the long feedback cycles. Judging whether someone performs good EA takes even longer than judging good application architecture. Even though the digital world forces shorter cycles, many EA plans still span three to five years. Thus, enterprise architecture can become a hiding ground for wanna-be cartographers. That's why enterprise architects *need to show impact* (Chapter 5).

FOOLS WITH TOOLS

Some enterprise architects associate themselves closely with a specific EA tool that captures the diverse aspects of the enterprise landscape. These tools allow structured mapping from business processes and capabilities, ideally produced by the business architects, to IT assets such as applications and servers.

 Make sure that your tools work for you, not the other way around!

Done well, such tools can be the structured repository that builds the bridge between business and IT architecture. Done poorly, they become a never-ending discovery and documentation process that produces a deliverable that's *missing an emphasis* (Chapter 21) and is outdated by the time it's published. Needless to say, such a deliverable provides little value.

Visit All Floors

My definition of EA also implies that some IT architects, who aren't enterprise architects, work at enterprise scope. These are largely the folks I refer to in this book. Because they are the technical folks who have learned to *ride the elevator* (Chapter 1) to the upper floors to engage with management and business architects, they are a critical element in any IT transformation.

How is being an "enterprise-scale architect" different from a "normal" IT architect? First, everything is bigger. Many large enterprises are conglomerates of different business units and divisions, each of which can be a multibillion-dollar business and can be engaged in a different business model. As things get bigger, you will also find more legacy: businesses grow over time or through acquisitions, both of which breed legacy. This legacy isn't constrained to systems, but also to people's mindsets and ways of working. Enterprise-scale architects must therefore be able to *navigate organizations* (Chapter 34) and complex political situations.

Performing true EA is as complex and as valuable as fixing a Java concurrency bug. There's enormous complexity at all levels, but the good news is that you can use similar patterns of thinking at the different levels. For example, software architects need to balance their system's granularity and interdependencies: a giant monolith is rather inflexible, whereas a thousand tiny services will be difficult to manage and can incur significant communication overhead. The exact same considerations apply to business architecture when considering the size of divisions and product lines. Lastly, EA also faces the same trade-offs when having to decide which systems should be centralized, which simplifies governance but can also stifle local flexibility. Architecture, if taken seriously, provides significant value at all levels.

Enterprises resemble a fractal structure: the more you zoom in or out, the more things look similar. The short film *Powers of 10*, produced in 1977 by Charles and Ray Eames for IBM, illustrates this beautifully: the film zooms out from a picnic in Chicago by one order of magnitude every 10 seconds until it reaches 10^{24}, showing a sea of galaxies. Subsequently, it zooms in until at 10^{-18} it shows the realm of *quarks*. Interestingly, the two views don't look all that different.

5

An Architect Stands on Three Legs

A Three-Legged Stool Does Not Wobble

A three-legged stool does not wobble

What do IT architects do? You could say that they are the people who make IT architecture, but that leaves you with having to define what architecture is, which we won't do until Part II. More interesting yet, what sets a *good* architecture apart from an average one? And what does an architect become after many successful years? A *penthouse resident* (Chapter 1)? Hopefully not! A chief technology officer (CTO)? Not a bad choice. Or do they remain a (more senior) architect? That's what famous building architects do, after all.

It's time to have a look at the progression of architects.

Skill, Impact, Leadership

When asked to characterize the seniority of an architect, I apply a simple framework: a successful architect must stand on three "legs":

Skill

> The foundation for practicing architects. It requires knowledge and the ability to apply it to solve real problems.

Impact

> The measure of how well an architect applies his or her skill to benefit the company.

Leadership

> Determines whether an architect advances the state of the practice.

This nomenclature maps well to other professional fields that rely on highly trained and experienced individuals. For example, in the medical field after studying and acquiring skill, doctors practice and treat patients before they go on to publish in medical journals and pass their learnings on to the next generation of doctors. The legal field works similarly.

Let's have a brief look at each "leg."

SKILL

Knowledge is like having a drawer chest full of tools. Skill implies knowing when to open which drawer and which tool to use.

Skill is the ability to apply relevant knowledge which can relate to specific technologies (such as Docker) or architectures (such as microservices architectures). Such knowledge can usually be acquired by taking a course, reading a book, or perusing online material. Most (but not all) professional certifications focus on verifying knowledge, partly because it's easily mapped to a set of multiple choice questions. Skill brings this knowledge to life by successfully applying it to specific problems. For example, defining the right domain boundaries and service granularity for a complex microservices architecture is a skill. Knowledge is like having a drawer chest full of tools. Skill implies knowing when to open which drawer and which tool to use.

IMPACT

Impact is measured by the benefit achieved for the business, usually in form of additional revenue or reduced cost. Faster times to market or the ability to incorporate unforeseen requirements late in the product cycle also positively affect revenue and therefore count as impact. Focusing on impact is a good exercise for architects to not drift off into PowerPoint-land. As I converse with colleagues about what distinguishes a great architect, we often identify *rational and disciplined decision making* (Chapter 6) as a key factor in translating skill into impact. This doesn't mean that just being a good decision maker makes you a good architect. You still need to know your stuff.

LEADERSHIP

The leadership leg acknowledges that experienced architects do more than make architecture. Mentoring junior architects can save a new generation of architects many years of learning by doing. Senior architects should also further the state of the field as a whole; for example, by sharing what they've learned or mental models they've developed. Such sharing can be done via numerous channels, including academic publications, magazine articles, teaching at university, teaching professional courses, speaking at conferences, or blogging.

 When someone with the title "senior architect" proposes to meet me, I tend to do a quick internet search for their name before I reply. If nothing much comes up, I have doubts as to how "senior" they are. It will also make it more difficult for them to get my time.

A Chair Can't Stand on Two Legs

Just as a stool cannot stand on two legs, it's important to appreciate the balance between the three aspects. Skill without impact is where new architects start out as students or apprentices. But soon it is time to get out into the world and make an impact—architects who don't make an impact don't have a place in a for-profit business.

Impact without leadership is a typical place for architects who are deeply ingrained in projects but "don't get out much." Such architects will plateau at an intermediate level, which is bad for them and their employer. The architects will likely hit a glass ceiling in their career because they won't be able to see beyond their current environment. Likewise, such an architect won't lead the company to much-needed innovative or transformative solutions, ultimately limiting their impact.

Many companies are penny-wise and pound-foolish by not placing sufficient emphasis on nurturing their architects. They fear that any distraction from daily project work will be unproductive. However, they miss out on growing world-class architects.

Mature companies, in contrast, go as far as formalizing the aspect of leadership as "give back": for example, IBM distinguished engineers and fellows are expected to demonstrate giving back to the community both internally (e.g., via mentoring) and externally (e.g., via conference presentations or publications).

Lastly, leadership without (prior) impact lacks foundation and might be a warning signal that an architect has become an ivory tower resident with a weak link to reality. This undesirable effect can also occur when the impact stage of an architect lies many years or even decades back: the architect might preach methods or insights that are no longer applicable to current technologies. Although some insights are timeless, others age with technology: putting as much logic as possible into the database as stored procedures because it speeds up processing is no longer a wise approach as databases often turn out to be the bottleneck in modern web-scale architectures. The same is true for architectures that rely on nightly batch cycles. Modern 24/7 real-time processing doesn't know any nighttime.

The Virtuous Cycle

But there's more to the three facets of being a good architect: each element contributes back to the other, as shown in Figure 5-1.

As an architect applies their skill to generate impact, they also learn what skills to prioritize to maximize that impact. Most likely you learned a lot of things that don't easily translate into daily life in corporate IT—the *Ackerman function* (Chapter 39) is one of my favorites. Given the rate of innovation in our field, being able to prioritize your learning time is a major asset. So, there's a symbiotic relationship between building up skill and applying it.

Figure 5-1. An architect's virtuous cycle

 Often, the best way to learn something is to apply it to a real-world problem. That's why my house is full of home automation. It's not that I really need all things to be automated; most of these were learning projects.

Exercising leadership further amplifies an architect's impact: 10 well-mentored junior architects will surely generate more impact than one senior architect. As architects, we know that scaling vertically (getting smarter) works only up to a certain level and can lead to a single point of failure (you!). Therefore, you need to *scale horizontally* (Chapter 30) by deploying your knowledge to multiple architects. The scarcity of good architects makes this step more important than ever.

Interestingly, though, mentoring not only benefits the mentee, but also the mentor. The old saying that to really understand something you need to teach it to someone else is most true for architecture. Likewise, *giving a talk or writing a paper* (Chapter 18) requires you to sharpen your thoughts, which often leads to renewed insight. Also, in a fast-moving world, mentors can receive *reverse mentoring*[1] about new technologies or approaches, which can often help *offload existing assumptions that no longer hold true* (Chapter 26).

Authoring books and sharing openly has given me access to the most amazing communities and has allowed me to have much more impact.

Lastly, sharing openly and demonstrating thought leadership offers another huge benefit: it can give you access to a powerful community of other thought leaders, which in turn makes you a better architect. Most tight-knit communities share certain expectations for their members. While usually not spelled out, they typically involve giving back to the community in the form of conference talks, authoring books or blog posts, or contributing to open source projects.

You Spin Me Right Round...

Experienced architects will correctly interpret this 1980s reference (others can resort to Wikipedia[2]) to mean that an architect doesn't complete the virtuous cycle just once. This is partly driven by ever-changing technologies and architectural styles. A person might already be a thought leader in relational databases, but they might need to acquire new skills in NoSQL databases. The second time around, acquiring skill is usually significantly faster because you can build on what you already know. After a sufficient number of cycles, we might in fact experience what the curmudgeons always knew: that there is really not much new in software architecture and that we've seen it all before.

Another reason to repeat the cycle is that the next time, our understanding can be at a much deeper level. The first time around, we might have learned how to do things, but only after the second time might we understand *why*. For example, it's likely no misrepresentation that writing *Enterprise Integration Patterns*[3] is a form of thought leadership. Still, some of the elements such as the pattern icons or the decision trees and tables in the chapter introductions were more accidental than based on deep insight. It's only now in hindsight that we

---

1 Jennifer Jordan and Michael Sorell, "Why Reverse Mentoring Works and How to Do It Right," *Harvard Business Review*, Oct. 3, 2019, *https://oreil.ly/bjAET*.

2 Wikipedia, "You Spin Me Round (Like a Record)," *https://oreil.ly/fDcRP*.

3 Gregor Hohpe and Bobby Woolf, *Enterprise Integration Patterns: Designing, Building, and Deploying Messaging Solutions* (Boston, MA: Addison-Wesley, 2003).

understand them as instances of a visual pattern language or pattern-aided decision approaches. Thus, it's often worthwhile to make another cycle.

Architect as Last Stop?

Even though architects have one of the most exciting jobs, some people might be sad to see that being an architect implies that you'll likely remain one for most of your career. I am not so worried about that. First, this puts you in a good peer group of CEOs, presidents, doctors, lawyers, and other high-end professionals. Second, in technically minded organizations, software engineers should feel the same: your next career step should be to remain a software engineer, except a senior one, or *staff engineer* or perhaps a *principal engineer*.

The goal is, therefore, to detach the job title of *software engineer* or *IT architect* from a specific seniority level.

 At many digital organizations the software engineer career ladder reaches all the way to the senior vice president level, with commensurate standing and compensation.

Some organizations even include a *chief engineer*, which, if you think about it, might be a better title than chief architect. Personally, I prefer to get better at what I like doing than trying to chase something else just for the title. Keep architecting!

6

Making Decisions

Deciding Not to Decide Is a Decision

(IT) Life is full of choices

You buy a lottery ticket and win. What a fantastic decision! You cross the road at night, on red, on a busy street, slightly intoxicated, and with your eyes closed, and arrive safely on the other side. Also a good decision? Doesn't sound like it. But what's the difference? Both decisions had positive outcomes. In the latter case, though, we judge by the risk involved while in the former we focus on the outcome, ignoring the ticket price and the (usually low) odds of winning. However, you can't judge a decision by the outcome alone, simply because you didn't know the outcome when you made the decision.

Here's another exercise: in front of you is a very large jar. It contains 1,000,000 pills. They all look the same, are all tasteless, and benign—except one, which will kill you instantly and painlessly. How much money does someone have to pay you to take a pill from this jar? Most people will answer 1 million dollars, 10 million dollars, or straight-out refuse. However, the same people are quite willing to cross the road on a red light (with their eyes open), which carries the same risk as swallowing a couple of pills. It'd be difficult to argue that the 30 seconds you saved by crossing on red would have earned you the equivalent of a few million dollars.

Humans are terrible decision makers, especially when small probabilities and grave outcomes like death are involved. Kahneman's book *Thinking, Fast and Slow*[1] shows so many examples of how our brain can be tricked, it can make you wonder how humanity could get this far despite being such terrible decision makers. I guess we had a lot of tries.

Making decisions is a critical part of an enterprise-scale architect's job. Being a good architect therefore warrants a conscious effort to becoming a better decision maker.

The Law of Small Numbers

Contrived examples make erratic or illogical behavior quite apparent. But when faced with complex business decisions, poor decision-making discipline often isn't as obvious.

 I attended weekly operations meetings that labeled weeks "good" or "bad" based on the number of critical infrastructure outages. I relabeled those weeks as "lucky" because lowering the number and severity of incidents in the long run is the real metric to observe.

Hoping for a week with fewer outages is the corporate IT equivalent of the (flawed) roulette strategy of "after five times black it's gotta be red!" My shocker version of highlighting such flawed thinking consists of a (fictitious) sequence of events during Russian Roulette: "click—I am a genius!—boom." Kahneman calls this "The law of small numbers"; people tend to jump to conclusions based on sample sizes that are way too small to be significant. For example, zero outages in a week are no cause for celebration in a large enterprise.

---

1 Daniel Kahneman, *Thinking, Fast and Slow* (New York: Farrar, Straus and Giroux, 2013).

Google's mobile ads team used rigid metrics for A/B testing experiments that affected ad appearance or selection. The dashboard included metrics to check click-through rates (more clicks = more money) but also to understand whether ads distract from the search results (users come for search, not ads). Each metric's confidence interval represented the range that 95% of sample sets would randomly fall into. If your experiment's improvement landed inside the confidence interval, you'd need to extend the experiment to get valid data before implementing the suggested change (for normal distributions, the confidence interval narrows with the square root of the number of sample points).

Alas, not all data leads to better decisions. When selecting a product, IT often compiles extensive requirement lists that are summed up into scores. However, when you pick the "winner" with a score of 82.1 over the "loser" with 79.8, it would be challenging to prove the statistical significance of this decision.

Still, numeric scores might be better than *traffic light* comparison tables that rate each attribute as "green," "yellow," or "red." A product might get "green" for allowing time travel but "red" for requiring planned downtime. Although this might make it look roughly equivalent to one with the opposite properties, I know which one I'd prefer.

 Traditional IT organizations often reverse engineer score charts from a specific outcome so that they have data to back up their preference.

Sadly, such comparison charts are reverse engineered from a preferred outcome. Others are designed to protect the status quo by demanding quirks only present in existing products.

 I have seen IT requirements analogous to demanding that a new car must rattle at 60 mph and have a squeaky door so that it can appropriately replace the existing one.

Bias

Kahneman's book lists many ways in which our thinking is biased. For example, *confirmation bias* describes our tendency to interpret data in such a way that it supports our own hypotheses. The Google Ad dashboard was designed to overcome this bias.

Another well-known bias is *prospect theory*: when faced with an opportunity, people tend to favor a smaller but guaranteed gain over the uncertain chance for a larger one: "A sparrow in the hand is better than the pigeon on the roof." When it comes to taking a loss, however, people are likely to take a (long) shot at avoiding the penalty over coughing up a smaller amount for sure. We tend to "feel lucky" when we can hope to escape a negative event, an effect called *loss aversion*.

 You have likely seen project managers avoid the certain loss in short-term velocity for performing a major refactoring because the payoff in system stability or sustained velocity is uncertain.

The following scenario shows how loss aversion tricks us into making irrational decisions. When you offer someone a coin toss that makes them pay $100 on heads but gives them $120 on tails, the expected return of taking the gamble is $10 (0.5 × –$100 + 0.5 × $120)—easy money. However, most people will kindly decline due to their loss aversion. Losing $100 to them feels worse than the chance to gain $120. Most people will only accept the offer when the payout is between $150 and $200.

Priming

Another phenomenon, *priming*, can influence decisions based on recent data we received. In the extreme case, when faced with enormous uncertainty, it can make us pick a number we recently heard or saw even if it's totally unrelated. This effect plays a role when many people answer one million dollars when faced with the one-million-pills example.

Priming is routinely used in retail scenarios. When you go to buy a piece of clothing—let's say a sweater—the store clerk is almost guaranteed to first show you something expensive, even outside your price range. A sweater for $399? It's made from cashmere and feels very soft and comfortable; tempting, but it's simply too expensive. But the almost-as-nice sweater for $199 seems a reasonable compromise, and you'll happily buy it. Next door, decent sweaters can be had for $59. You fell victim to priming, setting a context that influences your decision. Priming can even make you walk more slowly if your mindset is on elderly people.[2]

---

2 John A. Bargh, Mark Chen, and Lara Burrows, "Automaticity of Social Behavior," *Journal of Personality and Social Psychology* 71, no. 2 (Aug. 1996): 230-244.

William Poundstone's book *Priceless: The Myth of Fair Value*[3] shows that products that no one actually buys can shift purchasing behavior significantly, thanks to priming. When presented with a choice between a "premium" beer for $2.60 and a "bargain" one for $1.80, about two thirds of test subjects (students) chose the premium beer. Adding a third, "super-premium" beer for a whopping $3.40 shifted student's desire so that 90% ordered the premium beer and 10% the super-premium.

If we are such horrible decision makers, what can we do to get better at it? Understanding these pitfalls can help you avoid or at least compensate for them. However, mathematics can also help.

Micromort

One of the most interesting classes that I took at Stanford was Ron Howard's class on decision analysis, which was entertaining, thought-provoking, and challenging. Decision analysis helps us think rationally about our earlier jar-with-pills example. A one-in-one-million chance of dying is called one *micromort*. Taking one pill from the jar amounts to being exposed to exactly one micromort. The amount you are willing to pay to avoid this risk is called your *micromort value*. Micromorts help us reason about decisions with small probabilities but very serious outcomes, such as deciding whether to undergo surgery that eliminates lifelong pain but fails with a 1% probability, resulting in immediate death.

To calibrate the micromort value, it helps to consider the risks of different life activities: a day of skiing clocks in at between one and nine micromorts, whereas motor vehicle accidents amount to about 0.5 per day. So a ski trip can run you some five micromorts—the same as swallowing five pills. Is it worth it? You'd need to compare the enjoyment value you derive from skiing against the trip's cash expense plus the "cost" of the micromort risk you are taking.

So how much should you demand to take one pill? Most people's micromort value lies between $1 and $20. Assuming a prototypical value of $10, the ski trip that might cost you $100 in gas and lift tickets costs you an extra $50 in risk of death. You should therefore decide whether a day in the mountains is worth $150 to you. This also shows why a micromort value of $1,000,000 makes little sense: you'd hardly be willing to pay $5,000,100 for a one-day ski trip unless you are

---

3 William Poundstone, *Priceless: The Myth of Fair Value* (New York: Hill and Wang, 2011).

filthy rich! Lastly, the model helps you judge whether buying a helmet for $100 is a worthwhile investment for you if it reduces the risk of death in half.

The micromort value isn't the same for all people. It goes up with income (or rather, consumption) and goes down with age. This is to be expected as the monetary value you assign to your remaining life increases with your income. A wealthy person should easily decide to buy a $100 helmet, whereas a person who is struggling to make ends meet is more likely to accept the risk. As you age, the likelihood of death from natural causes unstoppably increases until it reaches about 100,000 micromorts annually, or almost 300 per day, by the age of 80. At that point, the value derived from buying a risk reduction of two micromorts is rather small.

Luckily, Ron Howard and Ali Abbas have captured the mathematics of decision making in their book *Foundations of Decision Analysis*.[4] The book isn't cheap, though, listing at around $200. Should you buy a book for $200 that could make you a better decision maker? Think about it...

Model Thinking

Decision models can go a long way toward making us better decision makers. Thanks to George Box, it's well known that "all models are wrong, but some are useful."[5] So, don't dismiss a model just because it makes simplifying assumptions. It's likely to help you make a much better decision than your gut. The best overview of models and their application I have come across is Scott Page's Coursera course on Model Thinking (*https://oreil.ly/qKWp3*). He also recently published the content in his book *The Model Thinker*.[6]

Decision trees are very simple models that help us make more rational decisions (see Figure 6-1). Suppose that you want to buy a car, but there's a 40% chance that the dealer will offer a $1,000 cash-back promotion starting next month. You need a car now, so if you defer the purchase, you'll need to rent a car for $500 for the coming month, even if the rebate doesn't come through. What should you do? If you buy now, you'll pay the list price, which we calibrate to $0 for simplicity's sake. If you rent first, you are down by $500 with a 40% chance

---

4 Ronald A. Howard and Ali E. Abbas, *Foundations of Decision Analysis* (Prentice Hall, 2015).

5 George Box, "Science and Statistics," *Journal of the American Statistical Association* (1976).

6 Scott E. Page, *The Model Thinker: What You Need to Know to Make Data Work for You* (New York: Basic Books, 2018).

to gain $1,000, so the expected value is 0.4 × $1,000 − $500 = −$100, lower than the list price. You should buy the car now.

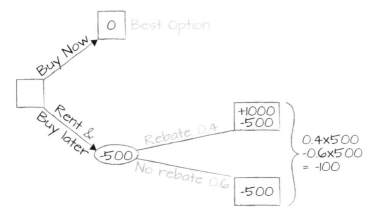

Figure 6-1. A decision tree helps you decide whether to buy a car now

Let's make the scenario a bit more interesting: assume that an insider offers to tell you whether the cash-back promotion happens next month or not. He asks $150 for this information. Should you buy it? Having this information, your new decision tree (see Figure 6-2) would allow you to buy now if you're told that there's no cash back (in 60% of cases) and to buy later if there is (in 40% of cases). Having information up front increases the expected value to 0.6 × 0 + 0.4 × (1,000 − 500) = $200. As your current best scenario (i.e., buying now) yielded a value of $0, it's worth paying $150 for the extra information.

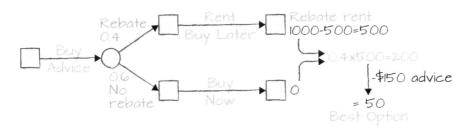

Figure 6-2. Should you pay someone to tell you whether there will be a rebate?

How do you know that the chance of the cashback is exactly 40%? You don't. But using the model helps you reason in face of uncertainty. You can rerun the model for a 50% likelihood and see whether your decision changes.

IT Decisions

Deadly pills, premium beers, and car dealer rebates—how do we bring our learnings back to IT decision making? Many IT decisions—especially those related to cybersecurity risks or system outages—share similar characteristics of small probability but severe downsides. Therefore, separating likelihood from impact and baselining probabilities can help remove emotion, resulting in more rational decisions. Maybe you even find it useful to define a concept of *microfail* for your systems: a one-in-a-million chance of a catastrophic system failure.

A classic case for decision making is system uptime. Suppose that a single server can achieve 99.5% availability, meaning that 99.5% of the time it will be available to your application's users. This means that over the course of an average month, which has 730 hours, the system can be "down" for 730 / 200 = 3.65 hours. That's not horrible, but also not great. 99.9% is generally considered a good uptime—the allowed downtime would be less than roughly 45 minutes per month. However, to achieve this, you generally need redundant hardware, meaning that you need a second set of servers ready to go in case your primary server fails. This will double your hardware cost, often require additional failover machinery, and in some cases also double your software license cost. Are three hours downtime less per month worth double the cost? Sounds like a perfect case for decision analysis!

Avoiding Decisions

With all this science behind decision making, what's the best decision? It's the one that you don't need to take! That's what Martin Fowler indicated when he observed that "one of an architect's most important tasks is to eliminate irreversibility in software designs."[7] Those are the decisions that don't need to be made or can be made quickly because they can be *easily changed later thanks to you having built-in options* (Chapter 9). In a well-designed software system, decisions aren't as final as when taking deadly pills from a jar.

---

7 Martin Fowler, "Who Needs an Architect?," *IEEE Software*, July/August 2003, *https://oreil.ly/djeuH*.

Question Everything

Wer Nicht Fragt, Bleibt Dumm!

The architect riddler

It's a common misconception that chief architects know everything better than "normal" architects—why else would they be the "chief"? Such thinking is actually pretty far from the truth. Hence, I often introduce myself as a person who knows the right questions to ask. Wrangling one more reference from the movie *The Matrix*, visiting the chief architect is a bit like visiting the Oracle: you won't get a straight answer, but you will hear what you need to hear.

Five Whys

Asking questions isn't a new technique and has been widely publicized in the "five whys" approach devised by Sakichi Toyoda as part of the Toyota Production System (*https://oreil.ly/h_aFt*). It's a technique to get to the root cause of an issue by repeatedly asking why something happened. If your car doesn't start, you should keep asking "why" to find out the starter doesn't turn because the battery is dead because you left the lights on because the beeper that warns you of parking with your lights on didn't sound because of an electronics problem. So, before you jump-start the car, you should fix the electronics to keep the problem from happening again. In Japanese the method is called *naze-naze-bunseki* (なぜなぜ分析), which roughly translates into "why, why analysis." I therefore consider the "five whys" more of a guideline to not give up too early—you surely didn't cheat if you identified the actual root cause with just four whys.

The technique can be quite useful but requires discipline because people can be tempted to inject their own preferred solutions or assumptions into their answers. I have seen people conducting root-cause analysis on production outages repeatedly answer the second or third question with "because we don't have sufficient monitoring" and the next one with "because we don't have enough budget." The equivalent answer from the car example would be "because the car is old." That's not root-cause analysis but opportunism or *excuse-ism*, a word that made it into the Urban Dictionary (*https://oreil.ly/CVz6U*), but not yet into *Merriam-Webster*.

Repeatedly asking questions can annoy people a bit, so it's good to have the reference to the Toyota Production System handy to highlight that this is a widely adopted and useful technique and not you just being difficult. It's also helpful to remind your counterparts that you are not challenging their work or competence, but that your job requires you to understand systems and problems in detail so that you can spot potential gaps or misalignments.

Whys Reveal Decisions and Assumptions

When conducting architecture reviews, "why" is a useful question because it helps *draw attention to the decisions* (Chapter 8) that were made as well as the assumptions and principles that led to those decisions. Too often, results are presented as "god-given" facts that "fell from the sky" or wherever you believe the all-deciding divine creator (the *real* chief architect!) resides. Uncovering the assumptions that led to a decision can provide much insight and increase the value of an architecture review. An architecture review is not only looking to validate the results but also the thinking and decisions behind it all. To emphasize this fact, one should request an architecture decision record[1] from any team submitting an architecture for review.

Unstated assumptions can be the root of much evil if the environment has changed since the assumptions were made. For example, traditional IT shops often write elaborate graphical configuration tools that could be replaced with a few lines of code and a standard software development tool chain. Their decisions are based on the assumption that writing code is slow and error prone, which no longer holds universally true as we learn once we overcome our *fear of code* (Chapter 11). If you want to change the behavior of the organization, you often need to *identify and overcome outdated assumptions first* (Chapter 26).

Coming back to *The Matrix*, the explanation given by the Oracle—"You didn't come here to make the choice, you've already made it. You're here to try to understand *why* you made it"—could make a somewhat dramatic but very appropriate opening to an architecture review.

A Workshop for Every Question

A clear and present danger of asking questions in large organizations lies in the fact that people often don't know, can't express, or are unwilling to give the answer. Their counterproposal is usually to hold a meeting, most likely a very long one, which is labeled as "workshop," with the purported goal of sharing and documenting the answer. In the actual workshop, though, it frequently turns out that the answer is unknown, leaving you with the job of answering your own questions. The team might also bring external support to defend against you asking too many undesired questions.

 Asking questions in traditional organizations might not get you insights but defensiveness to cover up the lack of decision discipline.

Soon, your calendar will be full of workshop invitations, allowing teams to blame you for being the bottleneck that slows their progress because you aren't available for their important meetings. And they aren't even lying! Such organizational behavior is an example of *systems resisting change* (Chapter 10).

---

1 Michael Nygard, "Documenting Architecture Decisions," Relevance, Nov. 15, 2011, *https://oreil.ly/1sniB*.

If your goal is to not just review architecture proposals but also to change the behavior of the organization, you need to take up this challenge and change the system. For example, you can redefine the expectations for architecture documentation and obtain management buy-in for doing so; for example, to increase transparency. If satisfactory documentation isn't produced before the meeting, the workshop must be canceled. If teams are unable to produce such documentation, you can offer them architects who perform this task on a project basis. The actual workshop becomes more effective when you moderate and work off a list of concrete questions. Cutting the scheduled time in half brings additional focus.

On the upside, running architecture documentation workshops and *sketching bank robbers* (Chapter 24) can give you an invaluable set of system documentation that you can later use as a reference. This effort requires *good writing skills* (Chapter 18) and adequate staffing, which you can obtain only by taking the *architect elevator* (Chapter 1) to the upper floors and clearly articulating the value of documenting system architectures. For example, such documents could allow faster staff ramp-up, reveal architectural inconsistencies, and allow rational, fact-based decision making, which in turn supports evolution toward a harmonized IT landscape. In top-down organizations, sometimes you need to lob things to the top so they can trickle back down.

No Free Pass

Occasionally, teams that are sent into architecture review would like to just obtain a "rubber stamp" for what they have done, and they aren't excited about you asking any questions at all. These are often the same candidates who answer the "why" questions with "because we have no time" after they purposefully waited until the very last minute. For such cases, I have a stated principle of, "You can avoid my review, but you cannot get a free pass." If management decides that no architecture review is needed because it doesn't see architecture as a first-class citizen, I'd rather avoid the review altogether than hold a show trial.

I see this as in line with my professional reputation: be tough but fair and make tasty hamburgers out of holy cows. My boss once summarized this in a nice compliment: she stated that she likes to have the architecture team involved because, "we have nothing to sell, no one can fool us, and we take the time to explain things well." This would make a nice mandate for any architecture team.

If you're wondering about the meaning of the German subtitle of this chapter, it's from the title song of the German version of *Sesame Street*, which rhymes nicely and goes "*Wieso, weshalb, warum, wer nicht fragt, bleibt dumm!*," which literally translates into "why? who doesn't ask, remains stupid!" Don't remain stupid!

PART II

Architecture

Defining architecture isn't an easy task—there appear to be almost as many definitions of IT architecture as there are practicing architects.

Beyond Software Architecture

Most software architecture definitions cite a system's elements and components plus their interrelationships. In my view, this covers only one aspect of architecture. First, IT architecture is much more than software architecture: unless you outsourced all your IT infrastructure into the public cloud, you need to architect networks, datacenters, computing infrastructure, storage, and much more. And even if you did, you still need a deployment architecture, a data architecture, and a security architecture. Second, defining which "components" you are focusing on constitutes a significant aspect of architecture.

 A manager once stated that he can't understand the many network issues despite all the network stuff "being there." His view was a physical one: Ethernet cables plugged into servers and switches. The complexity of network architecture, however, lies in virtual network segregation, routing, address translation, and much more. Different stakeholders see different parts of the architecture.

Three Kinds of Architecture

When speaking about architecture, people routinely refer to three quite different concepts, all of which relate to IT but are very different in nature:

1. A system's architecture, defined by its structure, as in "*microservices architecture*"

2. The act of defining a system's structure, as in "the *architecture committee*"

3. A team that is involved in defining architecture, as in "we're setting up *enterprise architecture*"

So, while every system has an architecture, not every organization has an architecture (unit) and even if it does, they may not get much architecture done.

To make things a little less confusing, when I mention "architecture," I generally refer to a system's properties. For organizational aspects, I speak about "architects"—it's based on humans after all.

There Always Is an Architecture

When speaking about a system's architecture, it's worth pointing out that all systems have one. You can't build anything out of several pieces that doesn't have any structure. Even clumping everything together into a giant monolith is an architecture decision. Once we come to this realization, statements like "we don't have time for architecture" aren't particularly meaningful. It's simply a matter of whether you consciously choose your architecture or whether you let it happen to you. History has shown that the latter approach invariably leads to the infamous *Big Ball of Mud*[1] architecture, also referred to as *shantytown*. Although that architecture does allow for rapid implementation without central planning or specialized skills, it also lacks critical infrastructure and doesn't make for a great living environment. Fatalism isn't a great enterprise architecture strategy, so I suggest you pick your architecture.

The Value of Architecture

Because there always is an architecture, an organization should be clear on what it expects from setting up an architecture function. Setting up an architecture team and then not letting it do its job—for example, by routinely subjecting architecture decisions to management decisions—is actually worse than intentionally letting things drift into a Big Ball of Mud: you pretend to define your architecture, but in reality you don't. Worse yet, good architects don't want to be in a place where architecture is seen as a form of corporate entertainment. If you don't take architecture seriously, you won't be able to attract and retain serious architects.

---

1 Brian Foote and Joseph Yoder, "Big Ball of Mud," Laputan.org, Nov. 21, 2012, *http://www.laputan.org/mud*.

IT management often believes that "architecture" is a long-term investment that will only pay off far into the future. Although this is true for some aspects—for example, managed system evolution over time—architecture can also pay off in the short-term, such as when you can accommodate a customer requirement late in the development cycle, when you gain leverage in vendor negotiations because you avoided lock-in, or when you can easily migrate your systems to a new datacenter location. Good architecture can also make a team more productive by allowing concurrent development and testing of components. Generally, good architecture buys you flexibility. In a rapidly changing world, this seems like a smart investment.

Principles Drive Decisions

Architecture is a matter of trade-offs: there rarely is one single "best" architecture. For example, the option to be able to move your application to the cloud likely increased cost and complexity. Architects therefore must take the context into consideration when making architectural decisions, because that context will help them weigh the trade-offs against one another.

Architects should also strive for conceptual integrity, that is, uniformity across system designs. This is best accomplished by selecting a well-defined set of architecture principles that are consistently applied to architectural decisions. Deriving these principles from a declared architecture strategy assures that the decisions support the strategy.

Vertical Cohesion

A good architecture is not only consistent across systems but also considers all layers of a software and hardware stack. Investigating new types of scale-out compute hardware or software-defined networks is useful, but if all your applications are inflexible monoliths with hardcoded IP addresses, you gain little. Architects therefore not only need to *ride the elevator* (Chapter 1) across the organization but also up and down the technology stack.

Vertical cohesion doesn't stop at technology, but also needs to consider the business architecture. For example, many IT decisions can't be made by IT alone but require input from the business and an understanding of the business structure and context.

Architecting the Real World

The real world is full of architectures, not just building architectures but also cities, corporate organizations, or political systems. The real world must deal with many of the same issues faced by large enterprises: lack of central governance, difficult to reverse decisions, enormous complexity, constant evolution, slow feedback cycles. That's why architects should walk through the world with open eyes, always looking to learn from the architectures they encounter.

ARCHITECTURE IN THE ENTERPRISE

When defining architecture in large organizations, architects need to know a lot more than how to draw UML diagrams. They need to be able to do the following, as well:

Chapter 8, Is This Architecture?
Distinguish whether something is architecture in the first place.

Chapter 9, Architecture Is Selling Options
Be able to sell options to the business.

Chapter 10, Every System Is Perfect...
Tackle complexity by thinking in systems.

Chapter 11, Code Fear Not!
Know that configuration isn't better than coding.

Chapter 12, If You Never Kill Anything, You Will Live Among Zombies
Hunt zombies so that they don't have their brain eaten.

Chapter 13, Never Send a Human to Do a Machine's Job
Automate everything and make the rest self-service.

Chapter 14, If Software Eats the World, Better Use Version Control!
Think like software developers as everything becomes software defined.

Chapter 15, A4 Paper Doesn't Stifle Creativity
Build platforms and set standards that don't stifle creativity.

Chapter 16, The IT World Is Flat
Navigate their IT landscape with an undistorted world map.

Chapter 17, Your Coffee Shop Doesn't Use Two-Phase Commit
Gain architecture insights from waiting in line at the coffee shop.

8

Is This Architecture?

Look for Decisions!

Would you pay an architect for this?

Part of my job as chief architect is to review and approve system architectures. When I ask teams to show me "their architecture," I frequently don't consider what I receive to be an architecture document. Their counter-question of "what do you expect?" isn't so easy for me to answer: despite many formal definitions, it isn't immediately clear what architecture is or whether a document really depicts an architecture. Too often we have to fall back to the "I know it when I see it" test famously applied by a US Supreme Court judge to obscene material.[1] We'd hope that identifying architecture is a more noble task than identifying

---

1 Wikipedia, "*Jacobellis v. Ohio*," Sept. 7, 2019, *https://oreil.ly/EwvpU*.

obscene material, so let's try a little harder. I am not a big believer in all-encompassing definitions but prefer to use lists of defining characteristics or tests that can be applied. One of my favorite tests for architecture documentation is whether it contains any nontrivial decisions and the rationale behind them.

Defining Software Architecture

So many attempts at defining *software architecture* have been made that the Software Engineering Institute (SEI) maintains a reference page (*https://oreil.ly/ 48Opd*) of these definitions.

Among the most widely used is this definition from Garlan and Perry, from 1995:

> *The structure of the components of a system, their interrelationships, and principles and guidelines governing their design and evolution over time.*

In 2000 the ANSI/IEEE Std 1471 chose the following definition (adopted as ISO/IEC 42010 in 2007):

> *The fundamental organization of a system, embodied in its components, their relationships to each other and the environment, and the principles governing its design and evolution.*

The Open Group adopted a variation thereof for TOGAF:

> *The structure of the components, their interrelationships, and principles and guidelines governing their design and evolution over time.*

One of my personal favorites is from Desmond D'Souza and Alan Cameron Wills's book on the Catalysis method:[2]

> *The set of design decisions about any system that keeps its implementors and maintainers from exercising needless creativity.*

The key point here isn't that architecture should dampen all creativity, but *needless* creativity, of which I witness ample amounts. It also highlights the importance of *making decisions* (Chapter 6).

---

2 Desmond F. D'Souza and Alan Cameron Wills, *Objects, Components, and Frameworks with UML: The Catalysis Approach* (Boston: Addison-Wesley Professional, 1998).

Architectural Decisions

These well-thought-out definitions aren't easy to work with, however, when someone walks up with a PowerPoint slide showing boxes and *lines* (Chapter 23), claiming, "This is my system architecture." The first test I tend to apply is whether the documentation contains meaningful decisions. After all, if no decisions needed to be made, why employ an architect and prepare architectural documentation?

Martin Fowler's knack for explaining the essence of things using extremely simple examples motivated me to illustrate the "architectural decision test" with the simplest example I could think of, drawing from the (admittedly limping) analogy to building architecture.

Consider the drawing of a house on the left side of Figure 8-1. It has many of the elements required by the popular definitions of systems architecture: we see the main *components of the system* (door, windows, roof) and their *interrelationships* (door and windows in the wall, roof on the top). We might be a tad thin, though, on *principles governing its design*, but we do notice that we have a single door that reaches the ground and multiple windows, which follows common building principles.

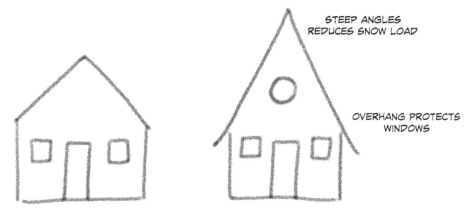

Figure 8-1. Is this architecture?

Yet, to build such a house I wouldn't want to pay an architect. This house is "cookie-cutter," meaning I don't see any nonobvious decisions that an architect would have made. Consequently, I wouldn't consider this architecture.

Let's compare this to the sketch on the right side of the figure. The sketch is equally simple, and the house is almost the same, except for the roof. This house has a steep roof and for a good reason: the house is designed for a cold climate where winters bring extensive snowfall. Snow is quite heavy and can easily overload the roof of the house. A steep roof allows the snow to slide off and be easily removed thanks to gravity, a pretty cheap and widely available resource. Additionally, an overhang prevents the sliding snow from piling up right in front of the windows.

To me, this is architecture: nontrivial decisions have been made and documented. The decisions are driven by the system context; in this case, the climate: it's unlikely that the customer explicitly stated a requirement that the roof not be crushed by snowfall. Additionally, the documentation highlights relevant decisions and omits unnecessary noise.

If you believe these architectural decisions were pretty obvious, let's look at a very different house in Figure 8-2.

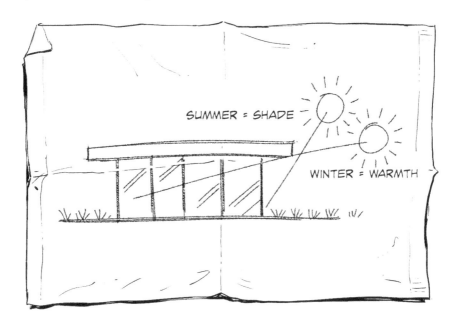

Figure 8-2. Great architecture on a napkin

This house in Figure 8-2 is quite different: the walls are made out of glass. While providing a stellar view, glass walls have the problem that the sun heats up the building, making it feel more like a greenhouse than a residence. The solution? Extending the roof well beyond the glass walls keeps the interior in the shade, especially in summer when the sun is high in the sky. In the winter, when the sun is low on the horizon, the sun reaches through the windows and helps warm the building interior. Again, the architecture is defined by a fairly simple but fundamental decision, documented in an easy-to-understand format that highlights the essence of the decision and the rationale behind it.

Fundamental Decisions Needn't Be Complicated

If you think the idea of building an overhanging roof isn't all that original or significant, try buying one of the first homes to feature such a design; for example, the Case Study House No 22 in Los Angeles by architect Pierre Koenig. It's easily in the league of most recognized residential building in Los Angeles or beyond (aided by Julius Shulman's iconic photograph) and surely isn't for sale. You can tour it, though, if you sign up far in advance. Significant architectural decisions may look obvious in hindsight, but that doesn't diminish their value. No one is perfect, though: UCLA PhD students have measured that the overhang works better on the south-facing facade than west or east.[3]

Fit for Purpose

The simple house example also highlights another important property of architecture: rarely is an architecture simply "good" or "bad." Rather, architecture is fit or unfit for purpose. A house with glass walls and a flat roof might be regarded as great architecture, but probably not in the Swiss Alps where it will collapse after a few winters or suffer from a leaking roof. It also doesn't do much good near the equator where the sun's path on the sky remains fairly constant throughout the year. In those regions, you are better off with thick walls, small windows, and lots of air conditioning.

Assessing the context and identifying implicit constraints or assumptions in proposed designs is an architect's key responsibility. Architects are commonly described as the people dealing with nonfunctional requirements. I generally

Architecture isn't good or bad, it's fit or unfit for a purpose.

---

3 P. La Roche, "The Case Study House Program in Los Angeles: A Case for Sustainability," in *Proc. of Conference on Passive and Low Energy Architecture* (2002).

refer to hidden assumptions as nonrequirements—*requirements that were never explicitly stated* (Part I).

Even the dreaded Big Ball of Mud (*http://www.laputan.org/mud*) can be "fit for purpose"; for example, when you need to make a deadline at all costs and can't care much about what happens afterward. This may not be the context you wish for, but just like houses in some regions have to be earthquake proof, some architectures have to be management proof.

Passing the Test

Having stretched the overused building architecture analogy one more time, how do we translate it back to software systems architecture? Systems architecture doesn't need to be something terribly complicated. It must include, however, significant decisions that are well documented and are based on a clear rationale. The word "significant" can be open to some interpretation and depend on the level of sophistication of the organization, but "we separate frontend from backend code" or "we use monitoring" surely have the ring of "my door reaches the ground so people can walk in" or "I put windows in the walls so light can enter."

Instead, when discussing architectures, let's talk about what isn't obvious. For example, "do you use a service layer and why?" (some people may find even this obvious) or "why are you spreading your application across multiple cloud providers?" A good test is whether the chosen option also has downsides—decisions without downsides are unlikely to be meaningful.

All meaningful decisions have downsides.

It's quite amazing how many "architecture documents" don't pass this relatively simple test. I hope our set of house sketches provides a simple and non-threatening way to provide feedback and to motivate architects to better document their designs and decisions.

9

Architecture Is Selling Options

In Uncertain Times It's Good to Have a Few Options

Options on sale

Quite frequently I am being asked about the value of architecture, sometimes out of actual curiosity, and at other times as a (welcome) challenge. Sadly, I also consistently find out just how difficult it can be to answer this seemingly harmless question in a succinct and convincing manner for a nontechnical audience. I thus consider having a good answer to this question a valuable skill for any senior architect.

 A colleague once suggested that an architect's key performance indicator (KPI) should be the number of decisions made. While decision making is a defining element of doing architecture, I had a feeling that making as many decisions as possible isn't what drives my profession.

Measuring an architect's contribution by the number of decisions they're making reminded me of trying to measure developers' productivity in lines of code written. That metric is widely known as a bad idea because poor developers tend to write verbose code with lots of duplication, whereas good developers find short and elegant solutions to complex problems. After a little bit of pondering, I remembered one of Martin Fowler's most popular articles that also involves decision making, but from a very different point of view.

Reversing Irreversible Decision Making

Many conventional definitions of software architecture include the notion of making difficult- (or expensive-) to-reverse decisions. Ideally, these decisions would be made early in the project to give the project a direction and avoid "analysis paralysis," the dangerous state in a project when requirements gathering drags on without any code being written. Making critical decisions early comes with a major challenge, though: the beginning of the project is also the time of highest ignorance because little is known about the project as well as the technologies to be used. Therefore, architects are generally expected to draw on their ability to abstract from their past experience to get those decisions "right." Consistent project cost and timeline overruns have hinted, though, that deciding the system structure early in a project is difficult at best, even for an *all-knowing architect* (Chapter 2).

Martin Fowler concluded some time ago that the opposite is actually true: "one of an architect's most important tasks is to eliminate irreversibility in software designs."[1] So, instead of entrusting all crucial decisions to one person, a project can be better off by *minimizing* the number of early and irreversible decisions. For example, choosing a flexible or modular design can localize the scope of a later change and thus minimize the extent of up-front decision making. Now one could posit that deciding on a modular design is a second-degree up-front decision—we'll come back to that point later.

The desire to make decisions up front is frequently driven by the project's surrounding structures and processes as opposed to technical needs. For example, time-consuming budget approval and procurement processes may require teams to make product selections well before development can start. Likewise, enterprise software and hardware vendors have a tendency to push for early

---

1 Fowler, "Who Needs an Architect?"

tooling decisions in order to secure a deal. They might promise unsuspecting IT management spectacular results, including reducing or removing the need for expensive programmers, if only their tool is chosen right from the start.

So if the organization is better off with an architect not making decisions, how do we eloquently articulate this to upper management?

Deferring Decisions with Options

Communicating to upper management becomes easier if you avail yourself of the business's concepts and vocabulary. Along the way you may even discover business concepts that lend themselves to a new way of looking at IT. Financial services present us with just that: options.

Decision making is a common activity in financial services, especially in stock trading. Buying shares in a company requires you to put up cash now in hopes of a future return—somewhat similar to *buying a new car* (Chapter 6), though the future price is unknown. Now, if you could travel into the future and see the stock price one year from now, making a decision would be very easy as long as you can still buy the stock at today's price. Time travel isn't available quite yet, but the example makes clear that being able to defer a decision while fixing the parameters has value. That's intuitive because you'll know more by the time the decision has to be made, allowing you to make a better decision.

 I tend to buy my ski passes on the day of my trip, as I'll have checked for good weather and snow conditions the night before. I choose to forgo a prepurchase discount for the value of being able to defer my decision.

The closest approximation to time travel in financial services is the concept of a financial *option*. An option is defined as "the right, but not the obligation, to execute a financial transaction at fixed parameters in the future." It's a lot simpler to understand with an example:

You may acquire the option to buy a stock for $100 (the "strike price") in a year's time (assuming a European option). After a year passes, it's trivial to decide whether to exercise this option: if the stock price trades higher than $100, you can instantly make money by exercising your option to buy the stock for $100 and selling it at a profit. If the actual stock price is less than $100, you let the option expire, meaning you don't use your right to buy at $100. Coincidentally, this doesn't mean buying the option was a bad decision (see Chapter 6).

An option allows you to defer a decision: instead of deciding to buy or sell a stock today, you can buy the option today and thus acquire the right to make that decision in the future.[2]

Good IT architecture can also offer options. For example, by coding in Java or another language that's widely supported you are offering an option to run that software on different operating systems, deferring that decision until a later date. Luckily, your option won't expire as long as Java keeps being supported on many platforms.

Options Have Value

The financial industry knows quite well that deferring decisions has value, and therefore an option has a price, C. There's a whole market for buying and selling options and other derivatives. Two very smart gentlemen, Fischer Black and Myron Scholes, scored a Nobel prize for computing the value of an option, a formula known as the Black-Scholes formula:[3]

$$C(S, t) = N(d_1)S - N(d_2)Ke^{-r(T-t)}$$

$$d_1 = \frac{1}{\sigma\sqrt{T-t}}\left[\ln\left(\frac{S}{K}\right) + \left(r + \frac{\sigma^2}{2}\right)(T-t)\right]$$

$$d_2 = d_1 - \sigma\sqrt{T-t}$$

There's a lot going on here, but we can see how a few key parameters influence the price. For example, a higher *strike price* (K) reduces the value of the option as we'd expect. We can also see that if the option is valid right now ($T = t$), the option price becomes the current price (S) minus the strike price (K).

So, it's nice to have mathematical proof that options have value: if architects sell options, that means they bring value!

---

2 You can also use options for selling shares, the so-called *put* options. These are commonly used to hedge against major drops in a stock price, essentially acting like an insurance policy for your investment.

3 Wikipedia, "Black–Scholes Model," *https://oreil.ly/2Zcml*.

An Architecture Option: Elasticity

Luckily, IT architects need neither complex formulas nor a Nobel prize. All you need to do is design your system such that it defers decisions. You accomplish that by providing options that can be exercised in the future.

A classic example is server sizing: before deploying an application, traditional IT teams would conduct a lengthy sizing study to calculate the amount of hardware required to run the application. Sadly, infrastructure sizing leads only to one of two possible outcomes: either too large or too small, which either results in wasted money or a poorly performing application. What a great opportunity to defer some decisions!

For this example, the option the architect creates is *horizontal scaling*, allowing compute resources to be added or subtracted at a later time. Clearly, this option has a value: infrastructure can be sized according to the application's actual needs and can grow (or shrink) as required. Also, this option isn't free given that the system has to be designed to be able to scale out; for example, by making application components stateless or by using a distributed database.

Essentially, you're paying for the option with increased complexity. Given that complexity is one of the primary factors slowing down system delivery, it's no small price to pay. Also, to take advantage of the application's scale-out capability, you likely need to deploy the application on an elastic cloud platform, which might lock you into a particular vendor. So, in effect you're paying for one option by giving up another.

 Architecture options are rarely free. For example, you may pay with increased complexity or loss of another option.

Just like financial options, architecture options also allow you to hedge your bets in case you want to limit your downside if a desired outcome doesn't materialize. For example, providing an abstraction from a vendor-specific interface can hedge against the vendor increasing license fees or going out of business.

Strike Prices

Now all the architect can do is offer the option for sale, describing the nature and price of the option. Someone has to decide whether to buy it. As mentioned a moment ago, making an application horizontally scalable or adding a layer of indirection isn't free, so while it might be good architectural practice, decision discipline teaches us to examine whether this option is actually needed.

The financial world sells options with different *strike prices*, which is the price you pay per share when you exercise the option in the future. It's easy to see (and reflected in the Black-Scholes formula) that options with a lower strike price command a higher up-front price: the lower the price to execute the option in the future, the higher your potential gain. It's useful to note that the option still has value even if the strike price is higher than today's price—after all, the price might increase in the future.

The effect translates easily into the earlier IT example: by migrating to a cloud provider we can lower the strike price for horizontal scaling to near zero, thanks to full automation. However, this reduction in strike price isn't free: you'll most likely pay with being locked into this specific provider's APIs, access control, account setup, and machine types. So, the strike price for switching providers will be high.

To reduce the strike price for switching cloud providers, you can build an abstraction layer that allows you to move your applications to any cloud provider by clicking a button. Container platforms make this feasible, but you also need to abstract all your storage, billing, and access control needs. You may also be bound by commercial agreements. So, aiming for a near-zero-cost cloud migration carries a huge up-front development cost: this is an expensive option to buy. Considering the low chance of needing to switch providers, this option might not be worth buying.[4]

 Minimizing the strike price—that is, switching cost from one vendor to another—is often seen as the architectural ideal, but it's rarely the most economical choice.

Alternatively, consciously managing your application's dependencies and deploying in containers might be a better balance. It carries a higher strike price—migrating will still incur some effort—but has a much lower up-front investment. Good architects offer a range of options at different strike prices and cost instead of aiming for a minimum strike price at all cost.

---

4 Gregor Hohpe, "Don't Get Locked Up into Avoiding Lock-in," MartinFowler.com (2019), *https://oreil.ly/jWDAW*.

Uncertainty Increases an Option's Value

Consequently, just as with financial markets, pricing and buying architecture options takes some consideration. There's a second factor, though, that has a major impact on the value of an option: uncertainty. The more uncertain about the future I am, the more value I derive from deferring a decision. For example, the option to scale horizontally isn't that valuable if my application is built for a small and constant number of users. However, if I am building an internet-facing application that could have 100 or 100,000 users, the option becomes much more valuable.

The same is true in the financial world: the Black-Scholes formula contains a critical parameter, σ ("sigma"), which indicates the volatility. You'll see this sigma squared in the numerator of the equation, indicating a strong correlation between volatility and option price.

The business not wanting to be involved in technical decisions leads to suboptimal decision making because IT alone can't judge the value of an option. Instead, it's the architect's job to translate technical options into meaningful choices for the business.

Therefore, architects who put up options for sale need to understand the context and its volatility. Most likely, such input needs to come from the business side and can't be made by IT alone. This implies that the business side stating that it doesn't want to be involved in technical decisions is a bad idea because it will lead to suboptimal decision making.

Time Is Fleeting

Another parameter influences an option's value: time. The time at which the option can be exercised—that is, the option's maturity date—is represented by the parameter T in the Black-Scholes formula, whereas the current time is identified as t. The further out the maturity is in the future, the higher its value. This makes intuitive sense because your uncertainty increases the further you are looking into the future, making the option more valuable.

Architects and project managers typically work under different time horizons and thus value the same option differently.

This effect can help explain why architects and project managers often debate the merit of architecture options: project managers typically have a shorter time horizon than enterprise architects, who need to assure architectural integrity over many years and sometime decades. Due to the different time horizons, each of them has a different perceived (and, in fact, calculated) value of the same option. Interestingly, during such arguments, both parties are making rational but different decisions because their input parameters differ. A model, such as the options model, can help reduce such arguments to differences in input parameters and thus lead to better decision making.

Real Options

The idea of applying options theory outside of financial instruments isn't just limited to IT and is referred to as *real options*.[5] Real options guide corporate investment decisions, such as acquisitions or buying real estate, and are commonly broken down into categories,[6] which map very well to software architecture and projects:

Option to defer
> The ability to make an investment, such as adding a feature, at a later time.

Option to abandon
> The ability to use or resell parts of a project in case the project as planned has to be abandoned. In IT architecture, this option can equate to building self-contained modules or services that can be salvaged for use in other projects.

Option to expand
> The ability to increase capacity; for example, to scale out an application by adding hardware.

Option to contract
> The ability to elegantly reduce capacity; for example, by using elastic infrastructure.

---

5 Stewart C. Myers, *Determinants of Corporate Borrowing* (Cambridge, MA: MIT Sloan School of Management, 1976).

6 Lenos Trigeorgis, *Real Options: Managerial Flexibility and Strategy in Resource Allocation* (Cambridge, MA: MIT Press, 1996).

Just like with *buying hot chocolate* (Chapter 17), we can learn from looking at the real world outside IT.

Arbitrage

In the financial world, markets are generally assumed to be efficient, meaning instruments are priced fairly according to their risk and expected return. Every once in a while, though, someone figures out a way to make immediate returns through arbitrage, an opportunity to profit at no risk. Architects should similarly look out for such opportunities where they can provide options at very low cost. For example, using an open source object-relational mapping (ORM) framework is both best practice and an inexpensive option to make switching database vendors easier.

Agile and Architecture

Some Agile developers question architecture's value because it was closely associated with a big, up-front-design approach that would look to make all decisions at the outset. Understanding architecture as providing options, you can easily see that the opposite is true. Both Agile methods and architecture are ways to deal with uncertainty, meaning that working in an Agile fashion allows you to benefit more from architecture.

 The value of both Agile methods and architecture increases with uncertainty, so they are friend, not foe.

Evolutionary Architecture

What should you do if meaningful options aren't known, or at least not known far enough in advance? In that case, you need an architecture that can evolve along with your increased understanding of technology and customer needs—an approach that's described as *evolutionary architecture.*[7] Just like in natural history, what sets evolution apart from a series of changes is a *fitness function* that guides change by examining how well a solution serves an intended purpose. Choosing the right fitness function can now become the evolutionary architect's

---

7 Neal Ford, Matthew McCullough, and Nathaniel Schutta, *Presentation Patterns: Techniques for Crafting Better Presentations* (Boston: Addison-Wesley Professional, 2012).

contribution, rather than choosing a specific architecture up front. If you feel that's an application of the well-known motto "all problems can be solved with one more level of indirection," you might be onto something.

Amplifying Metaphors

When I first shared the "selling options" metaphor with a senior financial services executive, the former head of asset management, he instantly embraced the metaphor and quickly concluded that higher volatility increases the value of an option. Translating this back into IT, he stated that in times of high uncertainty, as we are facing them today both in business and technology, the value of architecture options also increases. Businesses should therefore invest more into architecture.

Isn't it fantastic when a person from a different field adopts a metaphor and takes it to the next level?

10

Every System Is Perfect...

For What It Was Designed to Do!

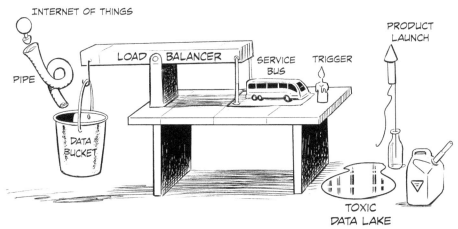

Analyzing system behavior

Much of what architects do is reason about the behavior of *complex systems*: systems that have many pieces and complex interrelationships. There's an entire field dedicated to such reasoning, called *systems thinking* or *complex systems theory*. While popular software architecture definitions focus on a system's components and interrelationships, systems thinking *emphasizes behavior* (Chapter 8). As architects, we should view structure simply as a means to achieve a desired behavior. Thinking in systems helps us do so.

Heater as a System

A residential heater provides a canonical example of a *system*, which we also look at when we realize that control is an *illusion* (Chapter 27). As demonstrated in Figure 10-1, a heating system's typical architecture diagram would depict the components and their relationships: a furnace generates hot water or air, a radiator or air duct delivers the heat to the room, and a thermostat controls the furnace. The structural/control system theory point of view, shown at the top of the figure, considers the thermostat the central element: it switches the furnace on and off as needed to regulate the room temperature.

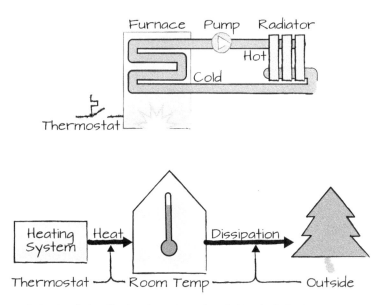

Figure 10-1. A structural view (top) and a systems view (bottom) of a heater

In contrast, the systems thinking point of view, at the bottom of Figure 10-1, focuses on the room temperature as the central variable and the reasons why it is influenced: the burning furnace increases the room temperature while heat dissipation to the outside reduces it. Heat dissipation depends on both the room and the outside temperature: in cold weather more heat dissipates through walls and windows. That's why smart heating systems increase the heating power in cold weather. In a way, systems thinking is a parallel universe that looks at the same system from a completely different angle, an angle that helps us better understand *why* we are building something.

Feedback Loops

Systems thinking helps us understand interrelated behavior; for example, feedback loops. The room thermostat establishes a negative feedback loop, which is typical for control systems: if the room temperature is too high, the furnace turns off, letting the room cool down again. Negative feedback loops usually aim to keep a system in a relatively stable state—the room temperature will still oscillate slightly depending on the hysteresis of the thermostat and the inertia of the heating system. The self-stabilizing range of most systems is limited, though: a heater cannot cool a room in the heat of summer or compensate for an open window during winter.

Positive feedback loops behave in the opposite way: an increase in one system variable fuels a further increase. We know the dramatic effects of such behavior from explosives (heat releases more oxygen to burn hotter), nuclear reactions (a classical "chain reaction"), or hyperinflation (a spiral of price and wage increases). Another positive feedback loop consists of more cars on the road leading to investments in roads as opposed to public transit, which makes it more compelling to commute by car. Likewise, rich people tend to have more investment options to achieve higher returns, leading to a "the rich getting richer" symptom, as for example described in Piketty's *Capital in the Twenty-First Century.*[1]

Positive feedback loops can be dangerous due to their "explosive" nature. Policies are often designed to counteract such positive feedback loops with negative ones; for example, by applying higher tax rates to higher incomes or by increasing gasoline tax while subsidizing public transit. However, it's difficult to balance out the exponential character of positive feedback loops. Thinking in systems helps us reason about such effects.

Organized Complexity

Gerald Weinberg[2] highlighted the importance of thinking in systems by dividing the world into three areas: *organized simplicity* is the realm of well-understood mechanics, such as levers or electrical systems consisting of discrete resistors and capacitors. You can calculate exactly how these systems behave. On the other end of the spectrum, *unorganized complexity* doesn't allow us to understand exactly what's going on, but we can model the system as a whole statistically because the behavior is unorganized, meaning the parts don't interrelate much. Modeling the spread of a virus falls into this category. The tricky domain is the one of *organized complexity*, where structure and interaction between

---

1 Thomas Piketty, *Capital in the Twenty-First Century* (Boston: Belknap Press, 2014).

2 Gerald M. Weinberg, *An Introduction to General Systems Thinking* (Dorset House, 2001).

components matter, but the system is too complex to solve it by using a formula. This is the area of systems. And the area of systems architecture.

System Effects

If we can't determine system behavior with mathematical formulas, how can systems thinking help us? Complex systems, especially systems involving humans, tend to be subject to recurring system effects or patterns. These effects explain why fishermen keep overfishing, depleting their own livelihood, and why tourists flocking to the same destination destroy exactly what attracted them. Understanding these patterns allows us to better predict system behavior and influence it. Donella Meadows's book *Thinking in Systems*[3] contains a list of common effects, including these typical ones:

- *Bounded rationality*, a term coined by Nobel laureate Herbert A. Simon, captures the effect that people will generally do what is rational, but only within the context that they observe. For example, if an apartment building has a central heating system without consumption-based billing, people will leave the heater on all day and open the windows to cool down the apartment as needed. Obviously, this is a giant waste of energy and leads to pollution, resource depletion, and global warming. However, if your bounded context is just that of the temperature in your apartment and your wallet, this behavior is the rational thing to do, whether you like it or not: keeping the heater running allows you to control the room temperature more easily as you avoid the inertia of the heating system having to warm up.

- The idea of the *tragedy of the commons* derives from the concept of *the commons*, a shared pasture in old Irish and English villages that was open to grazing by all the villagers' animals. As this common resource is free, villagers are incentivized to acquire more cattle to feed on the commons. Of course, as the commons is a finite resource, this behavior will lead to resource depletion and poverty; hence, the tragedy. One reason such a system doesn't self-regulate is delay: the effect of the wrong behavior will only become apparent when it is too late.

---

3 Donella H. Meadows, *Thinking in Systems: A Primer* (White River Junction, VT: Chelsea Green Publishing, 2008).

The complexity of these effects is underlined by the fact that Elinor Ostrom, the only woman to win the Nobel Prize in Economics, famously debunked[4] the concept of the *tragedy of the commons*.

Understanding System Behavior

Systems documentation, especially in IT, tends to depict the static structure but rarely the behavior of the system. Ironically, however, the system's behavior is what's most interesting: systems generally exist to exhibit a certain, desirable behavior. For example, the heating system was created to keep the temperature in your house at a comfortable level. Server infrastructure is made redundant to increase availability. In both cases the system structure is simply a means to an end.

The difficulty in deriving system behavior from its components can be illustrated by the heating system in my apartment, which supplies both floor heating and wall radiators with hot water

A system's structure is simply a means to achieve a desired behavior.

and comprises a handful of major components: the gas burner heats the water inside a primary circuit driven by a built-in pump. Two additional external pumps feed the hot water from the primary circuit to the floor heating and wall radiators, respectively. A misconfiguration caused the secondary pumps to not draw enough water, and therefore heat, from the primary circuit, which quickly overheated. This, in turn, caused the gas heater to shut off for a fixed duration, leading to a lack of heating power: naturally, the house cannot get warm when the heater is not burning. Because the house wouldn't warm up, the technician's intuition was to *increase* the burner's heating power. However, this only exacerbated the problem: the system wasn't able to move enough heat away from the primary circuit, so increasing the gas burner's power only overheated it faster. After almost a dozen attempts, the heating system still wasn't operating as designed, because the technicians might understand the individual system components but they are not comprehending the complex system behavior.

Seems a little complicated? For architects, this stuff is our daily bread and butter. Understanding complex interrelationships between system components

---

4 David Bollier, "The Only Woman to Win the Nobel Prize in Economics Also Debunked the Orthodoxy," *Evonomics*, July 28, 2015, *https://oreil.ly/9NaOH*.

and influencing them to achieve a desired behavior is what architects do. Often a good *diagram* (Chapter 22) will help.

Influencing System Behavior

Most of what users see from a system are events: things happening as a result of the system behavior, which in turn is determined by the system structure, that is often invisible. If the users are unhappy with those events, such as the heater shutting off despite the room being cold, they often try to inflict a change, such as setting the room thermostat higher, without analyzing or changing the system behind them. The book *Inviting Disaster*[5] provides dramatic examples of how misunderstanding a system led to major catastrophes such as the Three Mile Island nuclear reactor incident or the capsizing of the Deepwater Horizon drilling platform. In both cases, compromised system displays led operators to perform the very action that caused the disaster because they didn't understand the underlying system and its behavior from the events they observed. Their *mental model* deviated from the real system, causing them to make fatal decisions.

It has repeatedly been observed that humans are particularly bad at steering systems that have slow feedback loops, meaning those that exhibit reactions to changing inputs only after a significant delay. A classic example is MIT's "beer game" in which participants on average perform almost 10 times worse than the ideal scenario.[6] Overuse of credit cards is another classic example: people keep piling on debt until they are no longer able to pay even the interest and wonder how they got themselves into such a mess.

Also, humans who don't think about the system as a whole are prone to taking actions that have the opposite of the intended effect. For example, people react to overly full work calendars by setting up "blockers," which make the calendars even fuller. Instead, we need to understand and fix what causes the full calendars; for example, a misaligned organizational structure that requires too many alignment meetings. You can't fix a system by merely addressing the symptoms.

Understanding system effects can help you devise more effective ways to influence the system and thus its behavior. For example, transparency is a useful

---

5 James R. Chiles, *Inviting Disaster: Lessons from the Edge of Technology* (New York: Harper Business, 2002).

6 John D. Sterman, "Modeling Managerial Behavior," *Management Science*, Vol. 35, No. 3 (March 1989), *https://oreil.ly/wrtzb*.

antidote to the bounded rationality effect because it widens people's bounds. An example from Donella Meadows's book illustrates that having the electricity meter visible in the hallway caused people to be more conservative with their energy consumption without additional rules or penalties. Interestingly, systems thinking can be applied to both organizational and technical systems. We'll learn this, for example, when we scale an *organization* (Chapter 30).

John Gall's *Systems Bible*[7] gives a humorous but also insightful account of the ways in which systems behave, often against our intention or intuition.

Systems Resist Change

Changing systems is difficult not only because of their complex structure, but also because most of them actively resist change. Organizational systems' change resistance achieves longevity, for example, through well-defined processes, but presents a challenge when a shift in the environment requires the organization to change. Frederic Laloux[8] describes it as a key characteristic of *amber organizations*: they are built on the assumption that what worked in the past will work in the future, and it often served them well over thousands of years.

As described in Chapter 7, if you request better documentation for architecture reviews, "the system" might respond by scheduling lengthy workshops that drain your available time. If you increase pressure, the system will respond with subquality documentation that increases your review cycles. You must therefore get to the root of the problem and highlight the value of good documentation, properly train architects, and allocate time for this task in project schedules.

Most organizational systems have settled into a steady state over time and serve their purpose well enough. If the business environment demands a different system behavior, the system will actively resist by wanting to revert to its previous state. It's like trying to push a car out of a ditch: the car keeps rolling back until you finally get it over the hump. This system effect makes organizational transformation so challenging.

---

7 John Gall, *The Systems Bible*, Third Edition (Walker, MN: General Systemantics Press, 2002).

8 Frederic Laloux and Ken Wilber, *Reinventing Organizations: A Guide to Creating Organizations Inspired by the Next Stage in Human Consciousness* (Nelson Parker, 2014).

II

Code Fear Not!

Programming in a Poorly Designed Language
Without Tool Support Is No Fun

Who dares run this code?

Yoda, the wise teacher of Jedi apprentice Luke Skywalker in the *Star Wars* movies, knows that fear leads to anger; anger leads to hate; hate leads to suffering. Likewise, corporate IT's fear of code and the love of configuration can lead it down a path to suffering from which it is difficult to escape. Beware of the dark side, which has many faces, including vendors peddling products that "only require configuration," as opposed to tedious, error-prone coding. Sadly, most complex configuration really is just programming, albeit in a poorly designed, rather constrained language without decent tooling or useful documentation.

Fear of Code

Corporate IT, which is often driven by operational considerations, tends to consider code the stuff that contains all the bugs, causes performance problems, and is written by *expensive external consultants* (Chapter 38) who are difficult to hold liable because they'll have long moved to another project by the time the problems surface. Some IT leaders even proudly proclaim that they are a "proper business" and not a software development company, so they shouldn't bother with coding stuff.

 The most grotesque example of fear of code I have observed was corporate IT providing application servers as a shared service. Once you deploy code on them, you'd no longer receive operational support. It's like voiding a car's warranty after you start the engine—after all, the manufacturer has no idea what you will do to it!

Corporate IT's eternal fear of code plays to the advantage of enterprise vendors who offer configuration as the safe alternative to coding. As we shall see, that's a rather short-sighted proposition.

Good Intentions Don't Lead to Good Results

IT's aversion to coding originates from a good principle. Most enterprise IT rightly follows a *buy-over-build* strategy: buying commercial off-the-shelf (COTS) solutions not only saves IT departments time and money but also lets someone else worry about regular updates and security patches. Once purchased, solutions can be customized and configured to the enterprise's specific needs.

Likewise, common libraries and open source tools are a great way of reusing existing work. Open source tools are also often accompanied by an extensive community that can provide support and make technology adoption easier. For example, who would you want to write their own XML serializer? There's a library for that.

There's a catch, though...well, actually, two: first, if you expect to configure a piece of software that you bought, you are relying on the vendor having anticipated the need for your case of customization, meaning the vendor gave you the *option* (Chapter 9). Doing this well would mean the vendor has perfected big, upfront design, correctly anticipating all possible requirements, while the rest of us are still trying to become more *Agile* (Chapter 31). Second, configuration means working in an abstraction provided by the software vendor. Now, abstractions are generally a good thing because they allow you to get away from the nitty-gritty details, but some abstractions also come with downsides.

Levels of Abstraction: Simplicity Versus Flexibility

Raising the level of abstraction is one of the primary techniques that makes developers' lives easier. Thanks to abstraction, very few programmers still write assembly code, read single data blocks from a hard disk, or put individual data packets onto the network. This level of detail has been nicely wrapped behind high-level languages, files, and socket streams. These programming abstractions are very convenient and dramatically increase productivity: try doing without them!

If abstractions are this useful, you might legitimately wonder whether adding further abstraction layers could boost productivity even more. For example, you could use libraries or services for all business functions. Ultimately, you could do away with coding altogether and allow solution development simply by, let's say, configuration. If this sounds a bit too good to be true, that's because it is.

When raising the level of abstraction, you face a fundamental dilemma: how do you make a really simple model without losing too much flexibility? For example, if a developer needs rapid direct-access to any file location, the file stream abstraction actually gets in the way because it requires reading files sequentially. The best abstractions are therefore those that solve and encapsulate the difficult part of the problem while leaving the user with sufficient flexibility.

If an abstraction takes away too many or the wrong things, it becomes overly restrictive and no longer applicable. If it takes away too few things, it didn't accomplish much in terms of simplification and hence isn't very valuable.

Or as Alan Kay elegantly stated: Simple things should be simple, complex things should be possible.[1] *MapReduce*, a framework for distributed data processing, is a positive example: it abstracts away the gnarly parts of distributed data processing, such as controlling and scheduling many worker instances, dealing with failed nodes, aggregating data across nodes, and so on. But it nevertheless

1 Wikiquote, "Alan Kay," *https://oreil.ly/SBC39*.

leaves the programmer enough flexibility to solve a wide range of problems and was extremely widely used within Google.

When Are We Configuring?

So, if configuration promises us to abstract away the details of programming, we should look a little closer at the trade-offs that were made. But before we get there, it turns out that it's not even trivial to determine when something is configuration as opposed to coding. The notion of configuration is mostly made by conflating several, unrelated aspects:

- The representation (e.g., visuals versus text)
- Whether you provide data or instructions
- Whether you make changes before or after deployment

Let's dissect each of these a bit.

MODEL VERSUS REPRESENTATION

Coding abstractions such as libraries take away implementation details, but you're still coding, although against more powerful objects and methods. Enterprise software abstraction often comes in different packaging, a graphical user interface (GUI) that enables spiffy drag-and-drop demos, which make the whole exercise seem trivial.

At first sight, we might believe that painting a thin visual veneer over an existing programming model can provide a higher level of abstraction. Many business users might at first agree: typing in commands surely looks like coding, whereas drawing diagrams feels a lot more like PowerPoint. Unfortunately, that's an illusion: a GUI changes the *representation*, but not the underlying *model*. A complex model, such as a workflow engine that includes concepts like concurrency, synchronization, correlation, long-running transactions, compensating actions, and more, inherently carries heavy conceptual weight: there's a lot of stuff to consider. Wrapping it in pretty visual packaging can make it more appealing, but it won't remove this weight. If your synchronization bar is drawn in the wrong place, your workflow is just as broken as when making a coding mistake.

This isn't to say visual representations have no value. For example, representing visual workflows as graphs can be naturally expressive. But although they may reduce some of the initial learning curve, they generally don't scale very well: once applications grow, it becomes difficult to follow what's going on via a giant canvas of symbols. Zooming out means text won't be readable anymore.

Debugging and version control can also be a nightmare given that these tools mostly lack familiar *diff* functions.

To test whether the visuals are just a thin veneer or really a better model, I generally apply two tests when vendors provide a demo of visual programming tools:

- I ask them to enter a typo into one of the fields where the user is expected to enter some logic. Often this leads to cryptic error messages or obscure exceptions in generated code later on. This is "tightrope programming": as long as you stay exactly on the line, everything is well. One misstep and the deep abyss awaits you.

- I ask them to leave the room for two minutes while we change a few random elements of their demo configuration. Upon return, they would have to debug and figure out what was changed.

So far, no vendor has taken the bait; they presumably know that failure doesn't respect abstraction.[2]

CODE OR DATA? OR BOTH?

Leaving visuals aside, at which level of abstraction can we call something "configuration" versus "high-level programming"? We've seen that despite repeated vendor messaging, a visual user interface doesn't suffice. Many programmers will tell you that files in XML (or JSON or YAML) syntax are configuration. However, anyone who has programmed in XSLT, which uses XML syntax, can attest that this isn't configuration but heavy-duty declarative programming. There's nothing simple about it.

A better decision criterion could be whether what you provide to the system is executable or pieces of data. If the algorithm is predefined and you supply only a few key values, it may be fair to call this configuration. For example, let's assume a program needs to classify users of different ages into children, adults, and seniors. The code will contain a chain of if-else or a switch statement. A configuration file could now supply the values for the decision thresholds; for example, 18 and 65. This would fit our definition of configuration.

---

2 Gregor Hohpe, "Failure Doesn't Respect Abstraction," The Architect Elevator (blog), January 21, 2019, *https://oreil.ly/ejTmy*.

We might now conclude that changing those values is safe: typing in a number keeps you from having to understand programming language syntax and operator precedence. Alas, it doesn't save you from screwing up the program. If you accidentally enter the values 65 and 18, the program is likely to not work as expected. The exact program behavior in this case is impossible to predict as it depends on the way the algorithm is coded. If the program checks for children first, you may have declared everyone as a child, whereas if the program checks for seniors first, you may have made everyone a senior. So while configuration is safer, it isn't foolproof.

The distinction between code and data blurs further when the data you enter determines execution order. For example, the "data" you enter may be a sequence of instruction codes. Or the data may resemble a declarative programming language; for example, to configure a rules engine or even XSLT. Aren't coding instructions just data for the execution engine? Von Neumann[3] would have said so. Apparently, it's not so black and white.

DEPLOYMENT AT DESIGN-TIME VERSUS RUNTIME

Another way configuration is commonly distinguished from code is that we can change configuration after the application is deployed. This is certainly useful given that we can't foresee some parameters until runtime; for example, the number of *servers we need* (Chapter 9). The distinction is based on the underlying assumption, though, that changing code is something that's slow (because you have to rebuild and redeploy the whole application) and risky (because you may be introducing new defects). Microservices architectures and automated build-test-and-deploy chains put quite a few question marks behind these assumptions: they enable teams to rebuild, test, and deploy application code rapidly, repeatably, and with high quality.

 Rather than trying to anticipate changes for configuration, you may want to invest in your tool chain to allow incremental, rapid deployment.

This doesn't mean that configuration is useless, but it does mean that modern software delivery has given us other tools to achieve much of what configuration was intended to do. If we can make changes in the code, we don't have

---

3 Wikipedia, "von Neumann architecture," *https://oreil.ly/ilzNC*.

to decide *a priori* which parameters we allow to be configured later, leading to much simpler code. Plus, we benefit from a fast range of tools like version control, editor support, and automated testing.

 When enterprise vendors tout their configuration suites, I challenge them to speed up their software delivery model.

The lack of tooling makes the common assumption that configuration is safer, a questionable one. For example, "Configuration changes" have caused major outages at several cloud services providers.[4]

Higher-Level Programming

In many cases, what's being passed as configuration is really higher-level programming. For example, when composing distributed systems by connecting them via named message channels, "configuration" files often determine over which channel(s) a component communicates. Two components talk to each other when they use the same channel. Entering this data in local XML configuration files seems convenient, but it's prone to mistakes because a simple typo would mean that components don't communicate or are chained together in the wrong order.

Composing a messaging system isn't a matter of configuration, but a high-level programming model for the *composition layer* of the system. Treating the configuration files as first-class citizens by checking them into source control and by creating validation and management tools[5] can help debugging and troubleshooting enormously.

Configuration Programming

Whenever there's a choice to be made—in our case *programming* versus *configuration*—you can be assured that someone has found a compromise. In our case this would be *configuration programming*:[6] an approach that advocates the use of a

4 Benjamin Treynor Sloss, "An Update on Sunday's Service Disruption," Inside Google Cloud (blog), June 3, 2019, *https://oreil.ly/yaGr6*.

5 Gregor Hohpe, "Visualizing Dependencies," Enterprise Integration Patterns (blog), July 12, 2004, *https://oreil.ly/1j4-7*.

6 FOLDOC, "Configuration Programming," *https://oreil.ly/DkiVO*.

separate configuration language to specify the coarse-grained structure of programs. Configuration programming is particularly attractive for concurrent, parallel, and distributed systems that have inherently complex program structures.

Configuration Hiding as Code?

So, is there a good place for configuration? Yes, for example, injecting runtime parameters into highly distributed programs or setting up *cloud infrastructure* (Chapter 14) are great use cases for configuration. Oddly, much of these approaches run under the moniker *infrastructure as code* (IaC) these days, even though most of the tools really are configuration. Someone must have felt that *code* sounds more powerful than *configuation*.

Abstractions are a very useful technique, but believing that labeling something as "configuration" is going to eliminate complexity or the need to hire developers is a fallacy. Instead, think about whether this "configuration" is really higher-level programming. And in either case, make sure that it undergoes the same best practices of design, testing, version control, and deployment management that defines modern software delivery. Otherwise, you'd have created a proprietary, poorly designed language without tooling support. Then you would have been better off coding.

12

If You Never Kill Anything, You Will Live Among Zombies

And They Will Eat Your Brain

The night of the living legacy systems

Corporate IT lives among zombies: old systems that are half alive and have everyone in fear of going anywhere near them. They are also tough to kill completely. Worse yet, they eat IT staff's brains. It's like *Shaun of the Dead* minus the funny parts.

Despite being a reality in corporate IT, living legacy systems are becoming more difficult to justify in a world that's changing faster and faster. It's time to put some zombies to rest.

Legacy

Legacy systems are built on outdated technology and are often poorly documented but (ostensibly) still perform important business functions. In many cases, the exact scope of the function they perform is not completely known. Ironically, most legacy systems generate a lot of revenue because otherwise they would have been killed a long time ago.

 When discussing what sets modern "digital" companies apart from traditional ones, "lack of legacy" regularly comes up as a key factor.

Systems fall into the state of legacy because technology moves faster than the business: life insurance systems often must maintain data and functionality for decades, rendering much of the technology used to build the system obsolete. With a bit of luck, the systems don't have to be updated anymore, so IT might be inclined to "simply let it run," following the popular advice to "never touch a running system." Unfortunately, changing regulations or security vulnerabilities in old versions of the application or the underlying software stack are likely to interfere with such an approach.

Traditional IT sometimes justifies their zombies with having to support the business: how can you shut down a system that may be needed by the business? They also feel that digital companies don't have such problems because they are too young to have accumulated legacy. 150 Google developers attending Mike Feathers's talk about *Working Effectively with Legacy Code*[1] might make us question this assumption. Because Google's systems evolve rapidly, they also accumulate legacy more quickly than traditional IT. So it's not that they have been blessed with not having legacy—they must have found a better way of dealing with it.

Fear of Change

Systems become legacy zombies by not evolving with the technology. This happens in classic IT largely because *change is seen as a risk* (Chapter 26). Once again: "never touch a running system." System releases are based on extensive, often manual test cycles that can last months, making updates or changes a

---

1 Michael Feathers, *Working Effectively with Legacy Code* (Upper Saddle River, NJ: Prentice Hall, 2004).

costly endeavor. Worse yet, there's no "business case" for updating the system technology. This widespread logic is about as sound as considering changing the oil in your car a waste of money—after all, the car still runs if you don't. And it even makes your quarterly profit statement look a little better; that is, until the engine seizes.

Slogans like "Never touch a running system" reflect the belief that change bears risk.

A team from Credit Suisse described how to counterbalance this trap in its aptly titled book *Managed Evolution*.[2] The key driver for managed evolution is to maintain agility in a system. A system that no one wants to touch has no agility at all: it can't be changed. In a very static business and technology environment, this might not be all that terrible, but that's not the environment we live in anymore!

In today's environment, the inability to change a system becomes a major liability for IT and the business.

Hoping for the Best Isn't a Strategy

Most things are the way they are for a reason. This is also true for the fear of change in corporate IT. These organizations typically lack the tools, processes, and skills to closely observe production metrics and to rapidly deploy fixes in case something goes awry. They hence try to test for all scenarios before deploying and then running the application more or less "blind," hoping that nothing breaks. This behavior looks to maximize MTBF—the *mean time between failures*.

While increasing the time between failures is a worthwhile approach, focusing on MTBF alone has two major downsides. First, it slows down hardware provisioning and software deployment due to excessive up-front testing. It also leads to a situation where the response to an actual failure becomes "this wasn't supposed to happen." It's unlikely that those are the words you want to hear from an operations team.

---

2 Stephan Murer and Bruno Bonati, *Managed Evolution: A Strategy for Very Large Information Systems* (Berlin: Springer, 2011).

Such teams often ignore the other side of the equation: the *mean time to recovery* (MTTR). This metric indicates how quickly a system can recover from an error. Modern teams look at both aspects. As an analogy, you'd want to use fire-retardant materials but also a fire brigade that can be onsite in a few minutes. The top benchmark for incident response time I observed was at a large chemical factory where the fire brigade would be at the incident site in 45 seconds (!). Airports generally achieve two to three minutes.[3]

Traditional organizations "hope for the best" by relying on ways to maximize MTBF, whereas modern organizations also "prepare for the worst" by minimizing MTTR.

Reducing MTTR involves very different mechanisms such as high system transparency, version control, and automation. In fact, reducing MTTR is such a game changer for IT organizations that it's one of the four software delivery performance measures used by the authors of the book *Accelerate*.[4]

Version Upgrades

The zombie problem is not limited to systems written in PL/1 running on an IBM/360, though. Often updating basic runtime infrastructures like application servers, JDK versions, browsers, or operating systems scare the living daylights out of IT, causing version updates to be deferred until the vendor ceases support. The natural reaction then is to pay the vendor for extended support to avoid the horror scenario of having to migrate your software to a new version.

Often the inability to migrate cascades across multiple layers of the software stack: one cannot upgrade to a newer JDK because it doesn't run on the current application server version, which can't be updated because it requires a new version of the operating system, which deprecates some library or feature the software depends on.

I have seen IT shops that are stuck on Internet Explorer 6 because their software utilizes a proprietary feature not present in later versions.

---

3 Wikipedia, "Airport crash tender," *https://oreil.ly/e4DNF*.

4 Nicole Forsgren, Jez Humble, and Gene Kim, *Accelerate: The Science of Lean Software and DevOps: Building and Scaling High Performing Technology Organizations* (Portland, OR: IT Revolution, 2018).

Looking at the user interfaces of most corporate applications, you would find it difficult to imagine that they eked out every little bit of browser capability. They surely would have been better off not depending on such a peculiar feature and instead being able to benefit from browser evolution. Such a line of thought requires a conscious trade-off between optimizing for the short term versus *assuring long-term velocity* (Chapter 3).

Ironically, IT's widespread *fear of code* (Chapter 11) leads it down a dark and narrow road toward heavily customized frameworks. Version upgrades become very difficult and expensive to make, and another zombie grows. Anyone who has done an SAP upgrade can relate.

Run Versus Change

The fear of change is even encoded in many IT organizations that separate "run" (operating) from "change" (development), establishing that running software doesn't imply change. Rather, it's the opposite of change, which is done by application development—those guys who produce the flaky code IT is afraid of. Structuring IT teams this way will guarantee that systems will age and become legacy because no change could be applied to them.

You might think that by not changing running systems, IT can keep the operational cost low. Ironically, the opposite is true: many IT departments spend more than half of their IT budget on "run" and "maintenance," leaving only a fraction of the budget for "change" that can support the evolving demands of the business. That's because running and supporting legacy applications is expensive: operational processes are often manual; the software may not be stable, necessitating constant attention; the software may not scale well, requiring the procurement of expensive hardware; lack of documentation means time-consuming trial-and-error troubleshooting in case of problems. These are reasons why legacy systems tie up valuable IT resources and skills, effectively devouring the brains of IT that could be applied to more useful tasks; for example, delivering features to the business.

Planned Obsolescence

When selecting a product or conducting a request for proposal (RFP), classic IT tends to compile a list containing dozens or hundreds of features or capabilities that a candidate product has to offer. Often, these lists are created by external consultants unaware of the business need or the company's IT strategy. However, they can produce very long lists, and longer appears to be better to some IT staff, whose main motivation lies in demonstrating that the selection was "thorough."

To cite another car analogy, this is a bit like evaluating a car by having an endless list of more or less (ir)relevant features like "must have a 12V lighter outlet," "speedometer goes above 200 km/h," "can turn the front wheels," and then scoring a BMW versus a Mercedes for these. How likely this is to steer (pun intended) you toward the car you will enjoy the most is questionable at best.

One item routinely missing from such "features" lists is planned obsolescence: how easy is it to replace the system? Can the data be exported in a well-defined format? Can business logic be extracted and reused in a replacement system to avoid vendor lock-in? During the new product selection honeymoon, this can feel like discussing a prenup[5] before the wedding—who likes to think about parting ways when you are about to embark on a lifelong journey? In the case of an IT system, you better hope the journey isn't lifelong; systems are meant to come and go. So better to have a prenup in place than being held hostage by the system (or vendor) you are trying to part with.

If It Hurts, Do It More Often

How do you break out of the "change is bad" cycle? As mentioned earlier, without proper instrumentation and automation, making changes is not only scary but indeed risky. The reluctance to upgrade or migrate software is similar to the reluctance to build and test software often. Martin Fowler issued the best advice to break this cycle: "If it hurts, do it more often." Behind the provocative name sits the insight that deferring a painful task generally makes it disproportionately more painful: if you haven't built your source code in months, it's guaranteed not to go smoothly. Likewise, if the application server your software is running on is three versions behind, you'll have the migration from hell.

Performing such tasks more frequently provides a forcing function to automate some of the processes; for example, with automated builds or test suites. Dealing with migration problems will also become routine. This is the reason emergency workers train regularly; otherwise, they'll freak out in case of an actual emergency and won't be effective. Of course, training takes time and energy. But what's the alternative?

---

5 A prenuptial agreement often clarifies asset division in case of a divorce.

Culture of Change

Digital companies also have to deal with change and obsolescence.

 The going joke at Google was that every API had two versions: the obsolete one and the not-yet-quite-ready one. Actually, it wasn't a joke, but pretty close to reality.

Dealing with constant change is painful at times—every piece of code you write could break at any time because of changes in its dependencies. But living this culture of change allows Google to *keep up the pace* (Chapter 35), which is the most important of today's IT capabilities. Sadly, it's rarely listed as a performance indicator for project teams. Even Shaun knows that zombies can't run fast.

13

Never Send a Human to Do a Machine's Job

Automate Everything; What You Can't Automate, Make a Self-Service

Sending a machine to do a human's job

Who would have thought that you can learn so much about large-scale IT architecture from the movie trilogy *The Matrix*? Acknowledging that the Matrix is run by machines, it should not be completely surprising to find some nuggets of system design wisdom, though: Agent Smith teaches us that one should never send a human to do a machine's job after his deal with Cypher, one of Morpheus' human crew members, to betray and hand over his boss failed.

Automate Everything!

There's a certain irony in the fact that corporate IT, which has largely established itself by automating business processes, is often not very automated itself. Early in my corporate career, I shocked a large assembly of infrastructure architects by declaring my strategy as: "automate everything and make those parts that can't be automated a self-service." The reaction ranged from confusion and disbelief to mild anger. Still, this is exactly what Amazon et al. have done. And it has revolutionized how people procure and access IT infrastructure along the way. These companies have also attracted the top talent in the industry to build said infrastructure. If corporate IT wants to remain relevant, this is the way it ought to be thinking!

It's Not Only About Efficiency

Just like test-driven development is not a testing technique (it's primarily a design technique), automation is not just about efficiency but primarily about repeatability and resilience. A vendor's architect once stated that automation shouldn't be implemented for infrequently performed tasks because it isn't economically viable. Basically, the vendor calculated that writing the automation would take more hours than would ever be spent completing the task manually (the vendor also appeared to be on a fixed-price contract).

I challenged this reasoning with the argument of repeatability and traceability: wherever humans are involved, mistakes are bound to happen, and work will be performed ad hoc without proper documentation. That's why you don't send humans to do a machine's job. The error rate is actually likely to be the highest for infrequently performed tasks because the operators are lacking routine.

The second counter-example is disaster scenarios and outages: we hope that they occur infrequently, but when they happen, the systems better be fully automated to make sure they can return to a running state as quickly as possible. The economic argument here isn't about saving manpower but minimizing the loss of business during the outage, which far exceeds the manual labor cost. To appreciate this thinking, you need to understand *economies of speed* (Chapter 35). Otherwise, you may as well argue that the fire brigade should use a bucket chain because all those fire trucks and pumps are not economically viable given how rarely buildings actually catch fire.

Repeatability Grows Confidence

When I automate tasks, the biggest immediate benefit I usually derive is increased confidence. For example, when I wrote the original self-published version of the book in Markdown, I had to maintain two slightly different versions: the ebook version used hyperlinks for chapter references, whereas the print version used chapter numbers. After quickly becoming tired of manually converting between the formats, I developed two simple scripts that switch between print and epub versions of the text. Because it was easy to do, I also made the scripts idempotent, meaning that running a script multiple times caused no harm. With these scripts at hand, I didn't even worry a split-second about switching between formats because I could be assured that nothing would go wrong. Automation is hugely liberating and hence speeds up work significantly.

Self-Service

Once things are fully automated, users can directly execute common procedures in a self-service portal. To provide the necessary parameters—for example, the size of a server—they must have a clear mental model of what they are ordering. Amazon Web Services provides a good example of an intuitive user interface, which not only alerts you that your server is reachable from any computer in the world but even detects your IP address to make it easy to restrict access.

 When filling out the spreadsheet required to order a Linux server, I was told to just copy the network settings from an existing server because I wouldn't be able to understand what I need anyway.

Designing good user interfaces can be a challenging but valuable exercise for infrastructure engineers who are largely used to working in hiding on rather esoteric "plumbing." It's also a chance for them to *show the Pirate Ship* (Chapter 19), which is far more exciting than all the bits and pieces it's made out of.

 Self-service gives you better control, accuracy, and traceability than semi-manual processes.

Self-service doesn't at all imply that infrastructure changes become a free-for-all. Just like a self-service restaurant still has a cashier, validations and approvals apply to users' change requests. However, instead of a human having to re-enter a request submitted in free-form text or an Excel spreadsheet, when a self-service request is approved the workflow pushes the requested change into production without further human intervention and possibility of error. Self-service also reduces input errors: because free-form text or an Excel spreadsheet rarely perform validations, input errors lead to lengthy email cycles or pass through unnoticed. An automated approach gives immediate feedback to the user and makes sure the order actually reflects what the user needs.

Beyond Self-Service

Self-service portals are a major improvement over emailing spreadsheets. However, the best place for configuration changes is the source code repository, where approvals can be handled via *pull requests* and *merge* operations. Approved changes trigger an automated deployment into production. Source code management has long known how to administer large volumes of complex changes through review and approval processes, including commenting and audit trails. You should leverage these processes for configuration changes so that you can start to *think like a software developer* (Chapter 14). Because it seems that any good idea needs a buzzword these days, using a source repository to manage code and configuration is now referred to as "GitOps."

Most enterprise software vendors pitch GUIs as the ultimate in ease of use and cost reduction. However, in large-scale operations the opposite is the case: manual entry into user interfaces is cumbersome and error prone, especially for repeated requests or complex setups. If you need 10 servers with slight variations, would you want to enter this data 10 times by hand? Fully automated configurations should therefore be done via APIs, which can be integrated with other systems or scripted as part of higher-level automation.

 I once set a rule that no infrastructure changes could be made from a user interface but had to be done through version-controlled automation. This put a monkey wrench into many vendor demos.

Allowing users to specify what they want and providing it quickly in high quality would seem like a pretty happy scenario. However, in the digital world, you can always push things a little further. For example, Google's "zero-click search" initiative, which resulted in Google Now, considered even one user click too much of a burden, especially on mobile devices. The system should anticipate the users' needs and answer before a question is even asked. It's like going to

McDonalds and finding your favorite happy meal already waiting for you at the counter. Now that's customer service! An IT world equivalent may be autoscaling, which allows the infrastructure to automatically provision additional capacity under high load situations without any human intervention.

Automation Is Not a One-Way Street

Automation usually focuses on the top-down part; for example, configuring a piece of low-level equipment based on a customer order or the needs of a higher-level component. However, we will learn that *control can be an illusion* (Chapter 27) wherever humans are involved. Also, "control" necessitates two-way communication that references the current system state: when your room is too hot, you want the control system to turn on the air conditioning instead of the heater. The same is true in IT system automation: to specify how much hardware to order or what network changes to request, you likely first need to examine the current state. Therefore, full transparency on existing system structures and a clear vocabulary are paramount. In one case, it took us weeks just to understand whether a datacenter has sufficient spare capacity to deploy a new application. All order process automation doesn't help if it takes weeks to understand the current state of affairs.

If you manage to fully automate and make your infrastructure immutable, meaning no manual changes are allowed at all, you can start working under the assumption that reality matches what's specified in the configuration scripts. In that case, transparency becomes trivial: you just look at the scripts. While such a setup is a desirable end-state, it might take significant effort to consistently implement across a large IT estate. For example, legacy hardware or applications might not be automatable.

Explicit Knowledge Is Good Knowledge

Tacit knowledge is knowledge that exists only in employees' heads but isn't documented or encoded anywhere. Such undocumented knowledge can be a major overhead for large or rapidly growing organizations because it can easily be lost and requires new employees to relearn things the organization already knew. Encoding tacit knowledge, which existed only in an operator's head, into a set of scripts, tools, or source code makes these processes visible and eases knowledge transfer.

Tacit knowledge is also a sore spot for any regulatory body whose job it is to assure that businesses in regulated industries operate according to well-defined and repeatable principles and procedures. Full automation forces processes to be well defined and explicit, eliminating unwritten rules and undesired variation inherent in manual processes. As a result, automated systems are easier to audit for compliance. Ironically, classic IT often insists on manual steps in order to maintain separation of duty, ignoring the fact that manually approving an automated process achieves both separation of concerns and repeatability.

A Place for Humans

If we automate everything, is there a place left for humans? Computers are much better at executing repetitive tasks, but even though we humans are no longer unbeatable at the board game *Go*, we are still number one in coming up with new and creative ideas, designing things, or automating stuff. We should stick to this separation of duty and let the machines do the repeatable tasks without fearing that Skynet will take over the world any moment.

14

If Software Eats the World, Better Use Version Control!

When Your Infrastructure Becomes Software-Defined, You Need to Think Like a Software Developer

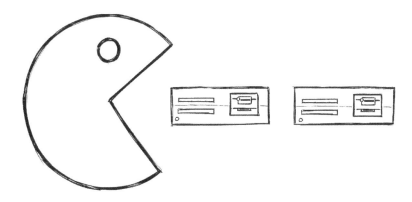

Software eats infrastructure

If software does indeed eat the world, it will have IT infrastructure for breakfast: the rapidly advancing virtualization of infrastructure from VMs and containers to *serverless* architectures turns provisioning code onto a piece of hardware into a pure software problem. While this is an amazing capability and one of the major value propositions of cloud computing, corporate IT's *uneasy relationship with code* (Chapter 11) and lack of familiarity with the modern development life cycle can make this a dangerous proposition.

SDX: Software-Defined Anything

Much of traditional IT infrastructure is either hardwired or semi-manually configured: servers are racked and cabled, network switches are manually configured with tools or configuration files. Operations staff, who endearingly refer to their equipment as "metal," are usually quite happy with this state of affairs: it keeps the programmer types away from critical infrastructure where the last thing you need is bugs and stuff like "Agile" development, which is still *widely misinterpreted* (Chapter 31) as doing random stuff and hoping for the best.

This is rapidly changing, though, and that's a good thing. The continuing virtualization of infrastructure makes resources that were once shipped by truck or wired by hand available via a call to a cloud service provider's API. It's like going from haggling in a car dealership and waiting four months for delivery just to find out that you should have ordered the premium seats after all to hailing an Uber from your mobile phone and being shuttled off three minutes later.

Virtualized and programmable infrastructure is an essential element to keeping up with the scalability and evolution demands of digital applications. You can't run an Agile business model when it takes you four weeks to get a server and four months to get it on the right network segment.

Operating system–level virtualization is by no means a new invention, but the "software defined" trend has extended to software-defined networks (SDNs) and full-blown software-defined datacenters (SDDC). If that isn't enough, you can opt for *SDX*—software-defined *anything*, which includes virtualization of compute, storage, network, and whatever else can be found in a datacenter, hopefully in some coordinated manner. Other marketing departments coined the term *infrastructure as code* (IaC), apparently oblivious to the fact their tools mostly accomplish it via *configuration, not code* (Chapter 11).

As so often, it's possible to look into the future of IT by reading Google's research papers describing its systems of five-plus years ago (the official paper on Borg,[1] Google's cluster manager, was published in 2015, almost a decade after its internal introduction). To get a glimpse of where SDN is headed, look at what Google has done with the so-called Jupiter Network Architecture.[2] If you are too busy to read the whole thing, this three-liner will do to get you excited:

> Our latest-generation Jupiter network [...] delivering more than 1 Petabit/sec of total bisection bandwidth. This means that each of 100,000 servers can communicate with one another in an arbitrary pattern at 10 Gb/s.

---

1 A. Verma et al., "Large-Scale Cluster Management at Google with Borg," Google, Inc., *https://oreil.ly/uGbf5*.

2 Amin Vahdat, "Pulling Back the Curtain on Google's Network Infrastructure," Google AI Blog, August 18, 2015, *https://oreil.ly/JWczw*.

Such capability can be achieved only by having a network infrastructure that can be configured based on the applications' needs and is considered as an integral part of the overall infrastructure virtualization.

The Loomers' Riot?

New tools necessitate a new way of thinking, though, to be useful. It's the old "a fool with a tool is still a fool." I actually don't like this saying because you don't have to be a fool to be unfamiliar with a new tool and a new way of thinking. For example, many folks in infrastructure and operations are far detached from the way contemporary software development is done. This doesn't make them fools in any way, but it prevents them from migrating into the "software-defined" world. They might never have heard of unit tests, continuous integration (CI), or build pipelines. They may have been led to believe that "Agile" is a synonym for "haphazard" and also haven't had enough time to conclude that immutability is an essential property because rebuilding/regenerating a component from scratch beats making incremental changes.

As a result, despite being the bottleneck in an IT ecosystem that demands ever-faster changes and innovation cycles, operations teams are often not ready to hand over their domain to the "application folk" who can script the heck out of the software-defined anything. One could posit that such behavior is akin to the Loomer Riots because the economic benefits of a software-defined infrastructure are too strong for anyone to put a stop to it.[3] At the same time, it's important to get those folks on board who keep the lights on and who understand the existing systems the best. So, we can't ignore this dilemma.

 If software eats the world, there will be only two kinds of people: those who tell the machines what to do and those for whom it's the other way around.

Explaining to everyone What Is Code?[4] can be a useful first step. Having more senior management role models who can code would be another good step. However, living successfully in a software-defined world isn't a simple matter of learning programming or scripting.

---

3 After the introduction of the power loom in the UK in the early 1800s led to widespread unemployment and reduction in wages among loomers, they organized to destroy this new type of loom.

4 Paul Ford, "What Is Code?" *BusinessWeek*, June 11, 2015, *https://oreil.ly/n2hmb*.

Software Developers Don't Undo, They Re-Create

A vivid example of how software developers think differently is *reversibility*; that is, the ability to quickly revert to a known stable state if a new configuration isn't working.

 When our team requested the ability to revert to a known good infrastructure configuration state from an infrastructure vendor, the response was that this would require an explicit "undo" script for each possible action, a huge additional investment in their eyes. Apparently, they didn't think like software developers.

With manual updates, reverting to a known good state is very difficult and time consuming at best. In a software-defined world, it's much easier. Experienced software developers know that if their automated build system can build an artifact, such as a binary image or a piece of configuration, from scratch, they can easily revert to a previous version. So, rather than explicitly undoing a change these developers reset version control to the last known good version, rebuild from scratch, and republish this "undone" configuration, as illustrated in Figure 14-1.

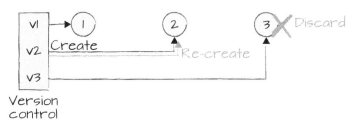

Figure 14-1. A traditional and a version-controlled mindset

This mindset stems from software being ephemeral—re-creating it from scratch isn't a major effort. By making infrastructure software-defined, it can also become ephemeral. This is a huge shift in mindset, especially when you consider the annual depreciation cost of all that hardware. But only thinking this way can provide the true benefit of being software defined.

In complex software projects, rolling things back is a quite normal procedure, often instigated by the so-called "build cop" after failing automated tests cause the build to go "red." The build cop will ask the developer who checked in the offending code to make a quick fix or simply revert that code submission. Configuration automation tools have a similar ability to regain a known stable state and can be applied to reverting and automatically reconfiguring infrastructure configurations.

Melt the Snowflakes

Software-defined infrastructure shuns the notion of "snowflake" or "pet" servers —servers that have been running for a long time without a reinstall, have a unique configuration,[5] and are manually maintained with great care.

"This server has been up for three years" isn't bragging rights but a risk: who could re-create this "pet" server if it does go down?

In a software-defined world, a server or network component can be reconfigured or re-created automatically with ease, similar to re-creating a Java build artifact. You no longer have to be afraid to mess up a server instance because it can easily be re-created via software in minutes.

Software-defined infrastructure therefore isn't just about replacing hardware configuration with software, but primarily about adopting a rigorous development life cycle based on disciplined development, automated testing, and CI. Over the past decades, software teams have learned how to move quickly while maintaining quality. Turning hardware problems into software problems allows you to take advantage of this body of knowledge.

---

5 Just like every snowflake is unique, "snowflake servers" are those that don't match a standard configuration.

Automated Quality Checks

One of Google's critical infrastructure pieces was a router, which would direct incoming traffic to the correct type of service instance. For example, HTTP requests for maps.google.com would be forwarded to a service serving up maps data, as opposed to the search page. The router was configured via a file consisting of hundreds of regular expressions. Of course, this file was under version control, as it should be.

 Despite rigorous code reviews, invariably someday someone checked a misconfiguration into the service router, which immediately brought down most of Google's services because the requests weren't routed to the corresponding service instance. Luckily, the previous version was quickly restored thanks to version control. Google's answer wasn't to disallow changes to this file, because that would have slowed things down. Rather, automatic checks were added to the code submit pipeline to make sure that syntax errors or conflicting regular expressions are detected *before* the file is checked into the code repository.

When working with software-defined infrastructure, you need to work like you would in professional software development.

Use Proper Language

One curiosity about Google is that no one working there ever used buzzwords like "big data," "cloud," or "software-defined datacenter" because Google had all these things well before these buzzwords were created by industry analysts. Much of Google's infrastructure was already software defined more than a decade ago. As the scale of applications grew, configuring the many process instances that were being deployed into the datacenter became tedious. For example, if an application consists of seven frontends, 1 through 7, and two backends, A and B, frontends 1 through 4 would connect to backend *A*, whereas frontends 5 to 7 would connect to backend *B*. Maintaining individual configuration files for each instance would be cumbersome and error prone, especially as the system scales up and down. Instead, developers generated configurations via a well-defined functional language called Borg Configuration Language (BCL) (*https://oreil.ly/ 2qfVz*), which supports templates, value inheritance, and built-in functions like map() that are convenient for manipulating lists of values.

While avoiding the trap of *configuration files* (Chapter 11), learning a custom functional language to describe deployment descriptors may not be everyone's cup of tea, but for software developers that's the natural approach.

When configuration programs became more complex, causing testing and debugging configurations to become an issue, folks wrote an interactive expression evaluator and unit testing tools. That's what software people do to solve a problem: solve software problems with software!

The BCL example highlights what a real software-defined system looks like: well-defined languages and tooling that make infrastructure part of the software development life cycle. GUIs for infrastructure configuration, which vendors often like to show off, should be banned because they don't integrate well into a software life cycle, aren't testable, and are error prone.

Software Eats the World, One Revision at a Time

There's much more to being software defined than a few scripts and configuration files. Rather, it's about making infrastructure part of your software development life cycle (SDLC). First, make sure your SDLC is fast but disciplined, and automated but quality oriented. Second, apply the same thinking to your software-defined infrastructure; or else you may end up with *SDA*, Software-Defined Armageddon.

15

A4 Paper Doesn't Stifle Creativity

A Solid Platform Gives Developers a Blank Sheet of Paper

Creativity knows no boundaries

Today's IT departments must meet two major but seemingly conflicting goals. First, the business environment puts pressure on IT spend, whereas digital disruptors require IT to increase the rate of change and innovation. One of IT's major cost levers is harmonization of the IT landscape: reducing the number of different applications and technologies in use provides better economies of scale, better negotiating power with vendors, and fewer skills requirements, which can be a major factor in times of skill scarcity.

At first sight, such an effort does seem at odds with innovation, though; how can a company be innovative if too many parameters are fixed? Doesn't innovation require freedom to experiment and questioning established norms and standards? Interestingly, some harmonization not only doesn't get in the way of innovation but actually boosts it.

Following a recurring theme from this book, we can once again get a hint from the real world: paper.

A4 Paper

One of the most well-known standards—at least outside the US—is the standard for paper sizes. The most common size of paper used around the world for printing or writing is A4 size paper. A4 paper sets a precise standard of 210 mm wide × 297 mm long for a sheet of paper. At first glance, setting such a standard may appear both arbitrary and constraining. On a second look, though, it's neither.

The family of DIN A paper sizes,[1] defined in 1922, are far from arbitrary. The ratio between length and width is always equal to the square root of 2. Thanks to this unique property, two sheets of a smaller size put next to each other along the long edge are the same size as a single sheet of paper of the next larger size. For example, two A4 papers make an A3 paper. And if you are out of A5 paper, you can fold a sheet of A4 paper in the center and tear it to receive two perfectly sized sheets of A5 paper. Pretty handy, huh?

But there's more. If two A4-size sheets make an A3-size sheet, and two A3 sheets make an A2 sheet, and so on, 16 A4 sheets make up an A0 size sheet. But how big should such a sheet be? Easy: one square meter, again with the edge dimensions having a square root of 2 relationship, resulting in a size of 841 mm × 1189 mm. So, if you ever wonder if 3 sheets of common "80 gram" paper require extra postage, you can quickly compute that each sheet weighs 1/16th of that of a square meter, which is 80/16 = 5 grams per the paper classification. For comparison, try calculating the weight of three letter size sheets of #20 paper in ounces.[2]

On top of all this, standardizing paper sizes eliminates the need to select from myriad paper sizes. It also stacks neatly and allows the use of same-size

---

1 *DIN* stands for *Deutsches Institut für Normung*, which is the current name of the German national institution that sets official domestic standards.

2 20 is the weight in pounds of a ream (500 sheets) of Bond paper, which measures 22 × 17 inches. Converting that to ounces per sheet is left as an exercise to the reader.

sleeves, envelopes, drawers, paper punches, and copiers, so you don't have to worry about any of those. A4-size paper is so ubiquitous that even my laptop is A4 size so that it will neatly fit into any briefcase that is designed to hold a sheet of paper.

Importantly, despite being rather prescriptive, the paper standard doesn't stifle creativity. You can still draw and write on it, whatever you prefer. I haven't seen a person who was unable to work on a blank sheet of paper due to its particular dimensions. It's fair to say that A4 paper actually *increases* creativity because it allows users to focus on the creative aspects—what they put on the paper, as opposed to dealing with paper format ecosystem entropy.

So, when we are standardizing IT components, we should look for a result that resembles paper formats: standardize what simplifies life and achieves economies of scale, but give users a blank sheet of paper to work on.

Product Standards Restrict, Interface Standards Enable

When IT departments are looking to harmonize their portfolio, they usually aim to *standardize products* (Chapter 32); for example, which databases or applications servers should be used across applications. Standardizing products reduces diversity and can save money by bundling purchasing power, a classic *economies of scale* (Chapter 35) maneuver: the bigger a company's spend on a particular product or vendor, the better a deal it can likely secure. However, unlike A4-size paper, such product standards do tend to limit developers' choices and are therefore quite unpopular.

The most successful technical standards in the world, in contrast, have been those that affect how products or components can be combined. We call such standards *interface standards* or *compatibility standards*. The most dramatic example of an interface standard that affects IT is the hypertext transfer protocol (HTTP). HTTP enabled the internet revolution because it allowed any browser to connect to any web server, implemented in any programming language or technology. As a result, parts became easily interchangeable and enabled independent evolution. For example, anyone could develop a higher-performing web server without having to replace all browsers.

Platform Standards

There's a useful and increasingly common approach that, done right, combines the benefits of interface and product standards to act more like A4-size paper than a corporate rule book. These standards are referred to as *platform standards* or simply *platforms*. Platform standards essentially split the IT into two parts: a lower layer that standardizes those elements that are unlikely to form a competitive differentiator and an upper layer of in-house-developed software that provides direct business value and competitive differentiation.

This concept of platforms has long been known to the car industry where multiple, outwardly distinct vehicle models share the same "infrastructure" of chassis, suspension, safety equipment, and engine options. Because these components require significant engineering effort and cost but are less visible to the end customer, it makes sense to reuse them across as many models as possible. Meanwhile, interior and exterior elements differ among models as they often serve as differentiating factors across market segments. For a nice model that allows plotting elements by how visible and how commoditized they are, I highly recommend Wardley maps.[3]

Back in IT, layering certainly isn't a new idea. If anything, it's one of the *oldest concepts to reduce complexity and achieve reuse* (Chapter 28). The best candidates for the lower layer are traditionally found in the networking and hardware environments. There are two reasons for this. First, for most enterprises, there's little business value in different types of processor architectures, networking equipment, monitoring frameworks, or application servers. Second, their *lower rate of change* (Chapter 3) makes it easier to standardize them into a common base layer.

Layers Versus Platforms

So, if platforms use layering, which is a well-known concept, what makes platforms different and interesting? At least three aspects spring to mind:

Self service

In traditional IT, the interaction between the layers occurred by means of *service requests or emailing spreadsheets* (Chapter 13), vaguely based on a model that the lower layers hold the power (that's governance, after all!) and the folks in the upper layer have to beg for access. Modern platforms, epitomized by cloud service providers, turn this concept on its head by allowing people in the upper layers to request services through online portals or APIs. It's customer centricity applied to IT services.

---

3 S. Wardley, "Wardley maps," Medium.com, March 7, 2018, *https://oreil.ly/bk3sL*.

Dividing line

> The dividing line between the IT layers used to be infrastructure versus applications, often even reflected in the organization's structure, where you'd find an application team and an infrastructure team. Cloud computing platforms have shifted the boundary dramatically and keep shifting it. For example, serverless computing shifts the platform all the way up to the code for a single function.

Center of gravity

> Modern platforms don't just focus on the compute runtime, such as network, servers, and storage as previous approaches did. They also include software delivery tool chains because they are a key element that defines *delivery velocity* (Chapter 3). They also often include monitoring and communication, such as service meshes. As a result, they offer applications a well-rounded ecosystem of services.

Done well, standardizing lower layers doesn't constrain what functionality can be delivered to the business. However, it relieves development teams from having to choose and operate a whole stack of software and hardware. It also channels developers' creative energy into those parts that generate business value as opposed to developing yet-another-persistence-framework. Interestingly, this matches my favorite definition of software architecture: design decisions that keep implementors from exercising *needless creativity* (Chapter 8).

 At a major financial services provider, we defined an Agile Delivery Platform that was a lot more than just a private cloud runtime; it included an on-premises source code repository, a containerized build tool chain, common monitoring and visualization, and security features. It became the de facto platform for new application delivery and sped up adoption of modern development techniques.

Digital Discipline

Digital companies are great examples of *high velocity necessitating discipline* (Chapter 31). They realized that strictness in some aspects actually boosts the rate of innovation. Often, this strictness comes in form of an A4-style platform. For example, Google, which is well-known for rapid innovation, has *very strict platform standards* (Chapter 32) for application deployment and operations: there's essentially one way to deploy an application, on one type of operating system, observed by one monitoring framework. Google found the exact level at which to abstract to allow people to innovate where it matters without exercising needless creativity.

 Google is a great example of enforcing strict platform standards that neverthe-less boost the speed of innovation.

Avoid the Skipping Stones

There's a very silly TV show called *Takeshi's Castle*, which makes contestants compete by enduring several rather sadistic exercises, much to the enjoyment of the audience. An all-time favorite is Skipping Stones, called "Dragon God Pond" in the Japanese original. The contestants are tasked with crossing a pond filled with a murky, rather uninviting liquid via a sequence of stepping stones. It wouldn't be funny, though, if there weren't a catch: most stones are solid, but some are merely floating pieces of Styrofoam. They are visually indistinguisha-ble, but designed to quickly give way to any unlucky contestant's misstep, result-ing in spectacular falls, which are best watched in slow motion.

Some platforms seem to make their customers play Takeshi's Castle—their components appear solid, but some suddenly give way. IT platforms give way by deprecating components, having inconsistent interfaces, or being poorly integra-ted. Needless to say that this isn't much fun for the contestant: you. So, don't build platforms that look like the Skipping Stones! Instead, follow a few critical aspects to assure that your platform is solid, but flexible enough to spur adoption and innovation:

Choose a useful level of abstraction
> Would standardizing pens and pencils still improve creativity or run the risk of stifling it? Useful standards are those that shield significant com-plexity but can be utilized by a wide range of tools: you can draw on A4 paper with pen, pencil, chalk, watercolor, and more, so it's a concrete stan-dard that allows many uses.

Constantly fine tune
> Nothing is eternal, especially in IT. The same holds true for IT standards. They need to be able to evolve along with the technology and new insights. Today's best innovation platform can be a road block in just a few years.

Keep it up to date

Although your customers may want your platform to be stable, they don't want it to be outdated or full of security holes because of lacking patches. Keep your product versions up to date!

Make it real

Standards that just exist on paper are unlikely to be followed. Therefore, make sure your standards come alive in ready-to-use tools and platforms. Many people may not care for A4 paper, but if it's the easy choice available in any store, they probably don't mind.

Reward compliance

You want to reward people who adopt the standards; for example, by offering lower prices, better service, or shorter provisioning times when compared to nonstandard solutions.

Cloud providers don't set standards just on paper, but provide an implementation that allows rapid delivery through self-service interfaces. Cloud platforms also continuously evolve and grow, making them excellent examples of solid platforms that enable innovation.

 One of the critical decisions making the Agile Delivery Platform a success was to regularly update the platform, against common practice (and advice from the infrastructure teams). The traditional approach, which would have required all application owners' agreement before updating, would have made the platform outdated within just a few months.

After initially mostly offering virtual machines as infrastructure as a service (IaaS), most cloud providers now offer platform as a service (PaaS) for applications and functions as a service (FaaS)/"serverless" for single code snippets. Focusing on common (de facto) standards like Docker for containers has fueled the creation of platforms and boosted the rate of innovation among platform users.

One Size Might Not Fit All Tastes

As powerful as platforms and standards are, establishing global standards can be harder than expected. For example, despite all the virtues of A4-size paper, so-called "letter-size" paper at 8.5 × 11 inches remains a standard in the United

States. Though Wikipedia describes its precise origin as "not known"[4]—the most credible hypothesis ascribes it to historical manufacturing by hand—a migration to DIN-sized paper appears unlikely. Until then, I'll have to use two different paper cartridges for my venerable HP LaserJet 4 and be frequently reminded to PC LOAD LETTER.[5]

---

4 Wikipedia, "Paper Size," *https://oreil.ly/et7UH*.

5 Wikipedia, "PC LOAD LETTER," *https://oreil.ly/ou-b8*.

16

The IT World Is Flat

Without a Map, Any Road Looks Promising

Living in the Middle Kingdom—by Kwong Hing Yen (江慶人)

Maps have been valuable tools for millennia, despite most of them, especially world maps, being quite badly distorted. The fundamental challenge of plotting the surface of a sphere onto a flat sheet of paper forces maps to make compromises when depicting angles, sizes, and distances—if the earth were flat, things would be much easier. For example, the historically popular *Mercator projection* provides true angles for seafarers, meaning you can read an angle off the map and use the same angle on the ship's compass (compensating for the discrepancy between geographic and magnetic north). The price to pay for this convenient property, which avoids distorting angles, is area distortion: the further away countries are from the equator, the larger they appear on the map. That's why Africa looks disproportionately small on such maps,[1] a trade-off that might

---

1 "The True Size Of Africa," Information Is Beautiful, Oct. 14, 2010, *https://oreil.ly/yeVps*.

be acceptable when navigating by boat: misestimating the distance is likely a lesser problem than heading into the wrong direction.

Plotting the surface of a sphere also presents the challenge of deciding where the "middle" is. Most world maps conveniently position Europe in the center, supported by 0 degree longitude (the *prime meridian*) going through Greenwich, England. This depiction results in Asia being in the "East" and the Americas being in the "West." The keen observer will quickly conclude that when living on a sphere, notions of West and East are somewhat relative to the viewpoint of the beholder. The same type of thinking likely motivated the residents of East Asia to historically put their country in the middle of the map and even name it accordingly: 中國, the "middle kingdom."

Although many centuries later we might regard such a world view as a tad self-centered, at the time it simply made practical sense: having the most detail about places that are near you makes putting your starting point in the middle of your map natural. It also roughly lines up the map boundaries with your travel limits.

IT landscapes are also vast, and navigating a typical enterprise's range of products and technologies can be equally daunting to sailing Cape Horn. Despite some similarities, each IT landscape tends to be its own planet, making universal IT world maps hard to come by. Aside from some useful attempts like the Big Data Landscape by Matt Turck (*https://oreil.ly/_yNxO*), enterprise architects therefore often rely on maps provided by their vendors.

Vendors' Middle Kingdoms

As chief architect of a large company, you'll quickly gather new friends: account managers, (presales) solution architects, field CTOs, and sales executives, to name a few. Their job is to sell their products to large enterprises like yours that rely heavily on external hardware, software, and services. It makes sense to buy systems that aren't a competitive differentiator or to lease them via a software as a service (SaaS) model. Creating an accounting system yourself is in most cases as valuable as creating your own electricity. It's important to have such things, but they won't give you any competitive advantage. So just as you're unlikely to benefit from operating your own power plant, you should also abstain from building your own accounting system.

Enterprise vendors are also an important source of information, especially for architects, as vendors keep close track of industry trends. Do keep in mind, however, that the information you are given might be skewed by the vendor's worldview. That's because enterprise vendors live in their own *middle kingdom*, generally depicting their home state disproportionately large and accepting a fair degree of distortion on the periphery. Distortion can take the form of vendors defining product categories or buzzwords by features that only their product has. For example, I have seen "Zero Trust" pegged to safe web browsing and "GitOps" tied to Kubernetes. Both are a stretch of imagination at best.

 I often joke that if you have no concept whatsoever of what a car is and only ever talked to one specific German automaker, you'd end up walking away with the firm belief that a star emblem on the hood is a defining feature of an automobile.

IT architects in large enterprises must therefore develop their own, balanced worldview so that they can safely navigate the treacherous waters of enterprise architecture and IT transformation. Vendors' distortion doesn't imply deception; it's largely a byproduct of the context people grew up in. If you develop databases, it's natural to view the database as the center of any application: after all, that's where the data is stored. Server and storage hardware are viewed as parts of a *database appliance*, whereas application logic becomes a *data feed*. Conversely, to a storage hardware manufacturer, everything else is just "data," and databases are lumped into a generic "middleware" segment. It's like me on my first trip to Australia considering a quick hop to New Zealand because I thought it was so super close. Realizing that it's still a good three-and-a-half-hour flight from Melbourne to Auckland proved that my world map is also distorted on the periphery.

Plotting Your World Map

To avoid falling into the "star on the hood" or the "it's all a database" trap, it's important that your architecture team first develops its own, undistorted map of the IT landscape—a great exercise for *enterprise architects* (Chapter 4). Luckily, the world of IT is flat, so it's a bit easier to plot on a whiteboard or a piece of paper. Your own map gives you a much better, product-neutral understanding and may, for example, illustrate that a car's drive train is much more relevant than the hood emblem.

 Any architect who carries a product name in their title likely carries the vendor's map as opposed to your own.

It's OK to draw the map piece-by-piece, starting, for example, where a new product needs to be set up or an old one replaced—*rate of change* (Chapter 3) is once again a good indicator for architecture. Another good starting point is where existing products represent critical differentiators for the company.

Drawing your map requires you to piece together information from various sources, which will often be distorted. Maybe one day we'll have an AI-driven application that can do this for enterprise architecture the same way smart-phones can stitch together multiple photos into a panorama. Until then, you have to collect information from vendors, blogs, industry analyst reports, and your infrastructure and development teams. Resist the temptation to simply ask your favorite two- or three-lettered enterprise supplier to make the map for you. For one, it will once again be distorted, and second, at today's rate of innovation many of them are outdated, as well.

When placing countries and territories on your map, focus on function and relationships as opposed to product names.

 Describing the architecture of a big data system as "Microsoft SQL Server" is no more useful than claiming the architecture of a house is "Ytong."[2] Both may be good choices, but neither describes the architecture.

Because IT architecture operates *between* the buzzwords and the product names, it's less concerned with the pieces than with how they are put together. This is why it's so important to look not only at the boxes but also the *lines* (Chapter 23).

Defining Borders

Where to place the "borders" in your map is a key aspect of doing architecture in the enterprise. Although we all like to think of boundary-free architecture, if we want to establish a meaningful map and vocabulary for our enterprise, we need to place some borders. For example, should our "data" continent be separated into data warehouses, data lakes, data marts, and databases? Would databases then break down into relational and NoSQL databases, which could further break down into graph databases, object stores, and so on? Would you want to distinguish managed cloud databases like DynamoDB or Spanner from other

---

2 Ytong is the name of a popular brand of aerated concrete bricks used in Europe for building construction.

databases? Would you want to separate operational databases from those used for analytics? There are many ways to slice, and defining these boundaries is a key element of doing architecture at an enterprise level. The word *reference architecture* even comes to mind, but you need to keep in mind that architecture isn't a copy-paste exercises. You need to define the continents and countries that are meaningful for your organization, your business strategy, and your business architecture, as illustrated in Figure 16-1.

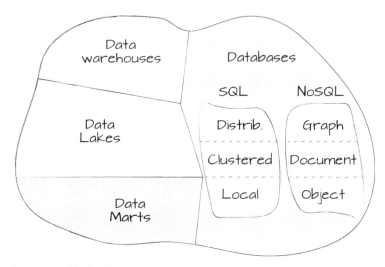

Figure 16-1. A plausible database continent

A colleague of mine conducted a thorough mapping exercise for application monitoring that includes black-box monitoring, white-box monitoring, troubleshooting, log analysis, alerting, and predictive monitoring. All are distinct but interrelated aspects of an application monitoring solution. Many vendors, especially those with a history in application performance monitoring, will also include performance testing because that's the middle of their map. Whether you want to do the same or whether it's part of the development tool chain is your decision.

 When I see most reference architectures, I feel that they ought to print a disclaimer at the bottom, similar to those used for movies: "Any similarities with real persons or systems is purely coincidental."

Charting Territory

As soon as your IT world map has undisputed borders, you can start populating "countries" with vendor products that may be in use or available on the market. The map will help you assess how well a vendor's product fits your map. Some products may not completely cover the gap, while others have significant overlap with solutions already in place.

> Placing products on an IT world map is a bit like playing Tetris: the piece that fits best depends on what you already have in place. This means that rather than picking the "best" product, you should select the one that fits best.

Most large IT organizations *govern their product portfolio* (Chapter 32) via a standards group. Standards reduce product diversity and allow enterprises to harvest economies of scale; for example, by bundling purchasing power. When defining standards, the world map can be an enormous help because it can determine what kind of standards you'll want and at which level you'd want to apply them. For example, defining different types of databases or data stores on your "database continent" can tell you whether you need a different standard for relational databases and NoSQL databases or whether you distinguish light-weight use cases from mission-critical ones. Having a good map is essential to navigating the complexity of vendor offerings.

> A vivid example of the difficulty of discussing product fit without a good map came up in a conversation about a web portal: a divisional IT manager using a shared web portal lamented the lack of documentation on port forwarding. The project's architect replied that a web server isn't part of their solution, assuming port forwarding is done in a web server. Much debate and confusion ensued because the division implemented port forwarding in an integrated network management tool, not in a web server. They used different world maps and continued to talk past each other for some time.

Looking at the map to get the proverbial "lay of the land" can help a lot to resolve misunderstandings. For example, a map might show that port forwarding is part of the concept of an *Application Delivery Controller* (ADC), which manages web traffic by including functions such as reverse proxying, load balancing, and also port forwarding. You can utilize a web server as ADC in simple cases or purchase an integrated product like *F5*.

Ironically, conducting the worthwhile exercise of plotting your own IT world map can be challenged by traditional IT managers as "academic." This can be especially amusing in Germany where IT management is littered with PhDs (not necessarily in any technical major) who carry the title "Dr." as part of their legal name. If *pragmatic* means "haphazard," I am happy to be in the "academic" camp: I am paid to think and plan, not to play product lottery.

Product Philosophy Compatibility Check

When plotting vendor offerings onto your map, it's not enough to just understand the vendor's current product portfolio, but also where it is headed—the world of IT never stands still. That's why I first like to understand whether a vendor's and our worldviews align.

Meeting with vendors' senior technical staff, such as a CTO, is most effective when discussing worldview and comparing maps because too many "solution architects" are just glorified technical salespeople, who navigate purely off the vendor's map, the "middle kingdom" so to speak. I need a world map, though.

 When an account manager starts the meeting with "please help us understand your environment," which roughly translates into "please tell me what I should sell to you," I typically preempt the exercise by asking the senior person about their product philosophy. It's a bit of a big word, but it's helpful in shifting the conversation to the vendor's world map.

I prefer to ask vendors two key questions to understand their world map:

- *What base assumptions did you have to make?* No one can operate on a completely empty map without borders, so the vendor must have made choices and picked boundaries. The answer to this question tells you where the edge of their map is.

- *What's the toughest problem you had to solve?* The answer to this question will tell you where the center of their map is.

Discussing what base assumptions and decisions are baked into a product gives you great insight into a vendor's world map (see Figure 16-2), both about the center and the edge (remember the IT world is flat, so it has edges).

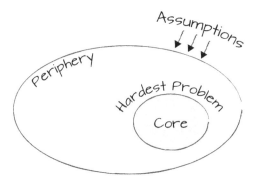

Figure 16-2. A product vendor's core and periphery

Naturally, this works only when talking to someone who is actually defining the vendor's corporate or product strategy. Looking at the company leadership page can help you identify the right people. Looking at the leadership's history can also help you understand "where they come from"; that is, under which assumptions they operate.

 When asking these questions of a monitoring vendor, it became clear that the core of their map was being able to monitor running applications without having access to the source code. This feature is particularly useful if you look at the problem from an operational point of view, especially if you work in *an organization that separates "change" from "run"* (Chapter 12). However, in a "you build it, you run it" environment where development teams are directly involved in operational aspects, this intellectual property would be less valuable. You can end up paying for something that you don't need. Understanding the vendor's world map can help you make better decisions.

Comparing world maps isn't about finding out which one is right and which one is wrong; it's about comparing worldviews. For example, I believe that a good programming language and a disciplined software development life cycle (SDLC) beats *"easy" configuration* (Chapter 11). That's because I come from a software engineer mindset. Other folks might be happy to not have to hassle with `git stash` and compilation errors and prefer the vendor's configuration tools.

Shifting Territory

While the real world is relatively static (continental drift is pretty slow and the trend of splitting countries in the '90s has also slowed down a bit), the world of IT is changing faster than ever. Because it's difficult for a vendor to change its product philosophy, you will likely encounter old products with a new coat of paint on top. Your job as an architect is to look through the shiny new paint and see whether there's any rust or filler underneath.

17

Your Coffee Shop Doesn't Use Two-Phase Commit

Learn About Distributed System Design While in the Queue!

Grande, durable, nonatomic, soy chai latte

When designing solutions, architects often look at technical solutions like ACID (Atomic, Consistent, Isolated, Durable) transactions and binary values in order to craft a well-defined and perfect system. In reality, though, designing complex systems isn't that easy, so there's one more source of design guidance that you should consider: the real world.[1]

---

1 This chapter was published (in slightly different form) in *IEEE Software*, Vol. 22, and *Best Software Writing*, ed. J. Spolsky (Apress).

Hotto Cocoa o Kudasai

You know you're a geek when going to the coffee shop gets you thinking about interaction patterns between loosely coupled systems. This happened to me on a trip to Japan. Some of the more familiar sights in Tokyo are the numerous Starbucks coffee shops, especially in the areas of Shinjuku and Roppongi. After stretching my limited Japanese skills by muttering *"Hotto Cocoa o Kudasai"* ("A hot chocolate, please"), I returned to my bubble of foreigner-ness and started thinking about how Starbucks processes drink orders.

Starbucks, like most other businesses, is primarily interested in maximizing throughput of orders because more orders equal more revenue. Interestingly, the optimization for throughput results in a concurrent and asynchronous processing model: when you place your order, the cashier marks a coffee cup with the details of your order (e.g., tall, nonfat, soy, dry, extra hot latte with double shot) and places it into the queue, which is quite literally a queue of coffee cups lined up on top of the espresso machine. This queue decouples cashier and barista, allowing the cashier to keep taking orders even if the barista is momentarily backed up. If the store becomes busy, multiple baristas can be deployed in a *competing-consumer* scenario,[2] meaning that they work off items in parallel without duplicating work.

Asynchronous processing models can be highly scalable but are not without challenges. Still waiting for my hot chocolate, I started thinking about how Starbucks dealt with some of these issues. Maybe we can learn something from the coffee shop about designing successful asynchronous messaging solutions?

Correlation

Parallel and asynchronous processing causes drink orders to be not necessarily completed in the same order in which they were placed. This can happen for two reasons. First, order processing time varies by type of beverage: a blended smoothie takes more time to prepare than a basic drip coffee. A drip coffee ordered last might thus arrive first. Second, baristas might make multiple drinks in one batch to optimize processing time.

Starbucks therefore has a correlation problem: drinks that are delivered out of sequence must be matched up to the correct customer. Starbucks solves the problem with the same "pattern" used in messaging architectures: a *correlation*

---

2 Gregor Hohpe, "Competing Consumers," Enterprise Integration Patterns, *https://oreil.ly/NShD-*.

identifier[3] uniquely marks each message and is carried through the processing steps. In the US, most Starbucks use an explicit correlation identifier by writing your name on the cup at the time of ordering, calling it out when the drink is ready. Other countries might correlate by the type of drink. When I had difficulties in Japan understanding the baristas calling out the types of drinks, my solution was to order extra-large "venti" drinks because they're uncommon and therefore easily identifiable, that is, "correlatable."

Exception Handling

Exception handling in asynchronous messaging scenarios presents another challenge. What does the coffee shop do if you can't pay? They will toss the drink if it has already been made or otherwise pull your cup from the "queue." If they deliver you a drink that's incorrect or unsatisfactory, they will remake it. If the machine breaks down and they cannot make your drink, they will refund your money. Apparently, we can learn quite a bit about error-handling strategies by standing in the queue!

Just like Starbucks, distributed systems often cannot rely on two-phase-commit semantics that guarantee consistent outcomes across multiple actions. They therefore employ the same error-handling strategies.

WRITE OFF

The simplest error-handling strategy is doing nothing. If the error occurs during a single operation, you just ignore it. If the error happens during a sequence of related actions, you can ignore the error and continue with the subsequent steps, ignoring or discarding any work done so far. This is what the coffee shop would do when a customer is unable to pay: discard the drink and move on.

Doing nothing about an error might seem like a bad plan at first, but in the reality of a business transaction, this option might be perfectly acceptable: if the loss is small, building an error correction solution is likely more expensive than just letting things be. When humans are involved, correcting errors also has a cost and might delay serving other customers. Moreover, error handling can lead to additional complexity—the last thing you want is an error-handling mechanism that has errors. So, in many cases "simple does it."

---

3 Gregor Hohpe, "Correlation Identifier," Enterprise Integration Patterns, *https://oreil.ly/NkR28*.

I worked for a number of ISP providers who would choose to *write off* errors in the billing/provisioning cycle. As a result, a customer might end up with active service but would not get billed. The revenue loss was small enough that it didn't hurt the business and customers rarely complained about getting free service. Periodically, they would run reconciliation reports to detect the "free" accounts and close them.

RETRY

When simply ignoring an error won't do, you might want to retry the failing operation. This is a plausible option if there's a realistic chance that a renewed attempt will actually succeed; for example, because a temporary communications glitch has been fixed or an unavailable system has restarted. Retrying can overcome intermittent errors, but it doesn't help if the operation violates a firm business rule. Starbucks will try to remake your beverage if it's not to your liking but they won't if the power is out.

When encountering a failure in a group of operations (i.e., "transaction"), things become simpler if all components are *idempotent*, meaning they can receive the same command multiple times without duplicating the execution. You can then simply reissue all operations because the receivers that already completed them will simply ignore the retried operation. Shifting some of the error-handling burden, i.e., detecting duplicate messages, to the receivers thus simplifies the overall interaction.

It's amazing how frequently a basic retry operation succeeds in systems that were built out of zeros and ones. The common saying that defines insanity as "doing the same thing over and over again and expecting different results" apparently doesn't apply to computer systems.

COMPENSATING ACTION

The final option to put the system back into a consistent state after a failed operation is to undo the operations that were completed so far. Such "compensating actions" work well for monetary transactions that can recredit money that has been debited. If the coffee shop can't make the coffee to your satisfaction, it will refund your money to restore your wallet to its original state.

Because real life is full of failures, compensating actions can take many forms, such as a business calling a customer to ask them to ignore a letter that has been sent or to return a package that was sent in error. The classic counterexample to compensating an action is sausage making. Some actions are not easily reversible.

Transactions

All of the strategies described so far differ from a two-phase commit that relies on separate *prepare* and *execute* phases. In the Starbucks example, a two-phase commit would equate to waiting at the cashier desk with the receipt and the money on the table until the drink is finished. Once the drink is added to the items on the table, money, receipt, and drink can change hands in one swoop. Neither the cashier nor the customer would be able to leave until this "transaction" is completed.

Using such a two-phase-commit approach would eliminate the need for additional error-handling strategies, but it would almost certainly hurt Starbucks's business because the number of customers it can serve within a set time interval would decrease dramatically. This is a good reminder that a two-phase-commit approach can make life a lot simpler, but it can also hurt the free flow of messages (and therefore the scalability) because it has to maintain stateful transaction resources across multiple, asynchronous actions. It's also an indication that a high-throughput system should be optimized for the happy path instead of burdening each transaction for the rare case when something goes wrong.

Backpressure

Despite working asynchronously, the coffee shop cannot scale infinitely. As the queue of labeled coffee cups gets longer and longer, Starbucks can temporarily reassign a cashier to work as a barista. This helps reduce the wait time for customers who have already placed an order while exerting *backpressure* to customers still waiting to place their order. No one likes waiting in line, but not yet having placed your order provides you with the option to leave the store and forgo the coffee or to wander to the next, not-very-far-away coffee shop.

Conversations

The coffee shop interaction is also a good example of a simple but common *conversation pattern*[4] that illustrates sequences of message exchanges between participants. The interaction between two parties (customer and coffee shop) consists of a short synchronous interaction (ordering and paying) and a longer, asynchronous interaction (making and receiving the drink). This type of conversation is quite common in purchasing scenarios. For example, when an order is placed on

---

4 Gregor Hohpe, "Conversation Patterns," Enterprise Integration Patterns, *https://oreil.ly/g-wvQ*.

Amazon, the short synchronous interaction assigns an order number, whereas all subsequent steps (charging credit card, packaging, shipping) are performed asynchronously. Customers are notified via email (asynchronous) when the additional steps complete. If anything goes wrong, Amazon usually compensates the customer (refunds payment) or retries (resends the lost goods).

Canonical Data Model

A coffee shop can teach you even more about distributed system design. When Starbucks was relatively new, customers were both enamored and frustrated by the new language they had to learn just to order a coffee. Small coffees are now "tall," while a large one is called "venti." Defining your own language is not only a clever marketing strategy but also establishes a *canonical data model*[5] that optimizes downstream processing. Any uncertainties (soy or nonfat?) are resolved right at the "user interface" by the cashier, thus avoiding a lengthy dialogue that would burden the barista.

Welcome to the Real World!

The real world is mostly asynchronous: our daily lives consist of many coordinated but asynchronous interactions, such as reading and replying to email, buying coffee, etc. This means that an asynchronous messaging architecture can often be a natural way to model these types of interactions. It also means that looking at daily life can help design successful messaging solutions. *Domo arigato gozaimasu!*[6]

---

5 Gregor Hohpe, "Canonical Data Model," Enterprise Integration Patterns, *https://oreil.ly/8SU8U*.

6 "Thank you very much!"

PART III

Communication

Architects don't live in isolation. It's their job to gather information from disparate departments, articulate a cohesive strategy, communicate decisions, and win supporters at all levels of the organization. Communication skills are therefore paramount for architects. Conveying technical content to a diverse audience is challenging, though, because many classical presentation or writing techniques don't work well for highly technical subjects. For example, slides with single words superimposed on dramatic photographs may draw the audience's attention, but they aren't going to convey the intricacies of your cloud computing platform strategy. Instead, architects need to focus on a communication style that emphasizes content, but in an engaging and approachable manner.

You Can't Manage What You Can't Understand

"You can't manage what you can't measure" is a common management slogan. However, for the measurements to be meaningful, you have to understand the dynamics of the system you are managing. Otherwise, you can't tell which levers you should pull to influence the *system behavior* (Chapter 10).

Understanding what you are managing becomes an enormous challenge for decision makers in a world in which technology invades all parts of personal and professional lives. Even though business executives aren't expected to code a solution themselves, ignoring technological evolution and capabilities invariably leads to missed business opportunities or missed expectations when IT systems don't deliver what the business needs. Managing complex technology projects by timeline, staffing, and budget considerations alone is no longer going to suffice in the digital world that demands ever faster *delivery of functionality at high quality* (Chapter 40).

Architects must help close the gap between technical knowledge holders and high-level decision makers by clearly communicating the ramifications of technical decisions on the business; for example, through development and operational cost, flexibility, or time-to-market. It's not only the "business types" who face challenges in understanding complex technology, though. Even architects and developers cannot possibly keep up with all aspects of intricate technical solutions, forcing them to also rely on easy-to-understand but technically accurate descriptions of architectural decisions and their implications.

Getting Attention

Technical material can be very exciting, but ironically more so to the presenter than to the audience. Keeping attention through a lengthy presentation on code metrics or datacenter infrastructure can be taxing for even the most enthusiastic audience. Decision makers don't just want to see the hard facts, but also be engaged and motivated to support your proposal. Architects therefore have to use both halves of their brain to not only make the material logically coherent but to also craft an engaging story.

Pushing (Less) Paper

The technical decision papers published by my team in the past yielded much praise, but also unexpected criticism like, "All you architects do is produce paper." You might want to preempt such criticism by reminding people that documentation provides value in numerous ways:

Coherence
>   Agreeing on and documenting design principles and decisions improves consistency of decision making and thus preserves the conceptual integrity of the system design.

Validation
>   Structured documentation can help identify gaps and inconsistencies in the design.

Clarity of thought
>   You can write only what you have understood.

Education
>   New team members become productive faster if they have access to good documentation.

History

Decisions (Chapter 8) are based on a specific context, which may have changed since. Documentation can help you understand that context.

Stakeholder communication

Architecture documentation can help steer a diverse audience to the same level of understanding.

Nevertheless there seems to be an unfounded resistance against writing documentation among development teams.

 If someone claims that writing their thoughts down is too much effort, I routinely challenge them that this is likely because they haven't really understood things in the first place.

Useful documentation doesn't imply reams of paper, rather the opposite: short documents are more likely to be read. That's why most technical documents that my teams write are subject to a five-page limit.

Isn't the Code the Documentation?

Never shy of arguments, some developers claim that the source code is their documentation. So writing anything down is just duplication, right? They might have a point as long as all audience groups have access to the code, the code is well structured, and tools such as search are available. Still, your source code is highly unlikely to explain your value proposition and your critical decisions to your executive sponsors. For that, you're going to want to take the *Architect Elevator* (Chapter 1) up to the penthouse, equipped with a crystal clear piece of documentation.

Generating diagrams and documentation from code can be useful, but the resulting visuals often struggle to help people see the forest for the trees. Also, they don't do a great job at explaining why things were done the way they are because they generally fail to place the appropriate emphasis. Defining what is "interesting" or "noteworthy" luckily remains a human task.

Choosing the Right Words

Technical writing is difficult, as evidenced by user manuals, which must rank as some of the most ridiculed pieces of literature, if we can even call them that. They might be surpassed in lack of empathy only by tax form instruction sheets.

Architects must therefore be able to engage readers who wasted years of their career perusing poorly written manuals and who may never want to read anything technical again outside of the occasional Dilbert comic. Careful choice of words and clean sentence structures go a long way toward assisting readers in grasping difficult concepts.

Communication Tools

This part helps overcome some common challenges of creating engaging technical communication and highlights that documentation can be a tremendously useful tool for architects:

Chapter 18, Explaining Stuff
> Helping management reason about complex technical topics requires you to build a careful ramp for the audience.

Chapter 19, Show the Kids the Pirate Ship!
> Excite your audience by showing not just the building blocks but also the pirate ship.

Chapter 20, Writing for Busy People
> Busy executives won't read every line you write, so make it easy for them to navigate your documents.

Chapter 21, Emphasis Over Completeness
> There's always too much to tell. Focus on the essence.

Chapter 22, Diagram-Driven Design
> Not only can a picture say more than a thousand words, but it can actually help you design better systems.

Chapter 23, Drawing the Line
> Your architecture doesn't just include a list of components, but also their relationships. You must draw a line.

Chapter 24, Sketching Bank Robbers
> Technical staff might struggle to create a good picture of a system, even though they know it best. Help them by sketching bank robbers.

Chapter 25, Software Is Collaboration
> Version control/continuous integration isn't just for software development. It's a key part of collaboration.

 nothing

18

Explaining Stuff

Build a Ramp for the Reader, Not a Cliff!

Build a ramp, not a cliff for the reader—by Miu Tsutsui

Martin Fowler occasionally introduces himself as a guy "who is good at explaining things." Although this certainly has a touch of British Understatement™, it also highlights a critically important but rare skill in IT. Too often technical people either produce an explanation at such a high level that it is almost meaningless or spew out reams of technical jargon with no apparent rhyme or reason.

Build a Ramp, Not a Cliff

A team of architects once presented a new hardware and software stack for high-performance computing to a management steering committee. The material covered everything from workload management down to storage hardware. It contrasted vertically integrated stacks like Hadoop and Hadoop Distributed File System (HDFS) against standalone workload management solutions like Platform Load Sharing Facility (LSF) (*https://oreil.ly/FQmQY*). In one of the comparison slides, "POSIX compliance" jumped out as a selection criteria. While this may be entirely appropriate, how do you explain to someone who knows little about filesystems what this means, why it is important, and what the ramifications are?

We often refer to learning curves as steep, meaning it is tough for newcomers to become familiar with, or "ramp up" on, a new system or tool. I tend to assume my executive audience is quite intelligent (you don't get that high up simply by brown-nosing and playing politics), so they can in fact climb up a pretty steep learning ramp. What they cannot do is climb up a vertical cliff. Building a logical sequence that enables the audience to draw conclusions in an unfamiliar domain can be "steep" but doable. Being bombarded with out-of-context acronyms or technical jargon constitutes a "cliff." "POSIX compliance" is a cliff for most people.

You can turn it into a ramp by explaining that POSIX is a standard programming interface for file access, which is widely adhered to by Unix distributions, thus reducing lock-in in case you're maintaining multiple Linux flavors. With this ramp, executives can reason that because they already standardized on a single Linux distribution, POSIX compliance doesn't add much value. It's also not relevant for vertically integrated systems like Hadoop, which include the filesystem.

By building a ramp out of just a few words, you managed to involve someone who isn't deeply technical in the decision-making process. The ramp might not take the audience into the depths of POSIX versions and Linux flavors, but it provides a mental model to reason within the scope of the proposed decision.

A steep ramp is suitable for a quick climb but becomes tiresome if you are trying to lead your audience up Mount Everest. Therefore, consider how high (or deep) your audience needs to go to reason about what is presented. When defining terms, define them within the context of your problem, highlighting the relevant properties and omitting irrelevant detail. For example, details about POSIX history and Linux Standard Base aren't pertinent to the decision above and should be omitted.

Mind the Gap

The ramp should not only provide a reasonable incline but also avoid gaps or jumps in logic. Experts often don't perceive these gaps because their mind silently fills them in. This is a phenomenal feature of our brain, but an audience not intimately familiar with the topic is likely to stumble over even a minor gap and lose track of the line of reasoning. This effect is known as the *curse of knowledge*: once you know something, it's very hard to imagine how someone else learns it.

At a discussion about network security, a team of architects presented their requirement that servers located in the untrusted network zone have separate network interfaces, so-called NICs, for incoming and outgoing network traffic to avoid a direct network path from the internet to trusted systems. They continued with a statement that the vendor's "three-NIC design" cannot meet their requirement. To me, this made no sense: why is a server with three network interfaces unable to support a design requiring two interfaces, one for incoming traffic and one for outgoing? The answer was "obvious" to those who are familiar with the context: each server uses one additional network interface each for backup and management tasks, bringing the number of required ports to four, which clearly exceeds three. Skipping this detail created a gap large enough for the audience (and me) to stumble.

How big a gap they are creating is difficult to judge for the presenter. That's the curse of knowledge. In the example above, just a few words or two additional labeled lines in the diagram would have been enough to bridge the gap. That, however, doesn't imply that the gap itself was small—it might have been narrow, but plenty deep.

Presenting your line of reasoning to a person not familiar with the topic and asking them to "teach back" what you explained to them, similar to *holding a pop quiz* (Chapter 21), can be a great help in finding gaps.

First, Create a Language

When preparing technical conversations, I tend to use a two-step approach: first I set out to establish a basic mental model based on plain vocabulary without product names or acronyms. Once equipped with this, the audience is able to reason in the problem space and to discern the relevance of parameters. This mental model doesn't have to be anything formal, it merely needs to give the audience a way to make a connection between the different elements that are being described.

In the aforementioned filesystem example, I would first describe how file access is composed of a layered stack spanning from hardware (i.e., disk), basic block storage (like a SAN) to filesystems, and ultimately the operating system, which hosts the applications on top. This explanation doesn't even occupy half a slide and would nicely fit into a picture of layered blocks (see Figure 18-1).

As a second step, I can use this vocabulary to explain that Hadoop is integrated from the application layer all the way down to the local filesystem and disks without any SAN or the like. This setup has specific advantages, such as low cost and data locality, but requires you to build applications for this particular framework. In contrast, standalone filesystems for high-performance computing, for example GPFS or pNFS, either build on top of standard filesystems or provide "adapters" that make the proprietary filesystem available through widespread APIs, such as POSIX.

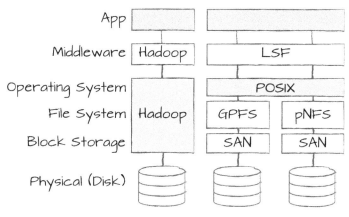

Figure 18-1. Comparing filesystems

You depict this in a diagram by having the Hadoop "stack" reach all the way from top to bottom, whereas other systems provide "seams," including POSIX compliance. The audience can now easily understand why the POSIX feature is important, but HDFS doesn't need to provide it.

Consistent Level of Detail

Determining the appropriate level of detail to support the line of reasoning is difficult. For example, we pretended "POSIX" is a single thing when in reality there are many different versions and components, the Linux Standard Base, and so on. The ability to draw the line at roughly the right level of detail is an important skill of an architect. Many developers or IT specialists love to inundate their audience with irrelevant jargon. Others consider it all terribly obvious and leave giant gaps by omitting critical details. As so often, the middle ground is where you want to be.

Drawing the line at the correct level of detail depends on you knowing your audience. If your audience is mixed, building a good ramp is ever more important because it allows you to catch up folks who aren't familiar with the details without boring those who are. The highest form is building a ramp that audience members already familiar with the subject matter appreciate despite not having learned anything new. This is tough to achieve but is a noble goal to aim for.

 Building a steep, but logical ramp allows those unfamiliar with the topic to get up to speed without boring those who are.

Getting the level of detail "just right" is usually a crapshoot, even if you do know the audience. At least as important, though, is sticking to a consistent level of detail. If you describe high-level filesystems on slide one and then dive into bit encoding on magnetic disks in slide two, you are almost guaranteed to either bore or lose your audience. Therefore, strive to find a line that maintains cohesion for reasoning about the architectural decision at hand, without leaving too many "dangling" aspects.

Algorithm-minded people would phrase this challenge as a graph partition problem: your topic consists of many elements that are logically connected, just like a graph of nodes connected by edges. Your task is to split the graph (i.e., to cover only a subset of the elements), while minimizing the number of edges (i.e., logical connections) being cut.

I Wanted to Have Liked To, but Didn't Dare Be Allowed

This poor translation of Karl Valentin's famous quote "*Mögen hätt' ich schon wollen, aber dürfen habe ich mich nicht getraut*" reminds me of the biggest challenge in explaining technical matter: too many architects believe their audience will never "get" their explanations, anyway. Some are also afraid that presenting technical detail will make them appear unfit for management. Therefore, even though they might have been able to, they're shying away from attempting to present technical concepts to a senior audience. In my view, this is a missed opportunity. I see every interaction with management also as a teaching opportunity. It's the basis for the *Architect Elevator*.

Every interaction with senior management is also a teaching opportunity. Use it!

Others go a step further and actually prefer to confuse management with random jargon, acronyms, and product names so that their "decisions" (often simply preferences or vendor recommendations) aren't unnecessarily put into question by the audience. This usually happens when technical teams, which see approval meetings as a nuisance rather than an opportunity to gather feedback, play off management's insecurity when it comes to technical topics.

I have a rather critical view of such behavior and generally advise management not to approve anything that isn't crystal clear to them. After all, if something isn't easily comprehensible, it's due to lack of clarity, not the audience.

Your role as an architect is to build a broad understanding of the ramifications of decisions and assumptions that were made. Without it, big problems are bound to pop up. For example, if a few years down the road an IT system can no longer serve the business needs, it is often due to a constraint or an invalid assumption that was made but never clearly communicated. Communicating decisions and explaining trade-offs clearly protects both you and the business.

19

Show the Kids the Pirate Ship!

Why the Whole Is Much More Than the Parts

This is what people want to see

When you look at the cover of a box of LEGOs you don't see a picture of each individual brick that's inside. Instead, you see the picture of an exciting, fully assembled model, such as a pirate ship. To make it even more exciting, the model isn't sitting on a living room table but is positioned in a life-like pirate's bay with cliffs and sharks—Captain Jack Sparrow would be jealous.

What does this have to do with communicating system architecture and design? Sadly, not much, but it should! Technical communication too frequently does the opposite: it lists all the individual elements in painstaking detail but forgets to show the pirate ship. The results are tons of boxes (and *hopefully some lines*; see Chapter 23), without a clear *gestalt* or overall value proposition.

Is this a fair comparison, though? LEGO is selling toys to kids, whereas architects need to explain the complex interplay between components to management and other professionals. Furthermore, IT professionals have to explain issues like network outages due to flooded network segments, something much less fun than playing pirates. I'd posit that the analogy holds and we can learn quite a few things from the pirate ship for the presentation of IT architecture.

Grab Attention

The initial purpose of the pirate ship is to draw attention among all the other competing toy boxes. While kids come to the toy store to hunt for new and shiny toys, many corporate meeting attendees are there because they were delegated by their boss, not because they want to hear your content. Grabbing their attention and getting them to put down their smartphones requires you to show something exciting.

Sadly, many presentations start with a table of contents, which I consider rather silly. First, it isn't exciting: it's like a list of assembly instructions instead of the ship. Second, the purpose of a table of contents is to allow a reader to navigate a book or a magazine. If the audience must sit through the entire presentation anyhow, there is no point in giving them a table of contents at the beginning.

Starting a presentation with a table of contents isn't useful, because the audience doesn't get to jump to Chapter 3. It also makes for a boring start: have you ever seen a movie that begins with the outline of its storyline?

The old adage of "tell them what you are going to tell them," which is vaguely attributed to Aristotle, certainly doesn't translate into a slide showing a table of contents. You are going to tell them how to build a pirate ship!

Build Excitement

The moment children and your audience look at the pirate ship, they should feel excitement. How cool is this? There are sharks and pirates, daggers and cannons, chests of gold, and the parrot. You can feel the story unravel in your head just as you are reading the list of play pieces. Why should PaaS, API gateways, web application firewalls, and build pipelines tell a less exciting story? It's a story of gaining speed in the treacherous waters of the digital world where automated tests and build pipelines keep you safe despite the fast pace. Automated deployments industrialize your delivery, and PaaS allows your fleet to grow and shrink as needed while you're trying to avoid running ashore in the vicious land of vendor lock-in. That's at least as exciting as a pirate story!

I am convinced that IT architecture can be much more exciting and interesting than people commonly believe. In an interview (*https://oreil.ly/79lq9*) with my friend Yuji back in 2004, I explained that software development is quite a bit more exciting than it appears on the outside—it is as exciting as you make it. If you regard software development as a pile of LEGOs, you haven't seen the pirate ship! People who find software and architecture boring or just a necessary tedium haven't scratched the surface of software design and architecture thinking. They also haven't understood that IT isn't any longer a means to an end but an innovation driver for the business. They consider IT as randomly stacking LEGO bricks, when in reality we are building exciting pirate ships!

Focus on Purpose

Coming back to the pirate ship, the box also clearly shows the purpose of the pieces inside. The purpose isn't for the bricks to be randomly stacked together but to build a cohesive, balanced solution. The whole really is much more than the sum of the parts in this case. It's the same with system design: a database and a few servers are nothing special, but a scale-out, masterless NoSQL database is quite exciting.

Alas, the technical staff who had to put all the pieces together is prone to dwell on said pieces instead of drawing attention to the purpose of the solution they built. They feel that the audience should appreciate all the hard work that went into assembling the pieces as opposed to the usefulness of the complete solution. Here's the bad news: no one is interested in how much work it took you; people want to see the results you achieved.

Pirate Ship Leads to Better Decisions

A pirate ship can do more than build excitement. It can also be a tool to make better decisions. My *Architect Elevator* workshops (*https://architectelevator.com/workshops/*) include an exercise to draw a system architecture. To see different ways of illustrating a common architecture, I picked a system that's quite well understood to most attendees, an application monitoring system. I hand each group of attendees about a dozen cards, each of which contains common monitoring components like log aggregator, time series database, thresholds, alerting, and ask them to draw an architecture containing these pieces.

Attendees will typically draw diagrams that put the components into a logical sequence; for example, by data flow, as demonstrated in Figure 19-1. Sometimes components are further grouped into major functions, such as data collection, data processing, and user interface. That's what architecture diagrams normally look like.

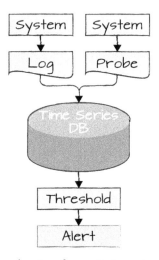

Figure 19-1. A typical architecture drawing of a monitoring system

After looking at such diagrams, I ask an innocent-sounding question: "What's this system's purpose?" Initially, attendees mention detecting anomalies and alerting someone. After some contemplation and prodding, the architects start to see the bigger picture. They correctly identify the real purpose of a monitoring system as maximizing system availability by minimizing system downtime. This is easily validated by assuming the opposite: the only time you don't need any monitoring is if you don't care about system availability.

Soon after, participants realize that the original picture shows only half the equation: a monitoring system is useful only if a detected problem can be analyzed and corrected. Based on this insight, they start to augment or redo the diagrams to show the pirate ship; that is, the main purpose, as depicted in Figure 19-2.

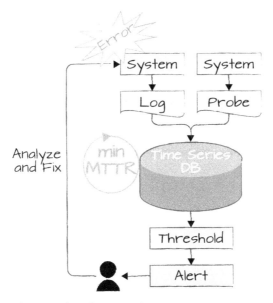

Figure 19-2. Showing the pirate ship of a monitoring system

They can now add the equivalent of the shark and the parrot by illustrating the purpose in the center of the diagram: minimize MTTR, the time from the error to recovery. As the MTTR spans the whole circle, we can think about both sides: how long does it take to detect an outage, and how long does it take to resolve it?

Thanks to the completed model, this aspect is apparent, and we can better reason about whether the company should invest in an upgraded monitoring system. Investing in a monitoring system that reduces the time to detect outages from half an hour to a few minutes thanks to better sensors and smarter analytics may seem like a good idea. If resolving an outage takes several hours, though, the picture changes: spending, for instance, half a million dollars to reduce the MTTR from 4.5 hours to 4.1 hours doesn't look that great anymore. Instead, you'd be looking to reduce the time spent resolving outages. This can be achieved, for example, by better transparency across systems or higher *levels of automation* (Chapter 13) that can quickly roll back the deployed software to an earlier, stable version. Drawing a better picture has *helped us make better decisions* (Chapter 22).

The Product Box

A successful concept similar to the pirate ship is the *product box*, one of Luke Hohmann's "innovation games" from his book of the same title.[1] This game asks participants to design a physical retail box for their product. To be appealing to potential buyers, such a box would want to show common usages and highlight benefits instead of just features.

 Thinking of your product like a retail item can help focus on tangible benefits instead of technical features.

If teams do well, they'll put an exciting pirate ship on the cover, as shown in Figure 19-3.

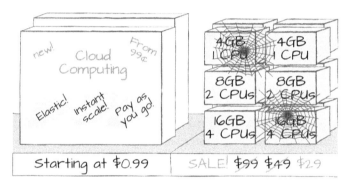

Figure 19-3. A product box for cloud computing

Designing the Pirate Ship

Drawing a pirate ship is generally a new, and occasionally uncomfortable, exercise for product and engineering teams. A few techniques can overcome initial hurdles.

---

1 Luke Hohmann, *Innovation Games: Creating Breakthrough Products Through Collaborative Play* (Boston: Addison-Wesley), 2007.

SHOW CONTEXT

The LEGO box cover image shows the pirate ship within a useful context, such as a (fake) pirate's bay. Likewise, the context in which an IT system is embedded is at least as relevant as the intricacies of the internal design. Hardly any system lives in isolation, and the interplay between systems is often more difficult to engineer than the innards of a single system. So you should show a system in its natural habitat.

Many architecture methods begin with a *system context diagram*. While well intentioned, too many times it fails to be useful because it aims for a complete system specification without *placing an emphasis* (Chapter 21). Such diagrams show an endless ocean, but not the pirate ship.

THE CONTENT ON THE INSIDE

LEGO toys also show the exact part count and their assembly, but they do so on a leaflet inside the box, not on the cover. Correspondingly, technical communication should display the pirate ship on the first page or slide and keep the description of the bricks and how to stack them together for the subsequent pages. Get your audience's attention, then take them through the details. If you do it the other way around, they might all be asleep by the time the exciting part finally comes.

CONSIDER THE AUDIENCE

Just like LEGO has different product ranges for different age groups, not every IT audience is suitable for the pirate ship. To some levels of management that are far removed from technology, you may need to show the little duckie made from a handful of LEGO DUPLO bricks.

Pack Some Pathos

Some might feel that excitement is a bit too frivolous for a serious workplace discussion. That's where you should look back at Aristotle, who gave us great advice on communicating, some 2,300 years ago (Figure 19-4). He concluded that a good argument is based on *logos*, facts and reasoning; *ethos*, trust and authority; and *pathos*, emotion! Most technical presentations deliver 90% logos, 9% ethos, and maybe 1% pathos. From that starting point, a small extra dose of pathos can go a long way. You just have to make sure that your content can match the picture presented on the cover: pitching a pirate ship and not having the cannons inside the box is bound to lead to disappointment.

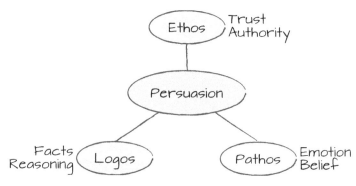

Figure 19-4. Three modes of persuasion

Play Is Work

While on the topic of toys: building pirate ships would be classified by most people as playing—something that is commonly seen as the opposite of work. Pulling another reference from the '80s movie archives reminds us that "all work and no play makes Jack a dull boy." Let's hope that lack of play doesn't have the same effect on IT architects as it had on the author Jack in the movie *The Shining* —he went insane and attempted to kill his family. But it certainly stifles learning and innovation.

Most of what we know we didn't learn from our school teachers, but from playing and experimenting. Sadly, most people seem to have forgotten how to play, or were told not to, when they entered their professional life. This happens due to social norms, pressure to always be (or appear) productive, and fear. Playing knows no fear and no judgment; that's why it gives you an open mind for new things.

 Playing is learning, so in times of rapid change architects need to play more.

If playing is learning, times of rapid change that require us to learn new technologies and adapt to new ways of working should re-emphasize the importance of playing. I actively encourage engineers and architects in my team to play. Interestingly, LEGO offers a successful method called *Serious Play* (*http://www.seriousplay.com*) for executives to improve group problem solving. They might be building pirate ships.

20

Writing for Busy People

Don't Expect Everyone to Read Word for Word

If you don't have time to read, look at the pictures

Most organizations are full of boring documents that remain largely unread. That doesn't mean that documentation is a bad idea. Done well, it's still the best vehicle to proverbially get everyone on the same page across a wide audience. Over time, brief but accurate technical position and decision papers have become a trademark of my architecture teams.

While the title of this chapter is a pun on the titles of popular books such as *Japanese for Busy People*, it intentionally implies an ambiguity that we are both writing for a busy audience and are busy authors as well.

Writing Scales

Sadly, writing takes much more effort than reading, but skimping on writing is penny-wise and pound-foolish because the written word has enormous advantages over the spoken word or slide presentations:

It scales
> You can address a large audience without gathering everyone in one room (podcasts, admittedly, can also accomplish that).

It's fast
> People read two to three times faster than they can listen.

It's searchable
> You can find what you want to read quickly.

It can be edited and versioned
> Everybody sees the same, versioned content.

So, writing pays off when you have a large (or important) enough audience. The biggest benefit, though, is Richard Guindon's insight that "Writing is nature's way of telling us how sloppy our thinking is." That alone makes writing a worthwhile exercise because it requires you to sort out your thoughts so that you can put them into a somewhat cohesive storyline. Unlike most slide decks, well-written documents are also self-contained, so they can be widely distributed without further commentary.

Quality Versus Impact

The catch with writing is that although you can to some extent force people to (at least pretend to) listen to you, it's much more difficult to force anyone to read your text. I remind writers that "the reader is by no means required to turn the page. They decide based on what they read so far."

Assuming the topic is interesting and relevant to the readership, I have repeatedly observed a nonlinear relationship between the quality of the writing and the attention it will receive, which is a good proxy metric for the impact of a technical paper. If the paper doesn't meet a minimum bar for quality—for example, because it is verbose, poorly structured, full of typos, or displayed in some ridiculous, difficult to read font—people won't read it at all, resulting in zero impact. I call this the "trash-bin" zone, named after the likely reader reaction. At the other end of the spectrum, additional impact from quality improvement ultimately tapers off as the document approaches the "gold-plating" zone.

So, you want to get the quality of your writing into the "sweet spot" and then focus on content instead of polishing further. While the sweet spot depends on the topic and the audience, I posit that the trash-bin zone is wider, and therefore more dangerous, than most developers believe. Key influencers—your most important readers—are very busy people and tend to shy away from anything that is more than a few pages long, perhaps unless it is from a high-paid consultancy, in which case they make someone else read it because they paid so much money for it.

 A senior executive once refused to read a paper because his first name was misspelled on the cover page. I think he was right.

For this impatient readership, clarity of wording and brevity aren't nice-to-haves: a lack thereof will quickly put your paper quite literally into the trash-bin zone. Blatant typos or grammar issues are like the proverbial fly in the soup: the taste is arguably the same, but the customer is unlikely to come back for more.

"In the Hand"—First Impressions Count

When Bobby Woolf and I wrote *Enterprise Integration Patterns*, the publisher highlighted the importance of the "in the hand" moment, which occurs when a potential buyer picks the book from the shelf to give a quick glimpse at the front and back cover, maybe the table of contents, and to leaf through. The reader makes the purchasing decision at this very moment, not when they stumble on your ingenious conclusion on page 326. This is one reason why we included many diagrams in that book: almost all facing pages contain a graphical element, such as an icon (aka "Gregorgram"), a pattern sketch, a screenshot, or a UML diagram: roughly 350 in total. We wanted to send a strong message to potential readers that it isn't an academic book, but a pragmatic and approachable one. Technical papers should do the same: use a clean layout, insert a handful of expressive diagrams, and, above all, keep it short and to the point!

To assess what a short paper will "feel" like to the reader without wasting printer paper, I zoom out my WYSIWYG editor far enough that all pages appear on the screen, as illustrated in Figure 20-1. I can't read the text anymore, but I can see the headings, diagrams, and overall flow; for example, the length of paragraphs and sections. This is exactly how a reader will see it when flipping through your document to decide whether it's worth reading. If they see an endless parade of bullet points, bulky paragraphs, or a giant mess, the paper will leave "the hand" quite quickly as gravity teleports it into the recycling bin.

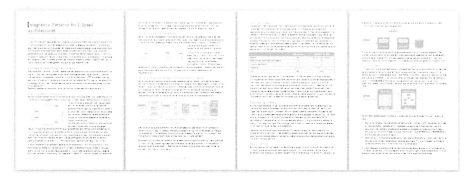

Figure 20-1. Zooming out from a technical paper

The Curse of Writing: Linearity

Text is linear: one word comes after the other, one paragraph after the previous. However, hardly any relevant technical topic is one-dimensional. One of the major challenges of technical writing (or speaking) is therefore to map a complex topic space into a linear storyline. For the algorithmically inclined, writing is a bit like coding a graph traversal problem: you can go *breadth-first* or *depth-first*. Breadth-first means that you cover all your topics at a high level, gradually descending down into the detail. Depth-first covers each topic in depth before moving on to the next topic.

A well-thought-out logical structure can help overcome this limitation. It's easier to traverse a tree than a complex graph with many loops. Barbara Minto captures the essence of this approach in her book *The Pyramid Principle*.[1] The "pyramid" in this context denotes the hierarchy of content; that is, a tree, not the *pyramids in IT* (Chapter 28).

---

1 Barbara Minto, *The Pyramid Principle: Logic in Writing and Thinking* (Upper Saddle River, NJ: Prentice Hall, 2010).

A Good Paper Is Like the Movie Shrek

Most animated movies have to entertain multiple audiences: the kids who love the cute characters plus the adults who had to shell out 30 bucks to take the family to the movies and spend two hours watching cute characters. Great animated movies like *Shrek* manage to address both audiences by including humor for kids *and* adults. The audiences might laugh at slightly different scenes but aren't distracted by each other.

Technical papers that address a diverse audience should aim to do the same. They need to supply technical detail while also highlighting important decisions and recommendations, so they can be read at two levels. A few simple techniques can help make reading your paper a little bit like watching *Shrek*:

Storytelling headings
> These replace an executive summary: your reader should get the gist of the paper just by reading the headings. Headings like "introduction" or "conclusion" aren't telling a story and have no place in a short paper.

Anchor diagrams
> These provide a visual cue for important sections. Readers who flip through a paper likely pause at a diagram, so it's good to position them strategically.

Sidebars
> These are the short sections that are offset in a different font or color, indicating to the reader that this additional detail can be safely skipped without losing the train of thought.

This way, executives can just read the headings and look at the diagram to get the essence of your paper in a minute or two (Figure 20-2). Most readers will read the paper but might skip the callouts, whereas specialists will pay particular attention to the detail in the callouts. This way, you can help break the curse of linearity a tiny bit by giving different readers different paths through the document.

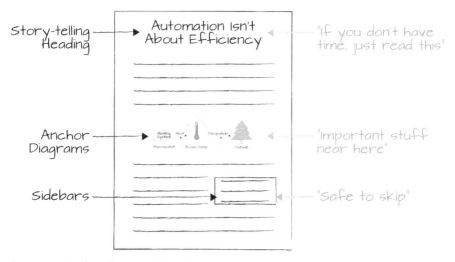

Figure 20-2. Breaking the curse of linearity

Making It Easy for the Reader

After a positive first impression, your readers will begin reading your paper. For advice on technical writing, I recommend the book *Technical Writing and Professional Communication*,[2] which sadly appears out of print but is widely available used. It covers a lot of ground in its 700 pages, including authoring different types of documents, such as resumes. I find the sections toward the end on parallelism and paragraph structure most helpful. Parallelism demands that all entries in a list follow the same grammatical structure; for example, all start with a verb or an adjective. A counterexample would be the left column of the following, with the right-hand side showing a better approach:

System A is preferred because:	System A is preferred due to:
• It's faster	• Performance
• Flexible	• Flexibility
• We want to reduce cost	• Economics
• Stable	• Stability

---

2 Leslie A. Olsen and Thomas N. Huckin, *Technical Writing and Professional Communication*, 2nd ed. (New York: McGraw-Hill, 1991).

Inconsistent writing uses too many of your reader's brain cells just to parse the text instead of focusing on your message. Taking the "noise" out of the language reduces friction and allows your reader to focus on the content. Parallelism is not only useful in lists but also in sentences; for example, when drawing analogies or contrasting.

Each paragraph should focus on a single topic and introduce that topic at the beginning, like this very paragraph: readers can glean from the first few words that this paragraph is about paragraphs. They can also rest assured that I don't start talking about lists halfway through, so if they already know how to write a good paragraph, they can safely skip this one. That's why "It is further important to note that in some circumstances one has to pay special attention to..." makes for a very poor paragraph opening.

Lists, Sets, Null Pointers, and Symbol Tables

Most programming languages support *sets*—i.e., unordered collections of elements—but books (and speeches) don't: every list has an order. Because you can't avoid it, you'd better choose the order consciously. Valid options are time (chronological), structure (relationships), or ranking (importance). Note that "alphabetical" and "serendipitous" aren't valid choices.

"How is this ordered?" has become a standard question I ask when reviewing documents containing a list or grouping.

Loose usage of the word *this* as a stand-alone reference is another pet peeve of mine; for example, stating that "this is a problem" without being clear what "this" actually refers to. Jeff Ullman cites such a "non-referential this" as one of the major impediments to clear writing, exemplified in his canonical example:[3]

> *If you turn the sproggle left, it will jam, and the glorp will not be able to move. This is why we foo the bar.*

Do we foo the bar because the glorp doesn't move or because the sproggle jammed? Programmers well understand the dangers of dangling pointers and

---

3 Jeff Ullman, "Viewpoint: Advising students for success," *Communications of the ACM* 52, No. 3 (March 2009).

Null Pointer Exceptions, but they don't seem to apply the same rigor to writing—maybe because your readers don't throw a stack trace at you?

Another fantastic piece of advice from Minto is the following:

> *Making a statement to a reader that tells him something he doesn't know will automatically raise a logical question in his mind [...] the writer is now obliged to answer that question. The way to ensure total reader attention, therefore, is to refrain from raising any questions in the reader's mind before you are ready to answer them.*

My translation for software engineers: when writing, assume that your readers use a single-pass compilation algorithm and don't have access to a complete symbol table. This means that forward references aren't allowed: you can only refer to terms and concepts that were already introduced. For the algorithmically minded, you'll need to do a topological sort on your topic graph. What if there's a circle? You'll get a stack overflow, just like your audience!

Following this simple advice will place your technical paper above 80% of the rest, because, sadly, the bar for technical documents is so low.

 An internal presentation once stated on the first slide: "only technology ABCD has proven to be a viable solution." When I asked for proof, it turned out that none existed due to "lack of time and funding." These aren't just wording issues, but fatal flaws. A reader no longer wants to see page 2 if they cannot trust page 1.

Lastly, make sure to avoid unsubstantiated claims. I refer to this phenomenon as the "hourglass presentation": it starts with a lot of buzzwords and promises, then becomes very narrow, and ends with bold requests for funding and headcount.

In der Kürze liegt die Würze[4]

In technical writing, your readers are not out to appreciate your literary creativity, but to understand what you are saying. Therefore, less is more when it comes to word count. Although Walker Royce[5] spends a good part of his book musing about English words, his advice on brevity and editing is sound. His paraphrased

---

4 Literally, "brevity gives spice," ironically translating into "short and sweet."

5 Walker Royce, *Eureka!: Discover and Enjoy the Hidden Power of the English Language* (New York: Morgan James Publishing, 2011).

citation from Zinsser[6] on the usage of "I might add," "It should be pointed out," and "It is interesting to note," hits the mark:

> *If you might add, add it. If it should be pointed out, point it out. If it is interesting to note, make it interesting.*

Royce also gives many concrete suggestions on how to replace long-winded expressions or "big" words with single, simple words, thereby not only reducing noise but also aiding non-native speakers.

If you are up to a more rigorous evaluation of properly linking words into sentences and you are willing to put up with a few tirades and snipes, I recommend Barzun's *Simple & Direct*,[7] which isn't simple, but pedantically direct.

Our team's internal editing cycles routinely cut word count by 20 to 30% despite including additional material or detail. To the first-time author this might be shocking, but Saint-Exupéry's adage that "perfection is achieved not when there is nothing more to add, but when nothing is left to take away" is especially true for technical papers (and good code for that matter). I actually edited this very chapter down by 15%.

When this type of cruel editing was first bestowed upon me by a professional copy editor, I felt that the document no longer sounded "like me." Over the years, I have come to appreciate that being crisp and accurate is a great way to have a technical paper sound like me. Longer, more personal pieces like this book allow some "slack" to help the reader keep attention after many pages.

Unit Testing Technical Papers

The most effective vehicle for improving technical papers is to hold a *writer's workshop*.[8] Such a workshop entails attendees discussing a paper, which they have read, while the author is allowed to listen but not to speak. This setup simulates someone reading and trying to understand a paper. The author must remain silent because they cannot pop out of their paper to explain to each reader what was really meant—a document must be self-contained. Because writer's

---

6 William Zinsser, *On Writing Well: The Classic Guide to Writing Nonfiction* (New York: Harper, 2006).

7 Jacques Barzun, *Simple & Direct* (New York: Harper Perennial, 2001).

8 Richard P. Gabriel, *Writers' Workshops & the Work of Making Things: Patterns, Poetry...* (Upper Saddle River, NJ: Pearson Education, 2002).

workshops are time intensive, they are best applied after the paper has gone through an initial review.

Technical Memos

A document doesn't need to be all encompassing—who reads an encyclopedia, anyway? Twenty years ago, Ward Cunningham defined the notion of a *technical memo*, a document that describes a particular aspect of the system, in his *Episodes* pattern language:[9]

> *Maintain a series of well formatted technical memoranda addressing subjects not easily expressed in the program under development. Focus each memo on a single subject. [...] Traditional, comprehensive design documentation [...] rarely shines except in isolated spots. Elevate those spots in technical memos and forget about the rest.*

Keep in mind, though, that writing technical memos is more useful, but not necessarily easier, than producing reams of mediocre documentation. The classic example of this noble idea gone wrong is a project wiki full of random, mostly outdated, and incohesive documentation. This isn't the tool's fault (the wiki was not quite coincidentally also invented by Ward); rather, it's due to a lack of *emphasis over completeness* (Chapter 21) by the writers.

The Pen Is Mightier Than the Sword, but Not Mightier Than Corporate Politics

Producing high-quality position papers can lead to an unexpected amount of organizational headwind. The word *perfection* is invariably used with a negative connotation by those who are poor writers or want to avoid sharing their team's work. Ironically, these are often the same departments that love to be entertained by colorful vendor presentations.

Other teams claim that their "Agile" approach spares them from any need to produce documentation, notwithstanding the fact that those teams have no running code to show either. Agile software development places the emphasis on producing working code that is worth reading, but multiyear IT strategy plans are

---

9 John Vlissides, James O. Coplien, and Norman L. Kerth, *Pattern Languages of Program Design 2* (Reading, MA: Addison-Wesley, 1996).

unlikely to manifest themselves in code alone. Alas, good documents seem to be even more difficult to find than good code.

Some corporate denizens actively resent writing clear and self-contained documents because they prefer to "tune" their story for each audience. Naturally, this approach *doesn't scale* (Chapter 30).

Writing good documents in an organization that is generally poor at writing can give you significant visibility, but it can also rock the political system.

 The first time I sent a positioning paper on digital ecosystems to senior management, a person complained to both my boss and my boss's boss about me not having "aligned" the paper with her.

Communication is a mighty tool, and some people in your organization will fight hard to control it. Pick your targets wisely.

21

Emphasis Over Completeness

Show the Forest, Not the Trees

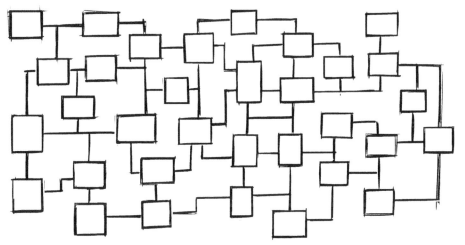

Can you spot the performance bottleneck in this database schema?

When sharing a diagram, you might receive feedback such as, "System ABC is missing." Even though it's well intentioned, completeness shouldn't be your architecture diagrams' primary goal. Rather, you should depict the appropriate scope. What's the right scope? One that's big enough to be meaningful, small enough to be comprehensible, and cohesive enough to make sense.

In large organizations, there's a constant danger of being overcome by the sheer size and complexity of the environment. So, putting some blinders on is allowed, and in fact encouraged.

Diagrams Are Models

When discussing architecture diagrams, it's good to remind ourselves why we draw them in the first place. Architecture diagrams are *models of reality* (Chapter 22). The most common model of reality we use in daily life is a map: maps help us decide where to go and how to get there. To do so, maps select a specific scope and emphasis. For example, a Chicago street map that shows only half of downtown would be awkward. However, including all of Lake Michigan wouldn't be very useful, just like adding Springfield at the same scale. A map designer chooses conscious boundaries and a conscious level of detail based on the map's intended purpose.

Models, whether maps or architecture diagrams, aren't about being right or wrong. In fact, *they're all wrong* (Chapter 6) because they aren't reality. The opening paragraph of William Kent's book *Data and Reality*[1] aptly reminds us: "Rivers do not have dotted lines in them and freeways are not painted red."

Instead of trying to make models right, you should think about whether your models are useful. To answer that question, though, you need to first know what the model's use, or purpose, is. For a model to be useful, it needs to help you answer a question or make a better decision. Otherwise, your diagram is just art, and having looked at thousands of architecture diagrams, my impression is that most architects aren't particularly gifted artists.

So, before setting out to draw a specific diagram or design a presentation slide, you must first decide which questions you are looking to answer. A broad "lay of the land" might be needed to *build your world map* (Chapter 16), but it isn't very useful as an architecture diagram. Think of it this way: a travel bureau will show you beaches and palm trees, not a map of the whole continent.

All models are wrong, but some are useful. To know which ones, you must first know which question you're trying to answer.

When deciding on a diagram's scope and boundaries, I am not always able to do so *a priori*. Sometimes, I need to have the diagram in front of my eyes to decide whether I prefer to split it into two. I therefore almost always work iteratively.

---

1 William Kent, *Data and Reality: A Timeless Perspective on Perceiving and Managing Information in Our Imprecise World*, 3rd ed. (Westfield, NJ: Technics Publications, LLC, 2012).

The Five-Second Test

Architecture diagrams or slides are designed to get a specific point across and therefore must place a clear emphasis. This distinguishes them from reference books or manuals, which aim to be comprehensive. Still, too many slides I see try to give the big picture as the best possible approximation of reality without knowing which part is actually worth looking at.

When faced with overly "noisy" slides, I tend to apply a strict but useful *five-second rule*, which isn't related to food safety:[2]

> *I show the audience a slide for a mere five seconds and ask them to describe what they saw. In most cases, the responses boil down to a few words from the headline and statements like "three yellow boxes and one blue barrel below." If you are aiming to convey a shared database pattern (https://oreil.ly/VQ2oP), you likely succeeded, but most authors will be disappointed to hear such a dramatic simplification of their precious content.*

Slides that don't pass this test are likely to confuse the audience when first shown: viewers' eyes will chase across the visuals, trying to discern what's important and what's the meaning of it all. During that time your audience isn't listening to you explaining the content because they're busy with the visuals. Of course, you will show the actual slide for more than five seconds, but first impressions count—for every slide you show.

 A useful presentation technique is to verbally introduce the concept of the next slide before actually showing it. The audience is more likely to listen because they're aren't distracted by the new visual and you're building up a bit of suspense. Naturally, this requires you to know which slide comes next rather than use the slides as a reminder what to talk about.

Some organizations create slides that try to act like documents, meaning they are also meant to be read as handouts. The resulting *slideument*, a term coined by Garr Reynolds,[3] is rarely a useful presentation and never passes the five-second test because there's way too much content on a slide. Sadly, most of them don't make a meaningful document either because it usually lacks a clear

---

2 Wikipedia, "Five-Second Rule," *https://oreil.ly/1Z397*.

3 Garr Reynolds, "*Slideuments* and the Catch-22 for Conference Speakers," Presentation Zen (blog), April 5, 2006, *https://oreil.ly/yw45r*.

structure and storyline. Interestingly, Martin Fowler realized that there's a use case for documents created in a presentation tool, for which he's coined the term *Infodecks*.[4] Nancy Duarte shows a similar approach with *SlideDocs*.[5] Both can be a useful communication medium when being read as opposed to being projected.

A Pop Quiz

I participate in many architecture reviews and decision boards. While such boards often exist due to an *undesirable separation of decision makers and knowledge holders* (Chapter 1), many large enterprises depend on them to harmonize their technical landscape and to gain an overview across many functional silos. The topics for these meetings can be fairly technical in nature, making me skeptical whether the audience is truly following along.

 A presentation pop quiz consists of blanking the presentation and having a member of the audience explain what they saw and understood. It's a test for the presenter, not the audience.

To test whether the decision body understands what they are deciding, I inject a pop quiz[6] into the presentation by telling the presenter to pause and blank the slide (hitting "B" will do this in PowerPoint) and asking who among the audience would like to recap what was said up to this point in their own words. Sadly, this exercise is more likely to trigger nervous laughter, frantic staring at the floor, and sudden checking of incoming emails as opposed to a good summary. As a result, I might ask the presenter to briefly recap the key points for everyone's benefit. It's also useful to highlight to the audience that this is a test for the presenter, not for them.

Simple Language

I don't exclude myself from the pop quiz. When replaying what the speaker said, I often intentionally use very simple language to make sure I really capture the essence.

---

4 Martin Fowler, "Infodeck," MartinFowler.com, Nov. 16, 2012, *https://oreil.ly/yvgTq*.

5 Nancy Duarte, "PowerPoint Presentations vs. Slidedocs," Duarte.com, *https://oreil.ly/MjKny*.

6 A pop quiz is a short test given by a teacher in class without prior announcement. It goes without saying that this is fairly unpopular with students.

In a presentation about network security architecture in the untrusted network zone, after watching a handful of rather busy slides, I summarized the speaker's statement as follows: "What worries you is the black line going all the way from top to bottom?" His resounding "yes" confirmed both that I had correctly summarized the issue and that the presenter took away an insight into how to better communicate this very aspect.

This technique might seem overly simplistic at first, but it validates that there is a solid connection between the model being presented (such as vertical lines depicting legal network paths from the internet to the trusted network) and the problem statement (direct paths pose a security risk). Removing all noise and reducing the statement down to the "black line" sharpens the message.

Diagramming Basics

If I had to name the number-one enemy of useful architecture diagrams, it would likely be Visio's default 10-point font size and skimpy line width, augmented by poor user judgment regarding component placement. It's really in the same league as PowerPoint's autosize feature that gives people an endless supply of bullet points to neutralize their audience. True, the tool isn't solely responsible, but Visio's default settings, which are tuned for detailed engineering schematics, lure the user into creating visuals that are unsuitable for projecting something evocative on the wall.

My advice for creating diagrams that can convey a clear message without dumbing down the content therefore starts with the following basic techniques.

AVOID THE ANT FONT

Text that isn't readable isn't adding value, so avoid *ant fonts*[7] unless you consider "I know you can't read this" an engaging introduction into a slide. Using sans-serif fonts of decent size and good color contrast will be appreciated in any presentation. I can't count the number of times I see slides that contain tiny fonts but consist of 50% empty space that could have been used for larger boxes and larger fonts, similar to Figure 21-1. Architecture diagrams aren't the place for minimalism—go bold.

---

7 Neal Ford, Matthew McCullough, and Nathaniel Schutta, *Presentation Patterns: Techniques for Crafting Better Presentations* (Boston: Addison-Wesley Professional, 2012).

Figure 21-1. Use the available space to make text easily readable

Most tools allow you to set defaults for line width and font sizes. Use them. Also, periodically zoom down the diagram on your screen to 25% to see what's still readable.

MAXIMIZE THE SIGNAL-TO-NOISE RATIO

Differences in elements that don't have meaning are nothing but distractions. Therefore, reduce visual noise; for example, by properly aligning elements and using a consistent form and shape (see Figure 21-2). It's also good to be careful with too much decoration, such as rounded corners, shadows, and so on—they can distract from the core message you're trying to convey. If things look different, make sure that this expresses meaning, as detailed in Chapter 23.

Figure 21-2. Make same things look the same

Great advice on placement, visual layout, and emphasis can be found in Nancy Duarte's book *slide:ology*.[8]

LET ARROWS POINT

One of the my most frequent maneuvers in presentation tools is to increase the size of arrowheads. If you use directed arrows to *express semantics* (Chapter 23), you're going to want them to be easily recognizable, as depicted in Figure 21-3. If direction isn't critical to understanding the diagram, omit the arrowheads to reduce noise.

Figure 21-3. If direction is important, make the arrowhead big enough to see

---

8 Nancy Duarte, *slide:ology: The Art and Science of Creating Great Presentations* (Sebastopol, CA: O'Reilly Media, 2008).

If your tool won't cooperate, place a triangle over the line; never let the tool be an excuse for poor diagrams. It's like the cook coming out of the kitchen and telling you that your meal isn't tasty because the farmer didn't grow tasty tomatoes. You're unlikely to be extraordinarily sympathetic.

LEGENDS ARE CRUTCHES

Although they're a standard feature in scientific circles and charts exported from Excel, a visual legend requires a viewer to correlate patterns or colors in a diagram with explanatory labels below or next to it. Having the label where the data is located is much easier to digest, as shown in Figure 21-4.

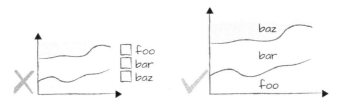

Figure 21-4. Label your data as opposed to making the reader read a legend

Therefore, use legends only when absolutely unavoidable. Most of the time you can remove clutter or increase the size of boxes to put the labels where they belong. I have redrawn stacked bar graphs exported from Excel export to have better control over sizing and labeling. The investment of a mere five minutes saved a room full of executives much time and effort in reading the data.

LAYER VISUALLY

As we already learned, a *good document reads like watching the movie Shrek* (Chapter 20). The same is true for diagrams, which might be required to illustrate complex interrelationships that lead to a particular *system behavior* (Chapter 10). They should nevertheless pass the *five-second test* by having a clear high-level structure that is visible first, augmented by additional detail that reveals itself later and doesn't interfere with the big picture. Figure 21-5 first reveals that the system consists of two identical zones, after which you can "zoom in" to see how each zone is internally composed.

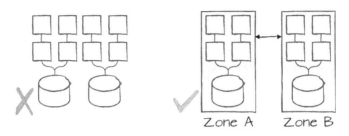

Figure 21-5. Give your diagrams a clear high-level structure

I occasionally use a *build slide* or *incremental reveal* for this purpose, acknowledging that there are strong opinions for and against such visual effects. I find build slides to work well as they give the viewer time to understand each element before adding the next batch. For this to work, let the new elements simply appear, avoiding any temptation to select one of those amazing spiral-twist-fade-rotate reveals.

If you layer a diagram perfectly, the visuals will reveal themselves incrementally. If you can't quite get there every time, incremental build slides are a reasonable substitute.

The Style of Elements

Most architects will develop their own visual style over time and can use it as a valuable branding tool. Many of my technical papers and diagrams are easily recognizable—for example, when sitting on someone's desk—thanks to a consistent set of colors and a bold, almost cartoon-like style that favors large lettering over subtle aesthetics.

My diagrams virtually always have *lines* (Chapter 23), but I keep the lines' semantics to two or at most three concepts. Each type of relationship that I depict with lines should be intuitive. For example, I might depict a data flow with broad, gray arrows, whereas control flow is shown in thin, black lines, as illustrated in Figure 21-6, which depicts the *Control Bus* pattern from *Enterprise Integration Patterns*.[9]

---

9 Hohpe and Woolf, *Enterprise Integration Patterns*.

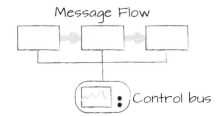

Figure 21-6. The Control Bus pattern illustrates line semantics

The line width suggests that a large amount of data flows through the system's data flow while the control flow is much smaller but significant. The best visual style, borrowed from advice on writing, is the one "that keeps solely in view the thought one wants to convey."[10]

Making a Statement

When preparing a slide or a document paragraph, the title sets the tone for a clear and focused statement. For most circumstances, I prefer titles that are full sentences because the title alone tells the essence of the story. Using this approach also assures that each slide or paragraph focuses on a single main statement.

I make an exception for keynote presentations to a large and diverse audience for which I use titles consisting of single words or short phrases like the *Architect Elevator* (Chapter 1). Such short titles mesh well with simple visuals that are truly a *visual aid* to me, the speaker, to draw the audience's attention and help them memorize the content via a visual metaphor.

For technical presentations that are prepared for a review or decision-making session, however, I prefer clear statements, with which one can either agree or disagree. These statements are much better represented as full sentences, akin to the *story-telling headings* (Chapter 20) in documents for busy people. In such cases, "Stateless services and automation support elastic scale-out" is a better title than "Server Architecture."

What you certainly want to avoid are verbose phrases or crippled sentences that confuse the reader but don't make any form of statement: "Server infrastructure and application architecture overview diagram (abstracted for simplicity's sake)." Trust me, I've seen even worse.

---

10 Barzun, *Simple & Direct.*

Twenty Slides, One Story

When structuring presentations, I realize that too many technical presentations tell one story per slide. While it's good to focus on one message per slide, the sequence of messages needs to form a cohesive story, as demonstrated in the bottom half of Figure 21-7. Interestingly, you can test this easily using PowerPoint's Outline View, which shows all slide headings in a sidebar.

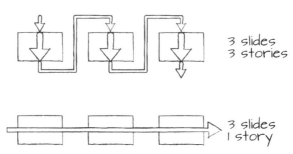

Figure 21-7. Telling one story supported by slides aids flow and saves time

Creating this cohesion not only makes a single story line for a more logical flow, it also drastically shortens the time needed to present. If each slide tells a new story, the speaker will easily spend half a minute looking at and introducing each slide. Multiply this by the typical 20 to 30 slides in a presentation, and you'll find that having a connected storyline can save you up 15 minutes. So, when someone worries that they don't have enough time for their content, I advise them to make sure that they have a single story.

For a good collection of slide decks that tell a story, I recommend a visit to *https://speakerdeck.com*.

Nothing Is Confusing in and of Itself

The closing advice I give to anyone creating documents and visuals that need to explain complex topics is the following: things might be complicated, but whether it's confusing, that's up to you.

22

Diagram-Driven Design

Cheating in a Picture Is Much Harder
Than Cheating in Words

Designing with Diagrams

Some years ago, the Crested Butte Enterprise Architecture Summit once again proved that sticking a bunch of geeks in a remote town can lead to creative results. In our case, the result was an A-to-Z list of 26 new development strategies, starting from activity-driven development (ADD) and ending on zero-defect development (ZDD). Domain-driven design (DDD) was dedicated to Eric Evans's fantastic book *Domain-Driven Design*.[1] However, another "DDD" sprang to mind: *diagram-driven design*, and it turned out that there's actually a serious idea behind the fun exercise.

Presentation Skills: More Than a Wide Stance

While working for Google in Japan, I created and taught a class on presentation skills for engineers, which included some common ideas of using strong, impactful visuals inspired by books like *Presentation Zen*.[2] Following my own advice equipped me with high-resolution graphics of confident managers, fuel gauges indicating that your mileage may indeed vary, shoes that apparently do not fit all, and so on. Still, however impactful fancy graphics may be, for most technical presentations a wide stance, deep voice, and Steve Jobs–like hand gestures (turtleneck optional) are unlikely to teach the audience how a multicloud strategy increases your system architecture complexity.

Instead, you need "meat": what design alternatives did the team have? How do they differ? What design principles made you choose one over the other? What are the main building blocks of the systems and *how do they interact* (Chapter 23)? How did you track down that performance bottleneck and what did you learn from it? When Garr Reynolds, the author of *Presentation Zen*, came to Google to talk about his book, he acknowledged that technical discussions often require detailed diagrams or even snippets of source code. He suggested to provide those as a handout instead of including it in the presentation to make it easier for the audience to read and digest them. Still, most technical presentations I see do contain source code or diagrams to explain technical concepts in detail, so we'd better figure out how to do so effectively.

Ed Tufte already ran bullet points through the grinder by blaming them for the inaction that led to the Space Shuttle *Columbia* disaster[3] upon re-entry (and he might not be wrong judging from the slides they put together). "Death by PowerPoint" was immortalized by a *Dilbert* comic strip as early as 2000. You can't fit a lot of source code on a slide either, especially if you are using a verbose

---

1 Eric Evans, *Domain-Driven Design: Tackling Complexity in the Heart of Software* (Upper Saddle River, NJ: Addison-Wesley, 2003).

2 Garr Reynolds, *Presentation Zen: Simple Ideas on Presentation Design and Delivery*, 3rd ed. (New Riders, 2019).

3 Edward Tufte, "PowerPoint Does Rocket Science: and Better Techniques for Technical Reports," Edward-Tufte.com, *https://oreil.ly/kDihX*.

language with checked exceptions. That leaves you with diagrams as your main communication vehicle for technical concepts.

Diagramming as Design Technique

Back at Crested Butte, we looked at our list and pondered whether some of our concoctions actually had meaning. Interestingly, as we discussed how to draw meaningful diagrams in a later session, I highlighted the importance of a consistent visual vocabulary, which would omit unnecessary details but highlight the essence of the *design decisions* (Chapter 8). During this discussion, we realized that to draw a good picture, you need to have a decent design in the first place. If reality is completely convoluted, it's hard to depict order in retrospect. Taking this thought a step further, we realized that good diagramming contributes to good system design in general. Diagram-driven design had become a reality!

When talking about diagram-driven design, I don't imply that we'd generate code from UML diagrams. I am pretty firmly rooted in Martin Fowler's *UML as Sketch*[4] camp, meaning UML is a picture to aid human comprehension, not a programming language or specification. If people don't quite agree, I refer to Grady Booch, who as co-creator of the UML remarked that "The UML was never intended to be a programming language."[5] Instead, I am talking about a picture that conveys important concepts—the proverbial big picture that does not get caught up in irrelevant details.

Designing with Diagrams

An excellent example of designing with diagrams is the book *Enterprise Integration Patterns* coauthored by Bobby Woolf and myself in 2003. The book defines a pattern language for designing asynchronous messaging solutions, which is represented both in text form and as a set of icons. The consistent visual style and the simple composition model of messaging solutions allows the visual language to become a design tool, as shown in the illustration from the book (Figure 22-1).

---

4 Martin Fowler, "UML as Sketch," MartinFowler.com, *https://oreil.ly/WLUgR*.

5 Mark Collins-Cope, "Interview with Grady Booch," *Objective View Magazine*, Issue 12, Sept. 12, 2014, *https://oreil.ly/HGc5j*.

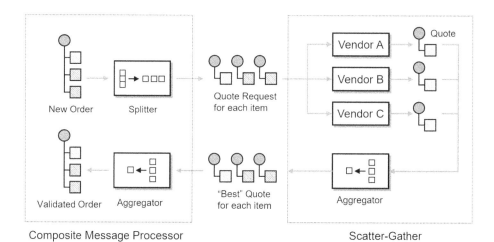

Composite Message Processor · Scatter-Gather

Figure 22-1. Designing with Enterprise Integration Patterns

The resulting diagrams aren't just illustrations but also help validate the design. For example, the visual language reminds you that for every splitting or distribution of messages, you need to aggregate them back later. It also validates a logical grouping of the elements.

One great historical example of diagram-driven design are the graphical train schedules created to plot trains' paths along two axes by distance (vertical) and time (horizontal). The faster a train moves, the steeper the line will drop. The lines on such charts intersect where trains running in opposing directions pass each other (see Figure 22-2). On a single-track railroad, you'd want to make sure that these occur at a station where there are two tracks and platforms. Having the train schedules laid out visually is a great design aid.

Well-known examples of these maps go back to Étienne-Jules Marey and his book *La Méthode Graphique* (1878). They are also featured prominently in Tufte's *The Visual Display of Quantitative Information*,[6] perhaps the standard text on charting and diagramming.

---

6 Edward R. Tufte, *The Visual Display of Quantitative Information* (Cheshire, CT: Graphics Press, 2001).

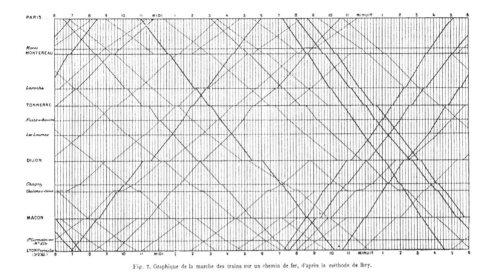

Fig. 7. Graphique de la marche des trains sur un chemin de fer, d'après la méthode de Ibry.

Figure 22-2. Visually designing train schedules

Diagram-Driven Design Techniques

Once you embrace diagramming as a design technique, you'll find several connections between good visual design and good system design, which we examine
in the following sections.

ESTABLISH A VISUAL VOCABULARY AND VIEWPOINTS

Good diagrams use a consistent visual language. A box means something (for
example, a component, a class, a process), a solid line something else (maybe a
build dependency, data flow, or an HTTP request), and a dashed line means
something else yet. No, you don't need a *Meta-Object Facility* and correctness-
proven semantics, but you need to have an idea what element or relationship you
are depicting how. Picking this visual vocabulary is important to define the architectural viewpoint you are going to concern yourself with, such as source code
dependencies, runtime dependencies, call trees, or allocation of processes to
machines.

Good design is often tied to the ability to think in abstractions. Diagrams are
visual abstractions and can be instrumental in this process.

LIMIT THE LEVELS OF ABSTRACTION

One of the most frequent problems I encounter in technical documents is a wild mix of different levels of abstraction (the same problem can be found in source code). For example, the way configuration data affects a system's behavior can be described like this:

> *The system configuration is stored in an XML file, whose "timetravel" entry can be set to either* true *or* false. *The file is read from the local filesystem or alternatively from the network, but then you need NFS access or to have Samba installed. It uses a SAX parser to avoid building the whole DOM tree in memory. The "Config" class, which reads these settings, is a singleton because...*

In these few sentences you learn about the file format, project design decisions, implementation detail, performance optimizations, and more. It's rather unlikely that a single reader is actually interested in this smörgåsbord of facts.

Now try to draw a picture of this paragraph! It will be nearly impossible to get all of these concepts onto a single sheet of paper.

Drawing a diagram thus forces us to clean up our thinking by considering one level of abstraction at a time. While drawing a picture doesn't automagically make the problem of mixing abstractions disappear, it puts it in your face much more bluntly than a meandering chain of prose, which from afar might not look all that bad. A well-known German proverb proclaims that *Papier ist geduldig* ("paper is patient"), meaning paper is unlikely to object to what garbage you scribble on it. Diagrams are a little less patient. If you do compare architecture diagrams to modern art, you'll want the Mondrian, not the Pollock.

REDUCE TO THE ESSENCE

Billboard-sized database schema posters, which include every single table, stick to a single level of abstraction but are still fairly useless because they try to convey reality without *placing an emphasis* (Chapter 21). When shrunken down to fit on a single presentation slide, they start to look like abstract art—something better placed in the museum than in architecture documentation.

Therefore, omit unimportant detail to concentrate on what's most relevant! The same is true for system design: it's important to know "what kind of thing" your system is; for example, by defining a *system metaphor* (Chapter 24).

FIND BALANCE AND HARMONY

Limiting the levels of abstraction and scope does not yet guarantee a useful diagram. Good diagrams lay out important entities such that they are logically grouped, relationships become naturally clear, and an overall balance and harmony emerges. If such a balance doesn't emerge, it may just be that your system doesn't have one.

> I once reviewed a relatively small module of code that consisted of a rather entangled mess of classes and relationships. When the developer and I tried to document this module, we just couldn't come up with a half-decent way to sketch what was going on. After a lot of drawing and erasing we came up with a picture that vaguely resembled a data-processing pipeline. We subsequently refactored the entangled code to match this new system metaphor. It improved the structure and testability of the code significantly, thanks to diagram-driven design!

A well-balanced diagram will show coupling, cohesion, and a high-level structure, concepts that equally help with good system design.

INDICATE DEGREES OF UNCERTAINTY

When looking at a piece of code, you can always figure out *what* was done, but it's much harder to understand *why* it was done. It can be even more difficult to understand which decisions were made consciously and which ones simply happened.

When creating diagrams, you have more tools at hand to express these nuances, so you should use them. For example, you can use a hand-drawn sketch to convey that your design is merely a basis for discussion. Once you have full agreement and want to convey that every detail is critical, you can use a visual style that resembles an engineering blueprint. Many books, including Eric Evans's, use this technique effectively. That's also the reason this book uses sketches: we are discussing architecture approaches and ways of thinking, not concrete tools and processes.

When drawing, consider the *precision versus accuracy* dilemma: "next week it will be roughly 15.235 degrees" doesn't make sense as it's precise but inaccurate. Don't make precise-looking slides if you know they aren't accurate.

Diagrams Are Art

Diagrams can (and should) be beautiful—little works of art, even. I am a firm believer that system design has a close relationship to art and (nontechnical) design. Both visual and technical design start with a blank slate and virtually unlimited possibilities. Decisions are often influenced by multiple, usually conflicting, forces. Good design resolves these forces to create a functional solution, which attains a good balance and some degree of beauty. This may explain why many of my friends who are great (software) designers and architects have an artistic vein or at least interest.

No Silver Bullet (Point)

Not all diagrams are useful as a design technique. Drawing a messy picture won't make your poor design any better. Beautiful *marchitecture* diagrams,[7] which have little to do with the actual system being built, are also of limited value. For many technical discussions, though, I have observed that drawing a good diagram greatly improves the conversation and the resulting design decisions. If you are unable to draw a good diagram (and it isn't due to lack of skill), it might just be because your actual system structure is not what it should be.

---

7 *Marchitecture* denotes marketing pictures disguised as architecture.

23

Drawing the Line

Architecture Without Lines Likely Isn't One

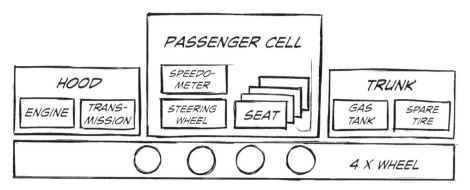

A functional architecture of a car

The sketch above depicts the architecture of a car. All the important components are there, including their relationships: the engine is under the hood; passenger seats are appropriately located inside the passenger compartment, close to the steering wheel; wheels are assembled nicely at the bottom of the car in the chassis. This diagram appears to fulfill most definitions of architecture (except my favorite one because I am looking for decisions; see Chapter 8).

However, it does precious little to help you understand how a car functions: could you omit the gas tank because it's far away from the engine, anyway? Are engine and transmission side by side under the hood by coincidence or do they have a special relationship? Does the car need exactly four wheels or will three also do? If you had to build the car in stages, what subset would make sense to assemble first? Would just the cabin with the seats be a good start? How can you distinguish a good car from a bad one? Which aspects are common in virtually all cars (e.g., the wheels being at the bottom) and which ones vary (Porsche 911, VW Beetle, or DeLorean owners would be quick to point out that their engine isn't under the hood)?

The picture doesn't really answer any of these questions. It depicts the location of the components, but it doesn't convey their relationships or function in the overall system "car." Even though the picture is factually correct and actually reasonably detailed, it doesn't allow us to reason much about the system it is describing, especially its behavior. Coincidentally, it might also not be a good example of *diagram-driven design* (Chapter 22).

Behold the Line!

The critical element that's missing in the picture are lines connecting the components. Without lines, it's quite difficult to represent rich relationships. The line is so important that boxes, labels, and lines suffice to make up Kent Beck's only half-joking Galactic Modeling Language.[1] Without lines, there wouldn't be much of a modeling language left. Also, as often stated, "the lines are more interesting than the boxes." Where does stuff usually go wrong? In the integration between two well-tested pieces. Where do I need to look to achieve strong or loose coupling? Between the boxes. How do I tell a well-structured architecture from a Big Ball of Mud?[2] By the lines.

The importance of lines is most easily understood from a simple example, illustrated in Figure 23-1.

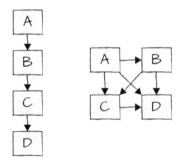

Figure 23-1. Without lines, an architecture diagram is rather meaningless

The system on the left and the system on the right are made from the same components, *A*, *B*, *C*, and *D*. Would the two systems have different properties

---

1 "Galactic Modeling Language," Wikiwikiweb, *https://oreil.ly/XT4IF*.

2 Neal Harrison, Brian Foote, and Hans Rohnert, *Pattern Languages of Program Design 4* (Boston: Addison-Wesley, 1999).

and behaviors? The system on the left has a neat, layered architecture, which provides clear dependencies and makes it easy to replace a component with a different one. It can also suffer from long latency because messages or commands have to travel through each component in sequence. Also, each component can become a single point of failure: if *C* fails, the chain is broken, and the system is unable to function.

The system on the right has almost the exact opposite properties: interdependencies are a bit messy, making it difficult to replace a component. However, the system provides shorter communication paths and is more resilient: if *C* fails, *A* can still talk to *D*.

Now imagine that this diagram had no lines. You would never know whether the system is built like the one on the left or the one on the right, resulting in a rather meaningless architecture diagram. Therefore, if I see an architecture diagram without any connecting lines, I am skeptical as to whether it qualifies as a meaningful depiction of an architecture. Unfortunately, many diagrams fail this basic test.

If I see an architecture diagram without lines, I am inclined to reject it because it won't convey the system's behavior.

The Metamodel

Stating that the diagram of the car doesn't show any relationships isn't quite true. The picture does contain two primary relationships between components:

Containment
One box is enclosed by another.

Proximity
Some boxes are close to one another, whereas others are farther apart.

Containment corresponds to real-world semantics in this drawing: seats are actually *contained* inside the passenger cell, and the hood (the engine compartment to be more precise) houses engine and transmission. Engine and transmission are also next to each other, giving them *proximity*, which underlines them sharing a strong relationship: one makes little sense without the other. But the *proximity* semantics in this picture are relatively weak: the gas tank and spare tire are also next to each other, but for the function of the car this doesn't have any meaning. The vague correspondence of proximity in the diagram to real-life proximity has no relationship to function and thus renders an odd mix of a logical and physical representation.

I routinely challenge diagrams that limit relationships between components to containment. Such diagrams make it difficult to reason about the system, as seen in the car example we looked at earlier. Reasoning about the system is one of the main purposes of drawing an (architecture) diagram, so we need to do better.

Diagrams that are based only on containment and proximity generally could have been just as easily represented as an indented bullet list: subbullets are contained by outer bullets and bullets next to each other are in proximity. In our example, you would end up with a list like this (showing only a portion to avoid *death by bullet points*):

- Hood
  — Engine
  — Transmission
- Passenger cell
  — Speedometer
  — Steering wheel
  — Four seats

In this case, the picture doesn't say the proverbial 1,000 words. The list and the picture are just different *projections* of the same tree structure. And people say intentional programming is difficult![3] You might like the picture better than the list, but you must be aware that both representations have the same richness, or poorness, of expression. The picture adds the size and shape of the boxes, which aren't represented in the textual list, but the semantics of size and shape in our example are unclear: all components are rectangles, but the wheels are circles. It's a crude approximation of reality, but for reasoning about the system it doesn't add much.

---

3 "Intentional Programming," Wikiwikiweb, *https://oreil.ly/5bGf-*.

The Semantics of Semantics

When I was told for the first time that "UML sequence diagrams have weak semantics," I was doubtful whether this rather academic statement had any relevance for me as a normal programmer. The short answer is: "yes, it does." Prior to UML 2, sequence diagrams depicted only one possible sequence of interactions between objects, albeit allowing for concurrency. They couldn't express the complete set of legal interaction sequences, such as loops (repeating interactions) or branches (either/or choices). Because loops and branches are some of the most fundamental control flow constructs, sequence diagrams' weak semantics rendered them essentially useless as a specification. UML 2 improved the semantics but at the cost of much reduced readability.

Why worry so much about the semantics of a diagram? The purpose of design diagrams or engineering drawings is to give viewers an understanding of the system, particularly the system behavior. A drawing is a model, so *it's by definition wrong* (Chapter 6). However, it can be useful; for example, by allowing the viewer to reason about the system. The visual elements, such as boxes and lines, must neatly map to concepts in the abstract model so that the viewer can build the model in their head. For the viewer to grasp the *meaning* of the drawing, the visual elements need semantics: semantics is the study of meaning.

Elements—Relationship—Behavior

Without lines, it is impossible to ascertain a system's behavior. It's like listing the ingredients for a meal without the recipe. Whether something tasty comes out primarily depends on the way it's prepared: potatoes can turn into French fries, gratin, boiled potatoes, mashed potatoes, baked potatoes, fried potatoes, hash browns, and more. A meaningful architecture diagram, therefore, needs to depict the relationships between components and provide semantics for these relationships.

Electric circuit diagrams provide a canonical example of system behavior that depends heavily on connections between components. One of the most versatile elements in analog circuitry is the operational amplifier, or *op-amp* for short. Paired with a few resistors and a capacitor or two, this element can act as a comparator, amplifier, inverted amplifier, differentiator, filter, oscillator, wave generator, and much more. The system's behavior, which varies widely, doesn't depend on the list of elements, but solely on how they are connected. In the world of IT, a database can act as a cache, ledger, file storage, data store, content store, queue, configuration input, and much more. How the database is connected to its surrounding elements is fundamental, just like the op-amp.

Architecture Diagrams

If you feel that this is about as much as one could and should say about a contrived sketch of a car, rest assured that I get to see many architecture diagrams without any lines. These diagrams do depict proximity, simply because some boxes have to be next to each other, but whether any semantics are tied to this fact remains unclear. If you are lucky, proximity represents a form of "layering" from top to bottom, which in turn implies a dependency from things on "top" to things "further down." In the worst case, proximity was defined by the order in which the author drew the boxes.

So-called "capability diagrams" or "functional architectures" are particularly likely to be devoid of lines. These diagrams tend to list (pun intended) capabilities that are needed to perform a certain business function. For example, to manage customer relationships you need customer channels, campaign management, a reporting dashboard, etc. The set of capabilities forms a "laundry list" of things that are needed, but we aren't closer to architecture than listing windows, doors, roof for a house. I, therefore, prefer such input to be represented as textual lists so that this distinction becomes clear. Wrapping text in boxes doesn't constitute architecture.

UML

Speaking of lines, UML has a beautiful abundance of line styles: in a class diagram, *classes* (boxes) can be connected through association (a simple line), aggregation (with a hollow diamond on one end), composition (a solid diamond), or generalization (triangle). Navigability can be indicated by an open arrow, and a dependency by a dashed line. On top of this, *multiplicities*—for example, a truck having four to eight wheels but only one engine—can be added to the relationship lines. In fact, UML class diagrams allow so many kinds of relationships that Martin Fowler decided to split the discussion into two separate chapters inside his defining book *UML Distilled*.[4] Interestingly, UML allows *composition* to be

---

4 Martin Fowler, *UML Distilled: A Brief Guide to the Standard Object Modeling Language*, 3rd ed. (Boston: Addison-Wesley Professional, 2003).

visually expressed through a line or as *containment*, that is, drawing one box inside the other.

With such a rich visual vocabulary, why invent your own? The challenge with UML notation is that you can appreciate the nuances of the relationship semantics between classes only if you have in fact read *UML Distilled* or the UML specification. That's why such diagrams aren't as useful when addressing a broad audience: the visual translation of solid diamond versus hollow diamond or solid line versus dotted line isn't immediately intuitive. This is where containment works well: a box inside another is easily understood without having to add a legend.

Beware of Extremes

As so often, the opposite of bad is also troublesome. I have seen diagrams in which elements have different shapes, sizes, colors, and border widths; connecting lines have solid arrows, open arrows, no arrows; are dotted, dashed, and of different color. These cases either result from sloppiness, in which case the visual variation has no meaning and is simply "noise," or from a metamodel that's so rich (or convoluted) that a diagram likely isn't the right way to convey it. The rule I apply is that any visual variation in a diagram should have meaning—in other words, semantics. If it doesn't, the variance should be eliminated to reduce visual noise, which only distracts the viewer and, worse yet, can cause the viewer to interpret this noise as semantics that were in fact never intended. Because you cannot look inside the viewer's head, such misunderstandings or misinterpretations are difficult to detect. In short: making all boxes the same size won't crimp your artistic talent, but it will make clear to the viewer that the model behind the diagram considers all boxes to have the same properties. It'll also help draw attention to the lines.

The standard text on charting and diagramming is Tufte's *The Visual Display of Quantitative Information*[5] plus his subsequent books. Although the books initially focus on display of numeric information, later volumes cover broader aspects, including many examples that package complex concepts into diagrams that remain crisp and easy to grasp.

---

5 Edward R. Tufte, *The Visual Display of Quantitative Information* (Cheshire, CT: Graphics Press, 2001).

24

Sketching Bank Robbers

Architects as Police Sketch Artists

That's what he looked like!

With a demanding job like that of an architect in a large IT organization, it's a healthy exercise to do more of those things you enjoy and fewer of those you don't enjoy. Of course, this requires you to know what you truly enjoy (and truly despise) in the first place—a task that can be a little more challenging than it sounds, especially for left-brained IT architects. The latter is generally more easily answered: in my case it's 8 a.m. meetings with no particular objective that end up in a monologue by the highest-paid person. The former usually takes a bit more reflection. Over the years, I have realized that one of my favorite work activities is to listen to system owners or solution architects describe their system, often in fragments, and to draw a cohesive picture for them. The most satisfying moment happens when they exclaim, "That's exactly what it looks like," without them having been able to draw the picture themselves. This exercise is also a great opportunity to learn about those system details that aren't documented anywhere.

Asking people to tell you about their system so that you can draw it for them may remind you of the old joke that describes *consultants* (Chapter 38) as those people who borrow your watch to tell you what time it is (and charge you a lot of money for it). Drawing expressive architecture diagrams, though, is a bit more involved than reading the time off a watch. It extracts people's knowledge and presents it in a way that they weren't able to create themselves.

Being able to build a system doesn't automatically mean the same person is gifted at representing it in an intuitive way. Therefore, helping such a person draw a picture of their system can be quite valuable. I liken this task to that of a police sketch artist.

Everyone Saw the Perpetrator

If a bank is robbed and you ask those people who saw the perpetrator to draw a picture, you'll likely end up with stick figures or very rough sketches. In any case, you won't get anything particularly useful even though the witnesses have a first-hand account of the person. Knowing something, being able to articulate it, and being able to draw it are three very different skills.

That's why a professional police sketch artist is usually brought in, especially in cases where security cameras could not get precise footage. The artist interviews the witnesses, asking them a series of questions that they can easily answer, such as "Was the person tall?" Based on the descriptions the artist draws the picture, frequently obtaining feedback from the witnesses. After initially giving trivial facts like "He was tall," people end up confirming, "He looked just like that!"

A Police Sketch Artist

A police sketch artist is a fairly specialized job whose education includes both art and human anatomy. For example, a police sketch artist will undergo training in dental and bone structure because they influence the appearance of the suspect. The same is true for *architecture artists*: they need to have a minimum level of artistic skill, probably not quite at the level of the criminal sketch artist, but they must also have the mental model and visual vocabulary to express architectural concepts.

Interestingly, sketch artists break down the problem and work with well-known "patterns": after initially asking very broad questions like "tell me about the person," the artist will guide the witness with these typical patterns, for example, ethnicity, or defining features such as nose, eyes, or hair. To exaggerate, they won't discover that the person had two ears, two eyes, and one nose (if they don't, that's certainly worth mentioning!), but they do drive toward discriminating and defining features, just like we do when we *try to tell whether something is architecture* (Chapter 8). In the world of IT, we would do the equivalent. For example, when looking at data storage, we'd ask if it's an RDBMS or a NoSQL DB, perhaps a combination, whether it uses caching, replication, and so on.

Sketching Architectures

When assuming the role of an "architecture sketch artist," I tend to combine two different approaches:

THE SYSTEM METAPHOR

First, I look for noteworthy or defining features; for instance, for the *key decisions* (Chapter 8). Is it a pretty vanilla website for a customer to review information, like a *customer information portal?* Or, is it rather a new sales channel, or even a piece of a cross-channel strategy? Is it designed to handle tons of volume, or is it rather an experiment that will see little traffic but must evolve very quickly? Or, is it a spike to test out new technologies and the use case is secondary? After I have established this frame, I start filling in the details.

I am a big fan of Kent Beck's notion of a system metaphor that describes what kind of "thing" the system is. As Kent wisely states in *Extreme Programming Explained*:[1]

> We need to emphasize the goal of architecture, which is to give everyone a coherent story within which to work, a story that can easily be shared by the business and technical folks. By asking for a metaphor we are likely to get an architecture that is easy to communicate and elaborate.

In the same book, Kent also states that "Architecture is just as important in XP [Extreme Programming] projects as it is in any software project," something

---

1 Kent Beck, *Extreme Programming Explained: Embrace Change* (Boston: Addison-Wesley, 1999).

to be kept in mind by folks who are *tempted to shun architecture because they are Agile* (Chapter 31).

Just like with *diagram-driven design* (Chapter 22), architecture sketching can also be a useful design technique. If the picture makes no sense (and the architecture sketch artist is talented), something might be inconsistent or wrong in the architecture.

VIEWPOINTS

As soon as I have a rough idea about the nature of the system, I let the metaphor drive which aspects or viewpoints to examine. This is where doing an *architecture sketch* differs from performing an *architecture analysis*. An analysis typically walks through a fixed, structured set of aspects, as defined for example by methods such as C4 (*https://c4model.com/*) or arc42 (*http://arc42.org/*). This is useful as a "checklist" to uncover missing aspects or gaps. In contrast, a police sketch artist doesn't want to draw the details of a person's trouser finishings (hemmed? cuffed?), but wants to highlight those characteristics that are unique or noteworthy. The same is true for the architecture sketch artist.

Following a fixed set of viewpoints always runs the risk of becoming a paint-by-numbers exercise in which one fills in every section of a template, but *forgets to place an emphasis* (Chapter 21) or omits critical points in the process. I therefore find the viewpoint descriptions in Nick Rozanski and Eoin Woods's *Software Systems Architecture*[2] useful because they don't prescribe a fixed notation, but highlight concerns and pitfalls. Nick and Eoin also separate *perspectives* from *views*. When sketching an architecture, you are most likely interested in a specific perspective, such as performance and security, that spans multiple viewpoints; for example, a deployment or functional view.

Visuals

Each artist has their own style, and to some degree architecture sketches will also differ. I am not a big fan of molding all system documentation into a single notation because we are not creating a system specification (that's in the code), but a sketch that gives humans a better vehicle to reason about the system. For me, it's important that every visual feature of the notation has meaning in the context, or

---

2 Nick Rozanski and Eoin Woods, *Software Systems Architecture: Working With Stakeholders Using Viewpoints and Perspectives*, 2nd ed. (Upper Saddle River, NJ: Addison-Wesley, 2011).

perspective, that we are analyzing. Otherwise, it's just noise. Of course, the diagram must not only show the components *but also their relationships* (Chapter 23).

The best diagrams are rich in expressiveness but don't require a legend because the notation is intuitive from the start, or because the viewer can learn the notation from simple examples and apply what they learned to more complex aspects of the diagram. This is very much how user interfaces work: no user wants to read a long manual, but they will use what they see to build a mental model and use it to set expectations for how more complex features should work. Why not think of a diagram as a user interface? You might feel that it lacks interactivity, and you are right, but viewers *navigate* complex diagrams very much like users navigate user interfaces.

Architecture Therapy

Grady Booch drew analogies between having teams depicting their architecture and family therapy,[3] which asks children to draw a picture of their family in a method referred to as Kinetic Family Drawings (KFD). The drawings give therapists insight into the family dynamics, such as proximity, hierarchy, or behavioral patterns. I have experienced the same with development teams, so you shouldn't outright discard their drawings as meaningless or incomplete, but derive insight into the team's thinking and hierarchy from them: is the database in the middle of it all? Maybe the schema designer is calling the shots in the team (I know a case of that happening). Are there many boxes, but no lines? Probably the team's thinking is focused on structural concerns but ignores system behavior. This is often the case when the architect is too far removed from code and operational aspects.

That's Wrong! Do It Again!

A common situation when sketching an architecture for someone else is them stating, "This is wrong!" This is a good thing; it means that you discovered a mismatch between your and their understanding. If you hadn't drawn it, you would have never realized. Also, if you assume you are a reasonable proxy for subsequent consumers of the diagram, you also saved them from the same misunderstanding. Therefore, sketching out architecture is almost always an iterative process. Bring an eraser.

---

3 Grady Booch, "Draw Me a Picture," *IEEE Software* 28, no. 1 (Jan./Feb. 2011).

25

Software Is Collaboration

Got Git?

Hello Peter, what's happening?

Much has (rightly) been said and written about the differences between IT architecture and classic building architecture, which we often refer to in our metaphors. For example, although buildings do evolve over time (just very slowly[1]), achieving high rates of change at low cost is something that brick-and-mortar objects can't do. But many things can, and it's not at all limited to software development.

Who Says Software Is for Computers Only?

Enterprises spend significant effort creating, revising, and sharing documents, be they *strategic plans, schedules, design documents, or status reports* (Chapter 30). Typically, these documents need input from multiple parties and undergo iterations and quality checks until they are released. Such artifacts are really a form of *software*—they surely aren't hardware, even though they may be printed on physical paper on occasion (witnessing someone print 25 copies of a large slide deck on digital transformation will forever be burned into my mind).

So, if documents are in fact software, if we want to optimize and accelerate our collaboration and communication, we might be able to learn a bit by looking at how software delivery teams, especially widely distributed open source teams, work.

Version Control

The one tool you won't be able to pry out of any developer's dead cold hands is *version control* (Chapter 14). Version control is the safety net that gives developers the confidence to move fast because they have the assurance that they can revert quickly in case they take a wrong turn. One of the most popular version control tools these days is Git. The model behind this software takes some getting used to, but once you adapt your flow, you'll never want to go back to anything else.

I wrote the precursor to this book in Markdown,[2] a simple text format. I used Git for version control and Dropbox for file synchronization with the publishing engine. After the book was published, I kept ideas for additional chapters (like this one) in a backlog. Without thinking too much about it, I reverted to writing the backlog in Microsoft Word as these chapters weren't done and weren't going to be published soon.

I instantly noticed that my rate of progress slowed down: should I remove or rewrite this paragraph? What if I change my mind later and want to keep it? I better make a copy and "park" it somewhere for later. By the way, where did I

---

1 Stewart Brand, *How Buildings Learn: What Happens After They're Built* (New York: Penguin Books, 1995).

2 A simple text-based language, originally intended to author web pages without having to learn HTML.

keep the latest version? Should I use the Track Changes feature instead? When working with text files and version control, I would not have spent a second on any of this because I'd be assured that I could revert to a prior version at any time. I'd also be able to see all the changes I made over time, so I could track progress easily.

Of course, I could have checked my Word documents into Git or a document management system like Microsoft SharePoint. However, two main factors would be missing: first, version comparison between Word files is much more laborious than on simple text files. Word's review mode tracks history but is much more geared toward minor revision changes as opposed to iterative creation of a document. More important, the build tool chain to produce the book works with Markdown files, so I would not enjoy the benefits of Continuous Integration, meaning I can create a preview copy of the book any time I make a change.

 Anyone who has looked at a corporate file server notices that I am not the only one who appreciates version control. You'll find 20-some copies of the same document, with the filename either suffixed with a version number, prefixed with the date (for easy sorting), tagged with the last author's initials to indicate branching, etc. Someone had the right idea but stumbled in the implementation.

Single Source of Truth

Version control is a powerful tool, if all team members look at the same version. Emailing documents around that are kept on local drives means that each person has their own source of truth, which is going to lead to friction in the best case and lost information in the worst. Therefore, version control must be coordinated among team members.

The most transformative change in collaboration patterns I have witnessed was the advent of Google Docs (then called "Writely") around 2006, and it wasn't due to my seven years of drinking Google Kool-Aid. Google Docs popularized a browser-based document editing model that allows multiple users to simultaneously edit the same document. Interestingly, when Google Docs first became available internally at Google for *dogfooding* (Chapter 37), its feature maturity resembled that of Microsoft Word 5.0 from 1989. Getting two bullet points to be the same size was already a challenge.

Still, being able to collaborate in real time on a shared document fundamentally changed the way people worked together. No time was wasted on maintaining, mailing, finding, or merging multiple versions of documents. Almost all "my version versus your version" discussions went away as it was clear that the team worked toward a single shared outcome. Adding collaborators became easy and natural. Having had to go back to sharing Word and Power-Point documents by email has been a rather frustrating experience.

Trunk-Based Development

Most version control tools allow *branching*. Branches are separate versions of the codebase, often used to develop a special feature that's not yet ready to be released. The major advantage of branching is that a person working in a branch can make many changes without having to worry about what else is going on. Alas, that freedom is usually short lived. Sooner or later, the branch must be "merged" back into the authoritative version, also called the *trunk*, following the analogy of a version "tree."

Unfortunately, while a person was working in the branch, time wasn't actually standing still: many other changes occurred to the documents or source code. As a result, merging becomes a rather unpleasant and often wasteful exercise: perhaps someone copyedited the paragraph that you just rewrote. That's wasted effort! Also, while you are working in your branch, no one else can benefit from what you have done. If branches remind you of locally stored document versions, you are onto something. A version control system where each person works in their own branch doesn't really help much in terms of collaboration.

As a result, many folks advocate *trunk-based development*,[3] an approach that mandates all changes going into a single authoritative version of the codebase or document. Naturally, doing so avoids any drift between different authors' versions.

However, how can you put unfinished work into the main version of a document? There are quite a few options:

- The most obvious but also most underused solution is to *break down big changes into a series of smaller tasks* (Chapter 30).
- Software teams use *feature toggles* to enable or disable a feature, allowing code to be integrated into the system but not yet available to users. The equivalent for presentations are hidden slides: you can happily work on those knowing that they won't be shown to the audience.

---

3 Paul Hammant et al., "Trunk Based Development," *https://trunkbaseddevelopment.com*.

- Making very short branches that last only a single day is also OK and won't break the trunk-based model. This way you can iterate and tinker and merge before you leave work.

Having code in the trunk doesn't mean it's instantly released to production. Many teams use separate release branches, which undergo additional review and testing. The equivalent for documents and presentations would be to cut a PDF at a known-good-state for subsequent distribution.

Always Be Ready to Ship

When collaborating on a slide deck, usually multiple authors contribute parts, which are then reviewed over the course of multiple iterations until it's considered good enough and meets the corporate style guidelines. The key question is when is something good "good enough"? To me, the most important elements of a presentation are the *key messages and the storyline they are woven into* (Chapter 20). Interestingly, both can be done well before painstakingly aligning all the boxes and converting graphics to the corporate color palette. A presentation with a solid storyline and simple graphics is also far more impactful than a half-finished one with fancy stock photographs, so we should work on those aspects first.

When working on slides, we can learn from modern software development techniques such as Agile development and DevOps, which aim to always have software that could be released if need be.

 I tend to ask my teams: "what if we had to present in one hour?" Do we have a core storyline and some essential slides to support it? When you are at that point, you can refine and improve slides with much less stress.

Always being ready to ship highlights the difference between working iteratively and incrementally.[4] Many people make slides incrementally and have only half a slide deck after half the time elapsed. They are not ready to present. Following the DevOps mindset nudges you to work iteratively, meaning you have a rough version of the whole story that you can share immediately if needed (see Figure 25-1).

---

4 Jeff Patton, "Don't Know What I Want, But I Know How to Get It," Jeff Patton and Associates website, *https://oreil.ly/biPNX.*

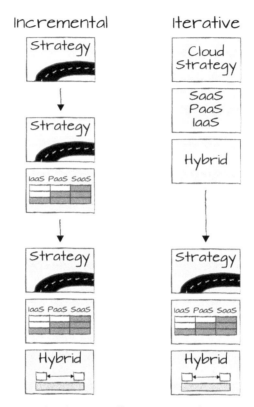

Figure 25-1. Building presentations incrementally versus iteratively

Style Versus Substance

Some folks might counter that even if a storyline is decent, presenting it in rough packaging means it "isn't ready" or even "not professional." I am a big fan of good design and spend a fair amount of time giving my stage presentations a clean and professional appearance. However, if I have to choose between a solid message and pretty pictures, I'd have to choose the message because I am an architect and not an artist—analogous to the Agile Manifesto's preference of running software over documents. Documentation is important, but if you can have only one or the other, you'd want to pick running software.

You'll encounter the same argument when working in formats like Markdown or simple collaboration tools. Because such systems aren't as full featured as desktop-publishing or word-processing tools, teams that are used to focusing on visuals over content often dismiss them as not meeting their needs, failing to realize that this is exactly what they need.

Transparency

On many software projects, you can see a monitor or a glowing orb that shows the project's current build status. Just by walking by, you can see how many builds have been made, how many are green (free of errors), and how many are red. Such a project is fully transparent, which builds trust outside the project and motivation within. The same level of transparency can be applied to any project; for example, showing how many servers were migrated out of an old datacenter over time or how many systems have become compliant with the IT security guidelines.

On a prior team we had a glowing LED display that showed the total number of pushes to our source code repository. Not only was it a great conversation piece, it also led to a minor celebration when four digits weren't sufficient anymore.

In an enterprise context, you are likely to encounter two major hurdles against such transparency. First, project managers prefer to "massage" their message carefully in status meetings instead of sharing it widely. Second, many teams don't have the relevant data ready at hand. Whereas the former is annoying, the latter is worse: how do they steer the project if they don't have the vital metrics at their fingertips?

Pairing

The most debated practice of modern software delivery is pair programming. However, when producing slides or documents, you'll find a joint working session to be much more productive than emailing redlined documents and comments back and forth.

I have seen slide review cycles that oscillate between review meetings, assigning tasks, people making changes (often misunderstanding what was discussed), and reconvening for weeks and months. If everybody sat in a room and developed the slides together, they could have been done in a few hours.

"Pairing" on slide decks—I call it "pair PowerPointing"—can save lengthy review and edit cycles and generally leads to better results.

Resistance

Of course, there's always resistance. *Star Wars* couldn't possibly have had nine episodes' worth of storyline without *The Resistance*. Besides purely politically motivated arguments against transparency, you may find that people consider working in text formats like Markdown to be "too technical."

I was once alerted by a large company's digital innovation branch that "Markdown is too technical." My initial reaction was to ask them whether it's the hash mark or the star that tripped them up...

More serious, you'll find that working with a version control system like Git is not to everyone's liking and carries a learning curve.

During my early days using Git I missed staging a new file. When I checked out an older branch, the file was still in my working directory (it wasn't under Git's control), so I concluded that I should delete it. When reverting to the original branch, I was shocked to find my file didn't come back. Thank God for hard drive backups.

When asking people to embrace version control, it's important to teach the concept of a version control system first; that is, a commit, a branch, etc., in the context of real work scenarios. It then becomes easier to get used to Git's occasionally quirky model. When they're past this hurdle, though, people will consider working without version control like driving without a seatbelt.

PART | IV

Organizations

Architects in the enterprise live at the intersection of the technical and business worlds. In fact, getting these two pieces to work together seamlessly is one of an *architect's key contributions* (Chapter 4). Therefore, a good architect needs to not only understand the interplay between system components, but also the interplay in a large and dynamic system that is known as *organization*.

Organizational Architecture: The Static View

The most common depiction of an organization's architecture is the organizational chart ("org chart"). These charts depict who reports to whom, and one can measure people's importance by how far they are from the CEO. Assuming you count from zero in good computer-science tradition, I am often at level two or three below a group CEO, a divisional CEO, and perhaps a COO in between. For an architect in a large organization, this isn't bad at all—many people find themselves at level 6 or 7.

Luckily, org charts have lines and thus pass our test for *architecture diagrams* (Chapter 23). Computer-science-educated folks may recognize an org chart as a tree, a noncyclical, connected directed graph with a single *root* (math folks consider trees to be undirected, but that's fine also). Alas, it's only showing part of the picture: depicting the static structure tells us little about how people interact to make the business work.

Organizational Architecture: The Dynamic View

An org chart depicts engineering, manufacturing, marketing, and finance departments as separate pillars of the organizational pyramid. However, in reality, engineering must design a product that can be easily and reliably manufactured, marketed to customers, and sold at a profit. How well organizations work is rarely defined by the organization's structure—most organizations will have the aforementioned functions—but by how they interact: how slow or fast are their development cycles; do they work in a Waterfall or an Agile model; who talks to customers, who, interestingly, aren't depicted in the org chart?

Coworkers also routinely talk to one another to solve problems without following the lines in the organizational pyramid. This is a good thing because otherwise managers would quickly become communication bottlenecks. In many cases the org chart shows the *control flow* of the organization—for example, to give budget approvals, whereas the *data flow* is much more open and dynamic. Ironically, the way people actually work with one another is rarely depicted in a diagram. Part of the reason might be that this data is difficult to gather; the other part could be that it doesn't look nearly as neat as the org chart pyramid.

When people coordinate and communicate electronically, the actual, dynamic organizational structure can be more easily observed. For example, if developers collaborate via a version-control system, we can analyze code reviews or check-in approvals to see the real collaboration taking place. Google had another interesting system that allowed you to see which persons are sitting nearby a given person. Because interaction and collaboration are often still based on ad hoc conversations, physical proximity can be a better predictor of collaboration patterns than the org chart structure.

The Matrix (Not the Movie)

In large organizations, people can have multiple reporting lines: a "dotted line" to their project or program manager, and a "solid line" to their department or "line manager." Such an arrangement is often part of a so-called *matrix organization* in which people report horizontally to the project and vertically to their manager. Or is it the other way around? If you find this a little confusing, you're not alone. High-performance delivery organizations generally shun such arrangements, making sure people are fully assigned to, and responsible for, a single project. I often jest that I want all people working on a project to be on the same boat without life vests and no rescue lines to other parts of the organization. A team needs a shared success or, if it so happens, shared failure. Don't worry, they are all able to swim.

Organizations as Systems

As architects, we know well how to design systems; for example, when to apply horizontal scaling, loose coupling, caching. We often are also trained in systems thinking (Chapter 9), which teaches us how to reason about the relationship between elements in a system and the overall system behavior, driven, for example, by positive or negative feedback loops. However, we often hesitate to apply such rational thinking to organizations because organizations have a very human face, which makes us feel bad if we degrade our nice and not-so-nice coworkers into the *boxes and lines* (Chapter 23) of some system architecture.

However, even though they're composed of individuals, large organizations behave much more like complex systems, including technical ones. Therefore, as architects we can apply our architectural mindset and rational systems thinking to large organizations in order to understand and influence them. It's a bit like a reverse engineering, debugging, and refactoring exercise.

Organizations as People

All rational reasoning aside, organizations are made up of individuals. We also shouldn't forget that for many of them work is just a small part of their lives: they have families to take care of, bills to pay, doctors to visit, home repairs to make, or hangovers from the party last night to overcome. Understanding organizations depends on understanding people's emotions and motivations. This can be a stretch for left-brain-type architects, but one they need to make. Consider this yoga for your brain.

Navigating Large Organizations

Dealing with organizations can be challenging for architects. However, many concepts that are well known in the context of architect systems can also be applied to understanding organizations:

Chapter 26, Reverse-Engineering Organizations
    To bring lasting change, you need to help organizations unlearn existing beliefs.

Chapter 27, Control Is an Illusion
    Command-and-control structures aren't a one-way street.

Chapter 28, They Don't Build 'Em Quite Like That Anymore
    Pyramids went out of vogue 4,500 years ago, but are still widely used in IT.

Chapter 29, Black Markets Are Not Efficient
> High-friction organizations breed black markets, which are dangerous.

Chapter 30, Scaling an Organization
> Experience in distributed systems design can be applied to organizations.

Chapter 31, Slow Chaos Is Not Order
> Slow-moving things can seem well coordinated when in reality they're just slow-motion chaos.

Chapter 32, Governance Through Inception
> Governance by decree is difficult and better done by planting ideas.

Reverse-Engineering Organizations

Learning Is Hard; Unlearning Is Much Harder

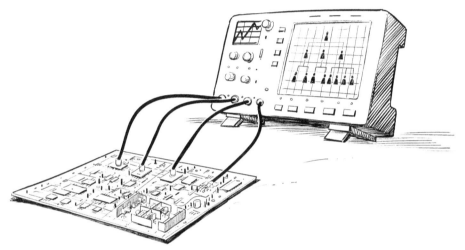

Attaching some probes to the organization

To change a system's observed behavior, you need to change *the system itself* (Chapter 10). For organizational systems, the systemic behavior is primarily guided by its culture. A significant portion of this culture derives from shared beliefs held by the organization's members. So, to permanently change an organization's observed behavior, you need to identify and change those beliefs.

Unfortunately, these shared beliefs aren't written down anywhere; there aren't any motivational posters for shared beliefs. Also, most people won't even be aware that they carry them. So, you'll need to apply one of your well-honed engineering skills: *reverse engineering.*

Dissecting IT Slogans

A good starting point for reverse-engineering an organization's hidden beliefs are popular slogans. Anyone who has worked in IT for a little bit surely has heard the saying *"never touch a running system"* (Chapter 12). Why would people not want to touch a system that's running? Apparently because they believe that change is risky: if you touch it, you might break it. Deeper down, they may also believe that fixing broken things is cumbersome, so it's better not to break them in the first place.

 The well-known IT slogan "never touch a running system" reflects the underlying belief that change is risky. And, worse yet, it also assumes that not changing anything bears no risk.

Importantly, though, there's an additional assumption behind this simple slogan: if you don't touch the system, all will be fine. This belief—that no change implies no risk, is worrisome. First, from an operational perspective, systems that aren't maintained will rot and, for example, use outdated libraries and operating systems that pose security risks. Also, in the digital world, which is constantly evolving, standstill is regress: competitors move ahead with frequent updates and rapid feature evolution. Ultimately, not changing can be fatal for organizations—consider Kodak, Blockbuster, or BlackBerry.

Second, you'll notice how simple slogans can become self-fulfilling prophecies. When you avoid changing a system for a long time this actually does increase the risk of change: important details will have been long forgotten, and undocumented manual steps increase the odds that something will go wrong. Such experiences confirm and fuel the belief.

Unknown Beliefs

Not all organizational beliefs manifest in slogans, though. In most cases, people might not even be aware that they carry certain beliefs until their assumptions are being challenged. I had that very experience at a Munich beer festival.

The well-known Munich Oktoberfest has a springtime cousin, the *Starkbier Fest* ("strong beer festival"). As the name suggests, this festival serves beer with an alcohol content about 50% higher than the Oktoberfest, in the same 1 liter jugs. Needless to say, "having a beer or two" can make the way home somewhat challenging. The more surprised I was when my younger colleague commented that he drove to the festival in a convertible to take advantage of the sunny weather. My immediate reaction was: "Are you out of your mind to drive to a beer fest?" His calm answer was, "No, I leave the car here."

Not only did I feel old, I also realized that I had been carrying a fundamental belief about cars: if you drive somewhere, you (hopefully) come back with the same car; otherwise, it would be difficult to go somewhere else tomorrow. What broke this assumption, which was useful in the past? Car sharing—the ability to pick up a car near your home, to rent it by the minute, and to leave it at your destination. Without ubiquitous smart phones, GPS, telematics, and other good stuff, my assumption was handy and never challenged; now it limited my thinking.

You can't just ask people what their beliefs are because most are unaware of them.

Because most people are unaware of the assumptions they hold, you can't just ask them what their beliefs are. If you had asked me about my beliefs about cars, I might have said that you must have liability insurance and fuel in the tank.

Beliefs Are Proven Until Disproven

Beliefs stick because people often have living proof or firsthand experience. When the environment changes, though, and the belief is no longer applicable, their past experience makes them reluctant to change.

Think of kids who learned that touching a stove top is a bad idea. Some of them learned this the very hard and painful way, others were told many times. They therefore embraced a useful belief that prevents accidents. Alas, the invention of the induction cooktop makes this belief obsolete: induction cookers heat pots directly through electromagnetic fields, leaving the cooktop surface relatively cool. You will find it difficult, though, to make children touch this new cooktop, because they learned their lesson well. The best way might be to touch the cooktop yourself to demonstrate the change.

 Because most people have living proof for their beliefs, just telling them otherwise is unlikely to succeed.

The same is true in IT: most IT folks will be able to tell you a story in which someone did touch a running system, causing it to fail, and needing operations teams to stay up 48 hours straight trying to get it back up and running. Simply telling people that they are wrong or that magically everything is different is unlikely to be successful. Trying to convince them that change isn't risky by spewing out buzzwords and acronyms like TDD, IaC, Git, and Spinnaker is like explaining to kids that an induction stove is safe to touch by citing Faraday's law. Instead, you might start by explaining the tenets of DevOps, such as deployment automation, version control, and automated testing. Also, making smaller changes reduces the risk of change. Better yet, you demonstrate the effect with a real software delivery project.

Unlearning Old Habits

Bringing change into an organization can easily stumble over existing, strongly held beliefs that are part of the existing culture. For example, selling Continuous Delivery to a person who equates change with risk is going to be quite a challenge. We therefore need to help the organization *unlearn* these old habits before lasting change can take hold. Learning new things isn't easy, but unlearning old habits, especially ones that served us well many times, is much more difficult.[1] It seems that replacing existing beliefs requires you to free up a memory slot in the brain first before you can program it again.

Common IT Beliefs

When trying to reverse-engineer existing beliefs, there's one ray of hope: many IT organizations hold similar beliefs because they were subject to the same learning, or *priming* (Chapter 6). Hence, the following list of beliefs can give you a head start:

SPEED AND QUALITY ARE OPPOSED ("QUICK AND DIRTY")

The so-called project management triangle is both one of the most popular and most dangerous tools in IT management because it purports that scope, time, and resources have a simple relationship. For example, twice as many people would be able to accomplish the same work in half the time. Worse yet, it assumes that by compromising quality, things can be sped up further.

While the triangle might work for simple, physical tasks, it surely doesn't work in software delivery where the opposite is often the case. For example, if a developer wanted to secretly sabotage a software project, a suitable way would be

---

1 Barry O'Reilly, *Unlearn: Let Go of Past Success to Achieve Extraordinary Results* (New York: McGraw-Hill, 2018).

to introduce subtle, hard-to-find bugs. How then, can lower quality speed things up?

Modern developers know that in software development the opposite effect takes place: we speed things up by automating them, which also *increases quality* (Chapter 40) and repeatability.

QUALITY CAN BE ADDED LATER

Classic software projects end with a "QA" phase, the quality assurance phase, which consists of a team of testers checking whether the deliverable is of high quality. Behind this common approach rests a fundamental belief that quality is something that can be added to an existing work product: if something of poor quality goes into QA, it comes out with higher quality.

Detecting bugs and reworking can improve some aspects of software, but it cannot correct fundamental deficiencies in the internal quality of a software system, such as its structure or testability. Those must be built in from the beginning. Methods such as shift-left testing[2] follow this approach.

This belief and the previous one are related. If you work under the assumption that quality is added at the end, compressing the schedule will most likely decimate the (manual) QA activity, actually resulting in lower quality.

ALL PROBLEMS CAN BE SOLVED WITH MORE PEOPLE OR MONEY

Also guided by the scope-resources-time triangle, some organizations assume that more people reduce time under constant scope.

There's a common saying that when a project manager in a typical bank tells the business that it's impossible to deliver the project in three months, the business responds by asking "how much more money do you need?"

Fred Brooks already documented four decades ago[3] that adding people requires onboarding and increases communication overhead, both of which will slow down a project. Also, large projects often come to a grinding halt due to excessive complexity. Adding more resources is likely to increase complexity, exacerbating the problem.

---

2 Wikipedia, "Shift-Left Testing," *https://oreil.ly/iotex*.

3 Fredrick P. Brooks, *The Mythical Man-Month: Essays on Software Engineering, Anniversary Edition* (Boston: Addison-Wesley Professional, 1995).

Therefore, if you want to speed up a project, look to reduce friction instead of adding more resources. If your car's (or your organization's) handbrake is set, you'll want to release the brake, not step harder on the gas pedal.

FOLLOWING A PROVEN PROCESS LEADS TO PROVEN GOOD RESULTS

Much of an organization's way of working is encoded in well-defined processes, which aim to reduce risk, control spending, and assure high-quality deliverables. Many large organizations even have entire departments whose job it is to define and update processes.

Even though most processes, such as approvals or budget reviews, are well intended, following them assures only one thing: that the process was followed. There's a big leap from someone checking a box or completing a task to actually achieving the desired result, such as reducing spend or assuring architecture compliance. Especially if processes are cumbersome, people will be inclined to just obtain the necessary process check marks without fulfilling the intention of the process, possibly leading to a flourishing *black market* (Chapter 29). Some organizations therefore police and audit for process compliance by investigating projects and their implementations, resulting in a *catch me if you can* kind of game.

Attempting to achieve desirable results via processes and check lists typically stems from a lack of transparency. If you can't see what a project does or what kind of code it develops, the next best thing you could do is to make sure a certain process was followed. Modern development and deployment practices such as central code repositories, automated code quality checks, automated policy checkers, and cloud runtimes provide a much higher level of transparency and allow much more effective compliance checks.

LATE CHANGES ARE EXPENSIVE OR IMPOSSIBLE

Did you ever wonder why a typical IT project has an endless list of requirements that appears to anticipate any possible use case or scenario for the next five years? It's based on a simple belief: the business has learned that late changes are expensive or even impossible.

 An old joke goes that IT tends to deliver only half of what it promised, so the business asks for twice as much in the hope that they get the right half.

This belief stems from IT service providers' common practice of charging large sums for late changes. Because they compete aggressively on the initial bid for a project, they compensate by charging astronomical sums for changes during project execution when the customer doesn't have a lot of alternatives. Even internal projects that are subject to budget approvals or are poorly architected might have reconfirmed this belief because they are difficult to change later.

Welcoming late changes is a key tenet of Agile development, dispelling this common belief. It's best illustrated by Mary Poppendieck's observation that "a late change in requirements is a competitive advantage."

AGILITY OPPOSES DISCIPLINE

Because Agile development welcomes change during a project, it is often seen as being at odds with stable processes. After all, change and stability are opposites of each other. Following this logic, some organizations even believe that in the absence of rigid steering and control mechanisms, things descend into utter chaos.

However, the opposite is true: Agile development is actually a very disciplined process because *speed and lack of discipline don't mix* (Chapter 31). Agile methods prioritize on delivering value early and maintain velocity through a rigid adherence to regular (re)planning and tracking of progress and quality, something often missing in traditional projects.

THE UNEXPECTED IS UNDESIRED

After spending a lot of time creating a plan, traditional organizations expect things to go according to their plan. Deviations from the plan or unexpected outcomes are undesired and considered a failure.

However, when something unexpected happens, the most learning happens. That's because the unexpected can tell you that you made a poor assumption or that an error was hidden in the system. Therefore, successful businesses run experiments to verify or falsify a hypothesis. Either way, the outcome implies learning and isn't a failure at all. This means that traditional enterprises learn less, which is dangerous in a world that's constantly changing.

Rather than avoid deviations, enterprise should identify valuable hypothesis that they can test quickly and cheaply. Therefore, minimizing the cost of experimentation is a better goal than minimizing deviation.

Reprogramming the Organization

Given how strongly existing beliefs influence an organization's ability to transform, how do you best go about identifying and changing them? There is no magic three-step recipe, but you can combine several behaviors to tackle them:

Observe carefully
> You can't just ask people about their beliefs, because most of the time they aren't even aware of them. Instead, observe how people behave and look for unusual or unexpected decisions. Then, consider which belief would make such a decision appear rational.

Ask questions
> Keep asking people (Chapter 7) why they would choose a particular option to uncover what drives their behavior.

Explain carefully
> Acknowledge the usefulness of their belief in the past, but explain what has changed since then.

Define new beliefs
> Because it's difficult for people to unlearn things, establish clear new beliefs that can replace the old ones.

Be patient
> Change takes time (Part V).

Your goal isn't to turn everyone's belief system upside-down but to identify and dislodge those beliefs that impede the change you are trying to bring. Reverting too many beliefs will make folks insecure and confused.

Handed-Down Beliefs

Whereas most beliefs stem from actual experience, others are handed down through generations. A classic (unconfirmed) story of beliefs taking a life of their own involves monkeys, water, and bananas: several primates were in a cage with bananas hung in the middle. As soon as any monkey would reach for the tempting bananas, all monkeys would be sprayed with cold water, something they weren't particularly fond of. Every now and then, a monkey was replaced with a new one. If the new arrival would reach for the bananas, the others would be quick to hold them back because they knew what was going to happen. Even after all the original monkeys have been replaced and none of the resident monkeys have ever been sprayed with water, the best practice of "don't touch the bananas" lives on.

This story isn't based on scientific evidence, but sometimes it does feel that despite all the technical advances we have made, our basic behavior hasn't evolved that much from reaching for bananas.

27

Control Is an Illusion

It's When You're Told Exactly What You Want to Hear

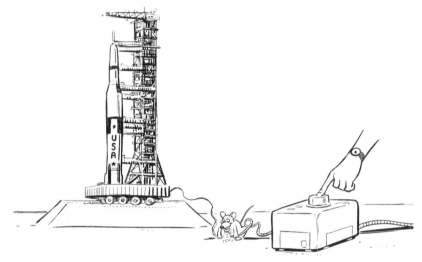

Who's in control here?

While working in Asia, I've become accustomed to sharing a few of my personal details before presenting to a group of people. I like the idea because it didn't have the flavor of bragging about professional accomplishments; rather, it gives the audience an impression about the speaker's background to better understand what shaped their thinking. In a presentation to a group of CEEMA (the Central-Eastern Europe, Middle-East, and Africa region) COOs and CIOs, I once opened with a slide summarizing my core beliefs in the form of the pin buttons that many people used to wear in the 1980s.

The one slogan that received immediate attention was "Control is an illusion." Even more attention was paid to my explanation: "You feel that you have control when people tell you exactly what you want to hear." Perhaps this wasn't the kind of control these senior executives wanted to have over their business.

The Illusion

How can control be an illusion? "Having control" is based on the assumption that a direction set from top down is actually being followed and has the desired effect. And this can be a big illusion. How would you know that it does, if you are simply sitting at the top, pushing (control) buttons instead of working alongside the staff? You can rely on management status reports, but then you make a major assumption that the presented information reflects reality. This might be yet another big illusion.

Steven Denning uses the term *semblance of control*[1] in contrast to *actual control* for this phenomenon in large organizations. A more cynical version would be to claim that the inmates are running the asylum. In either case, it's not the state you want your organization to be in.

Control Circuits

A brief look at control theory sheds some light on where the illusion originates. Control circuits, such as a room thermostat, keep a system in a stable condition —in this example, keeping a room at a constant temperature. They do so based on sensors and feedback: the thermostat senses the room temperature and turns the furnace on when the room is cold. When the desired temperature is reached, it turns off the furnace.

The feedback loop compensates for external factors such as the outside temperature or someone opening the window. This runs counter to many project planning approaches that attempt to predict all factors up front and then look to execute according to plan. It's like running the heater for exactly two hours and then blaming the cold weather for the room not being warm enough. Embarrassingly, a cheap thermostat can give us better control than some project managers.

A Two-Way Street

Jeff Sussna describes the importance of feedback loops in his book *Designing Delivery*,[2] drawing on the notion of *cybernetics*. While most people think of cyborgs and terminators when they hear the term, cybernetics is actually a field

---

1 Steve Denning, "Ten Agile Axioms That Make Managers Anxious," *Forbes*, June 17, 2018, *https://oreil.ly/DnIes*.

2 Jeff Sussna, *Designing Delivery: Rethinking IT in the Digital Service Economy* (Sebastopol, CA: O'Reilly, 2015).

of study that deals with "control and communication in the animal and the machine." Such control and communication is almost always based on a closed signaling loop.

When we portray large organizations as "command-and-control" structures, we often focus only on the top-down steering part, and less on the feedback from the "sensors." But not using the sensors means one is flying blind, possibly with a feeling of control, but one that's disconnected from reality. It's like driving a car at night without headlights and turning the steering wheel with no clue where the car is actually headed—a very dumb idea. It's shocking to see how such behavior, which borders on absurdity, can establish itself in large organizations.

Problems on the Way Up

Even if an organization uses sensors—for example, by obtaining the infamous status reports—not all is necessarily well. Anyone who has heard the term *watermelon status* understands: these are the projects whose status is "green" on the outside but "red" on the inside, meaning that they are presented as going well but in reality suffer from serious issues. Corporate project managers and status reporters aren't straight-out liars, but they might be overly optimistic or take some literary license to make their project look good. "700 happy passengers reach New York after *Titanic*'s maiden voyage" is also factually correct, but not the status report you'd want to get.

Observing how much trust some senior executives place in PowerPoint slides might make you believe that it not only has a built-in spell checker but also a lie detector. Digital companies are generally suspicious of fabricated presentations and "massaged" messages, but instead believe in hard data, preferably rendered in live metrics dashboards.

 Google's Mobile Ads team in Japan reviewed the performance of all ad experiments, run as A/B tests, every week, and decided which experiments should be accepted into production, which ones should be rejected, and which ones needed to run longer in order to become conclusive. The decisions were based on hard user data, not projections or promises.

Working based off of hard data can be frustrating because getting a solution running doesn't yet earn you much praise: that's expected anyway. Praise comes once your solution receives attention and traffic from actual users—data that's much harder to fabricate.

Smart Control

Some control circuits take in more feedback signals and refine how they drive the system. For example, some heating systems measure the outside temperature to predict energy loss through windows and walls. Google's Nest thermostat takes it a step further: it takes in additional information, such as the weather forecast (the sun helps warm the house), and when you are usually home or away. It also learns about the inertia of the heating system, which can lead to overheating the house due to heat capacity left in the radiators when the furnace is switched off. Nest is thus called a "learning" or "smart" thermostat; it takes in additional signals and optimizes what it does based on that feedback. It would be fantastic if we could apply that label to more project managers.

Saupreiß, ned so Damischer

When people speak about command-and-control structures, they are quick to cite the military, which, after all, is run by commanders. The military organization most equated with stodginess and "iron discipline" is the Prussian army. For people living in Bavaria, in Germany's southern region, Prussia is externalized in the concept of the *Preiß*, a not-so-friendly term referring to people born north of their state.

Ironically, the Prussian military understood very well that one-way control is merely an illusion. Carl von Clausewitz wrote a 1,000-page tome, *On War*, in the early 1800s, in which he cites sources of *friction*: the external gap between desired and actual outcomes (uncertainty) and the internal gap between plans and the actions of an organization.

In his book *The Art of Action*,[3] Stephen Bungay extends this concept into three gaps, as illustrated in Figure 27-1: the *knowledge gap* between what you'd like to know and actually do know, the *alignment gap* between plans and actions, and the *effects gap* between what you expect your actions to achieve and what actually happens.

---

3 Stephen Bungay, *The Art of Action: How Leaders Close the Gaps between Plans, Actions and Results* (London: Nicholas Brealey Publishing, 2010).

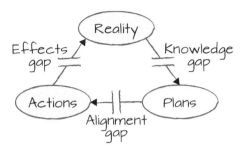

Figure 27-1. The three gaps that can make control an illusion (adapted from Bungay)

You can recognize organizations that believe they can close these gaps by the methods they apply. They try to close the knowledge gap by generating thick requirements documents, which are often outdated by the time they are completed. They try to tackle the alignment gap by developing extensive project plans and micro-managing according to them. Lastly, the effects gap is a bit more difficult to close. Such organizations try nonetheless, either through the aforementioned watermelon status reports or by using *proxy metrics* (Chapter 40), things that are easily measured but don't quite reflect reality. Essentially, these organizations create their own reality, or illusion.

 Many IT organizations believe they can close the knowledge, alignment, and effects gaps, an approach that has been disproven some 200 years ago.

Unlike some IT organizations, the Prussians already knew that the gaps couldn't be eliminated. Instead, they accepted the gaps and adjusted their management style accordingly, replacing a concrete order with the concept of *Auftragstaktik*, best translated as "mission command" or "directive." Understanding the purpose of the mission enabled the troops to adjust to unforeseen circumstances (knowledge or effects gaps) without having to report back to central command. This would save valuable time and lead to better decisions in the local context.

The difference between an order and a mission command becomes clear with a simple example. Suppose that a small platoon is given the order to take a hill. As it climbs up the hill, the soldiers realize that there's no resistance at all and progress easily. Should they march to the top? If they have been given a simple command, they'll do so. This might be correct if the intent, the *Auftrag*, was to take the hill as a strategic position. However, if the intent was to attack troops positioned on the hill, advancing to the top makes little sense.

Auftragstaktik doesn't mean people are left to do whatever they deem appropriate. It's based on discipline, but *active discipline*, one that respects the commander's intentions, as opposed to *passive obedience*, which demands blind execution. Also, when deciding on an action, teams pull from a well-defined repertoire of tactics that are well known and extensively trained.

So, the *Preißn* weren't so stodgy after all and were possibly ahead of many modern IT departments.

Actual Control: Autonomy

Ironically, it turns out that giving teams decision autonomy actually increases control as it accepts the gaps and avoids operating in an illusion. But be careful: many organizations equate autonomy to "everyone does what they think is best." Now, unfortunately, that's not autonomy, that's *anarchy*: whether we like it or not, anarchists do what they believe is right.

Everyone doing what they think is best isn't autonomy, it's anarchy.

How can large-scale IT organizations establish autonomy without falling into anarchy? In my experience, it requires the interplay between three elements (see Figure 27-2):

Enablement

It may sound trivial, but first you need to enable people to perform their work. Sadly, corporate IT knows many mechanisms that *disable* people: HR processes that restrict recruiting, approval processes that take weeks to provision servers, *black markets* (Chapter 29) that are inaccessible to new hires. Just like a thermostat connected to a furnace with a plugged gas line won't do much good, high friction negates autonomy. In IT, platforms such as cloud computing can enable employees and at the same time assure consistency in "tactics" as they provide a common set of tools to select from.

Feedback

Autonomous teams can make better decisions because they have the shortest *feedback cycles* (Chapter 36). This way, they can learn fast and improve. This works only if teams see the consequences for their decisions. If the thermostat is mounted in another room than the radiator, there's no control circuit.

Strategy

To make good decisions, teams need to be able to distinguish which decisions are good. They therefore need to have specific goals; for example, revenue generated or quantifiable user engagement. These goals aren't specific commands but overall objectives to be achieved. A thermostat is useful only if someone sets the desired temperature.

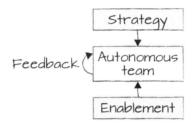

Figure 27-2. Strategy, feedback, and enablement separate autonomy from anarchy

This system won't work if you omit one or more elements: strategy without enablement will lead to zero progress but lots of frustration. Autonomy without strategy or feedback will resemble anarchy as teams can't judge the appropriateness of their decisions. And enablement without strategy will only make anarchy more efficient. For example, the Spotify Squad Model[4] found that increasing alignment on a common strategy supports increasing autonomy.

---

4 Henrik Kniberg, "Spotify Engineering Culture (part 1)," Spotify Labs, March 27, 2014, *https://oreil.ly/d3MAI*.

Many *enterprise architecture teams* (Chapter 4) set direction without being responsible for the consequences. Applying the logic that lack of strategy and feedback leads to anarchy implies a rather disconcerting outcome.

Another insight might surprise traditional organizations that are looking to give teams more autonomy: autonomous teams need better management. Managing nonautonomous teams is comparatively easy: they'll largely do as told. Autonomous teams, in contrast, require *leadership*: they need to be told the overall intent and goals. So, ironically, organizations that are looking to increase autonomy in their teams might need to strengthen management first.

Autonomous teams need better management.

Controlling the Control Loop

Even though a control circuit's job is to keep a system in a steady state without someone having to monitor it, observing the circuit's behavior can still be useful in a larger context, meaning we shouldn't blindly trust the autopilot. For example, if the air filter in a forced-air heating system becomes clogged or the furnace collects soot, it will take longer to warm the house under otherwise identical conditions. A "dumb" thermostat will simply run the heater longer, covering up the issue. A smart control system, in contrast, can measure the length of the thermostat duty cycle; for instance, how long the furnace runs to reach or maintain a certain room temperature. If this duty cycle extends, the controller can give a hint that the system is no longer operating as efficiently as before. Therefore, a control loop shouldn't be a black box; instead, it should expose health metrics based on what it has "learned."

Advanced cloud features like server autoscaling, which are able to absorb sudden load spikes without human intervention, are handy, but they can also mask serious problems. For example, if a new version of the software performs poorly, the infrastructure might attempt to autocompensate this problem by deploying more servers. You might just find out a bit later via your monthly bill.

In control theory, observing the behavior of a control loop is considered an "outer loop" that observes the behavior of the inner control loop and can trigger adjustments to the system.

28

They Don't Build 'Em Quite Like That Anymore

No One Lives in a Foundation

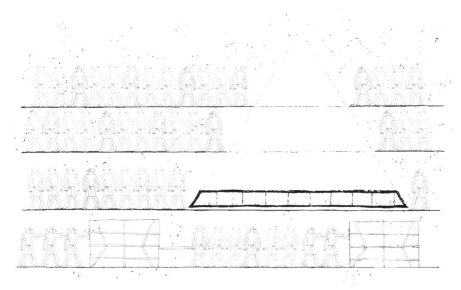

The Great Pyramid at 30% completion: effort completion, that is

The great pyramids are impressive buildings and attract hordes of tourists even several millennia after their construction. The attraction results not only from the engineering marvel, such as the perfect alignment and balance, but also from the fact that pyramids are quite rare. Besides the US one-dollar bill, you'll find them only in Egypt, Central America, and IT organizations!

Why IT Architects Love Pyramids

Pyramids are a fairly common sight in IT architecture diagrams and tend to give architects, especially the ones nearer to the penthouse, a noticeable sense of satisfaction. In most cases, the pyramid diagram indicates a layering concept with a base layer that includes functionality commonly needed by the upper layers. For example, the base layer could contain generic functions, while the next layer up would contain industry-specific functions, followed by functionality for specific business functions, and being topped off with *customer-specific configuration* (Chapter 11).

Layering is a very popular and useful concept in systems architecture because it constrains dependencies between system components to flow in a single direction, as opposed to a *Big Ball of Mud* (Chapter 8). Depicting the layers in the shape of a pyramid suggests that the upper layers are much smaller and more specialized than the base layers, which provide most of the common functionality.

IT is enamored with this model because it implies that a large portion of the base layer code can be shared or acquired given that it's identical across many businesses and applications. For example, a better Object-Relational Mapping (ORM) framework or a common business component such as a billing system are unlikely to present a competitive advantage and should simply be bought. Meanwhile, necessary and valuable customizations can be performed in the "tip" with relatively little effort or by lesser-skilled labor. The analogy is consistent with the pyramids of Giza, where the top third of the pyramid's height makes up only roughly 4% of the material.

Organizational Pyramids

The other place littered with pyramids are slide decks depicting organizational structures, where they refer to hierarchical structures. Almost all organizations are hierarchical: multiple people from a lower *tier* report to a single person on the next upper tier, resulting in a directed *tree* graph, which, when the root is placed on the top, resembles a pyramid. Even "flat" organizations tend to have some hierarchy, as a single person generally acts as a chairman or CEO. Such a setup makes sense because directing work takes less effort than actually conducting the work, meaning an organization needs fewer managers or supervisors than workers (unless they are *trying to buy love*; see Chapter 38). Having fewer leaders also helps with consistent decision making and setting a single strategic direction.

No Pyramid Without Pharaoh

Still, there's a good reason why the Egyptians abandoned the idea of building pyramids some 4,500 years ago: the base layers of a pyramid require an enormous amount of material. It's estimated that the Great Pyramid of Giza consists of more than two million blocks weighing in at several tons each. Assuming workers toiled day and night over the course of one decade, they would have had to lay an average of three large limestone blocks per *minute*. Three quarters of the material had to be laid for the first 50 meters of height alone. Even though the result is undoubtedly impressive and long lasting, it can hardly be called efficient.

The economics of building pyramids can function only if there's an abundance of cheap or forced labor (historians still debate whether the pyramids were built by slaves or paid workers) or a pharaoh's unbelievable accumulation of wealth. In addition to resources, one also needs to bring a lot of patience. Building pyramids doesn't mix well with *economies of speed* (Chapter 35). Some of the pyramids in Egypt weren't even finished during the pharaoh's lifetime.

No One Lives in a Foundation

Functional pyramids as we find them in IT system designs face another challenge: the folks building the base layer not only need to move humongous amounts of material, they also must anticipate the needs of the teams building the upper layers. That's a lot more difficult to do in IT pyramids *where things tend to evolve over time* (Chapter 3).

Building an IT pyramid purely from the bottom up incurs several problems:

- First, the lower layers alone don't provide much value to the business—they are merely a foundation for more things to come. The result is a large investment with a slow return of value, not something a typical business is looking for.

- It also negates the Agile principle of "use before reuse." Building a base layer means designing functions to be reused later without first actually using them. This can be a guessing game at best.

- Lastly, it also dangerously ignores the *Build-Measure-Learn cycle* (Chapter 36) of learning what's needed from observing actual usage. What if the business expected a different pyramid?

No one likes to live in a foundation. Therefore, delivering only a base layer has limited business value.

Not limited to pyramids but applicable to any layered system is the challenge of defining the appropriate *seams* between the layers. Done well, these seams form abstractions that hide the complexity of the layer below while leaving the layer above with *sufficient flexibility* (Chapter 11). It's not easy to find examples that work well—like abstracting packet-based network routing behind data streams (*sockets*)—but when implemented well, this enables major transformations like the internet. Normal IT teams can't expect to be quite that lucky.

Building Pyramids from the Top

If you're determined to build an IT pyramid, the best way to do so is from the top down. This is not something you can do with real pyramids, but software does allow us to defy gravity in this case. When I mention "top down," I am referring to the way the pyramid is constructed, not the way the project is managed. Ironically, "top-down management" leads to pyramids being built bottom up.

To build an IT pyramid from the top, you start with a specific application or service that delivers customer value, thus assuring *use* before considering *resue* and avoiding the dangerous notion of "reusable." When multiple applications can utilize a specific feature or functionality, you can let the related components "sift down" into a lower layer of the pyramid, making them more broadly available. Building the pyramid this way ensures that the base layer contains functionality that's actually needed as opposed to functions that some people, often the *enterprise architects* (Chapter 4) far away from actual software development, believe might be needed somewhere, sometime.

"Reusable" can be a dangerous word. It describes components that were designed to be widely used but aren't.

Anticipating some needs ahead of time, such as the much-mentioned ORM framework, is fine. So is building some of the pyramid base layers like operating systems. In many ways, cloud computing is a massive base layer, but one with very nice seams.

Building pyramids from the top can lead to some amount of duplication; for example, if two independent development teams build similar functionality that's not yet part of the base layer. Transparency across teams—for example, by using a common source code repository or a common service registry—can help detect such duplication early. While too much duplication may be undesired, we must keep in mind that *avoiding duplication isn't free* (Chapter 35).

 I have seen base services layers that force a consumer to make many remote calls even to execute a simple function. This approach was chosen by the base-layer architects because it ostensibly provides more flexibility. The first client developer coding against this interface described his experience in quite unkind words, citing well-known issues such as sequencing, partial failure, and main-taining state. The base-layer team's retort was a new *dispatcher* layer on top of their service layer to "enhance the interaction." The team was building the pyra-mid from the bottom up.

Building the pyramid from the top down also typically results in much more usable APIs (programming interfaces) into the lower layers. Because in the lay-ered model the consumers of the lower layers live on top, building APIs from the top equates to being customer centric: rather than guessing what your customers (other development teams in this case) might want, you derive it from actual use.

Celebrating the Base Layer

Building pyramids is popular in IT for another reason: the completion of the pyr-amid's base layer provides a *proxy metric* for actual product success. It allows teams to claim major progress without any meaningful validation of business impact.

It's analogous to developers' love of building frameworks: you get to devise your own requirements, and upon delivery of those requirements, you declare success without any actual user having validated the need nor the implementa-tion. In other words, designing pyramid base layers allows *penthouse architects* (Chapter 1) to claim that they are connected to the engine room without facing the scrutiny of actual product development teams or, worse yet, real customers.

 The folks highest up in the organizational pyramid love to design the bottom layers of the IT system pyramid, far away from actual users.

It's ironic that the folks highest up in the organizational pyramid love to design the bottom layers of the IT system pyramid. The reason is clear: building successful applications is more difficult than generic and unvalidated base layers. Unfortunately, by the time the bluff becomes apparent, the penthouse architects are almost guaranteed to have moved to another project.

Living in Pyramids

While IT building pyramids can be debated, organizational pyramids are largely a given: we all report to a boss, who reports to someone else, and so on. In large organizations, we often define our standing by how many people are above us in the corporate hierarchy. The key consideration for an organization is whether they actually *live* in the pyramid; in other words, whether the lines of communication and decision making follow the lines in the hierarchy. If that's the case, the organization will face severe difficulties in times that favor *economies of speed* (Chapter 35) because pyramid structures can be efficient, but they are neither fast nor flexible: decisions travel up and down the hierarchy, often suffering from a *bottleneck in the coordination layer* (Chapter 30).

Luckily, many organizations don't actually work in the patterns described by the org chart but follow a concept of *feature teams*, *tribes*, or *squads*. These organizational elements typically have complete ownership of an individual product or service: decisions are pushed down to the level of the people actually most familiar with the problem. This speeds up decision making and provides shorter feedback loops.

Some organizations are looking to speed things up by overlaying *communities of practice* over their structural hierarchy, bringing people with a common interest or area of expertise together. Communities can be useful change agents, but only *if they are empowered and have clear goals* (Chapter 27). Otherwise, they run the risk of becoming *communities of leisure*, a hiding place for people to debate and socialize without measurable results.

We should wonder, then, why organizations are so enamored with org charts that they adorn the second slide of almost any corporate project presentation. My hypothesis is that static structures carry a lower semantic load than dynamic structures: when presented with a picture showing two boxes, *A* and *B*, connected by a line, the viewer can easily derive the model: *A* and *B* have a relationship. One can almost imagine two physical cardboard boxes connected by a string wire. Dynamic models are more difficult to internalize: if *A* and *B* have multiple lines between them that depict interaction over time, possibly including conditions, parallelism, and repetition, it's much more difficult to imagine the reality the model is trying to depict. Often, only an animation can make it more intuitive. Hence, we are more content with static structures even though understanding a *system's behavior* (Chapter 10) is generally much more meaningful than seeing its structure.

It Always Can Get Worse

Running an organization as a pyramid can be slow and inhibit feedback cycles, which are needed to drive innovation. However, some organizations have a pyramid model that's even worse: the inverse pyramid. In this model, a majority of people manage and supervise a minority of people doing actual work. Besides the apparent imbalance, the inevitable need of the managers to obtain updates and status reports from the workers is guaranteed to grind progress to a halt. Such pathetic setups can occur in organizations that once *depended completely on external providers* (Chapter 38) for IT implementation work and are now starting to bring IT talent back in-house. It can also happen during a crisis, such as a major system outage, which gets so much management attention that the team spends more time preparing status calls than resolving the issue.

A second antipattern ironically occurs when organizations attempt to fix the issues inherent in their hierarchical pyramid setup. They supplement the existing top-down reporting organization (often referred to as a *line organization*) with a new *project organization*. The combination is typically called a *matrix organization* (for once, this isn't a movie reference) as people have a horizontal reporting line into their project and a vertical reporting line into the hierarchy. However, organizations that are not yet flexible and confident enough to give project teams the *necessary autonomy* (Chapter 27) are prone to creating a second pyramid, the project pyramid. Now employees struggle not only with one but with two pyramids.

Building Modern Structures

If pyramids aren't the way to go, how should you build systems, then? I view both systems and organizational design as an iterative, dynamic process that's driven by the need to deliver business value. When building IT systems, you should add new components only if they provide measurable value. Once you observe a sizable set of common functions, it's good to push those down into a common base layer. If you don't find such components, that's also OK. It simply means that a pyramid model doesn't fit your situation.

29

Black Markets Are Not Efficient

But They Reveal How Things Actually Get Done

I got anythin' you need, bro

A common complaint about large organizations is that they are slow and mired in processes that are *designed to exert control* (Chapter 27) as opposed to supporting people in getting their work done quickly. For example, I used to be allowed to make technical decisions involving tens of millions of dollars, but I had to obtain management approval to purchase a $200 plane ticket. By the time I got the approval, often the fare had increased.

Most organizations consider such processes as crucial to keeping the organization running smoothly. "What would happen if everyone did what they wanted?" is the common justification. Most organizations never dare to find out, not because they fear chaos and mayhem, but because they fear that everything will be fine, and the people creating and administering the processes will no longer be needed.

Black Markets to the Rescue

Ironically, beneath the covers of law and order, such organizations are intrinsically aware that their processes hinder progress. That's why these organizations tolerate a "black market" where things get done quickly and informally without following the self-imposed rules. Such black markets often take the innocuous form of needing to "know who to talk to" to get something done quickly. You need a server urgently? Instead of following the standard process, you call your buddy who can "pull a few strings." Setting up an official "priority order" process, usually for a higher price, is fine. Bypassing the process to get special favors for those who are well connected is a black market.

 If the answer to "how long does it take to get a server?" is "it depends on who's asking," then you have a black market.

Another type of black market can originate from "high up." While it's not uncommon to offer different service levels, including "VIP support," providing senior executives with support that ignores the very process- or security-related constraints imposed by the executives in the first place is a black market. Such a black market appears, for example, in the form of executives sporting sexy mobile devices that are deemed too insecure for employees, notwithstanding the fact that executives' devices often contain the most sensitive data.

Black Markets Are Rarely Efficient

What these examples have in common is that they are based on unwritten rules and undocumented, or sometimes secret, relationships. That's why black markets are rarely efficient, as you can see from countries where black markets constitute a major portion of the economy: black markets are difficult to control and deprive the government of much-needed tax income. They also tend to circumvent balanced allocation of resources: those with access to the black market will be able to obtain goods or favors that others cannot. Black markets therefore stifle economic development because they don't provide broad and equal access to resources. This is true for countries as much as large enterprises.

Black markets stifle innovation because they don't provide equal access to resources. The digital world democratizes access, which is exactly the opposite.

In organizations, black markets often contribute to *slow chaos* (Chapter 31), in which the outside of the organization appears to be disciplined and structured, but the reality is completely different. They also make it difficult for new members of the organization to gain traction because they lack connections into the black market, presenting one way *systems resist change* (Chapter 10).

Black markets also cause inefficiency by forcing employees to learn the black-market system. Knowing how to work the black market is undocumented organizational knowledge that's unique to the organization. The time it takes employees to learn the black market doesn't benefit the organization and presents a real but rarely measured cost. Once acquired, the knowledge doesn't benefit the employee either, because it has no market value outside of the organization. Ironically, this effect can contribute to large organizations tolerating black markets: it aids employee retention because much of their knowledge consists of undocumented processes, special vocabulary, and black-market structures, which ties them to the organization.

Worse yet, black markets break necessary feedback cycles: if procuring a server is too slow to compete in the digital world, the organization must resolve the issue and speed up that process. Circumventing it in a black-market fashion gives management a false sense of security, which often goes along with fabricated heroism: "I knew we could get it done in two days." Amazon can get it done in a few minutes for a hundred thousand customers. The digital transformation is driven by *democratization*; that is, giving everyone rapid access to resources. That's exactly the opposite of what a black market does.

You Cannot Outsource a Black Market

Another very costly limitation of black markets is that they cannot be outsourced. Large organizations tend to outsource commodity processes like human resources or IT operations, exactly the areas that are subject to black market economies. Specialized outsourcing providers have better economies of scale and lower cost structures, partly because they follow officially established processes. Because services are now performed by a third-party provider, and processes are contractually defined, the unofficial black market bypass no longer works. Essentially, the business has subjected itself to a *work-to-rule* slowdown. Organizations that rely on an internal black market, therefore, will experience a huge loss in productivity when they outsource part of their service portfolio.

Beating the Black Market

How do you avoid running the organization via a black market? More control and governance could be one approach: just like the DEA cracks down on the black market for drugs, you could identify and shut down the black-market traders. However, one must recall that the IT organization's black market isn't engaged in trading illegal substances. Rather, people circumvent processes that don't allow them to get their work done. Knowing that overambitious control processes caused the black market in the first place makes more control and governance an unlikely solution. Still, some organizations will be tempted to do so, which is a perfect example of doing exactly the *opposite of what has the desired effect* (Chapter 10).

 You can't eliminate black markets with more control and governance. After all, those are the very mechanisms that caused the black market in the first place.

The only way to avoid a black market is to build an efficient "white market," one that doesn't hinder progress but enables it. An efficient white market reduces people's desire to maintain an alternate black-market system, which does take some effort after all. Trying to shut down the black market without offering a functioning white market is likely to result in resistance and substantial reduction in productivity.

Self-service systems are a great tool to starve black markets because they remove the human connection and friction by giving everyone equal access, thus democratizing the process. If you can order IT infrastructure through a self-explanatory tool that provides fast provisioning times, there's much less motivation to do it "through the back door." Automating undocumented processes is cumbersome, though, and often unwelcome because it can highlight the *slow chaos* (Chapter 31).

Feedback and Transparency

Black markets generally originate as a response to cumbersome processes, which result from process designers prioritizing reporting and control: inserting a checkpoint or *quality gate* at every step provides accurate progress tracking and valuable metrics. However, it makes people using the process jump through an endless sequence of hurdles to get anything done. That's the reason I have never seen a single user-friendly HR or expense reporting system. Forcing the people designing processes to use them for their own daily work can highlight the amount of friction the processes create and thus provide a valuable feedback loop (Chapter 27). This means no more VIP support but support that's good enough for everyone to use. Wouldn't everyone like to be treated like a VIP? Similarly, HR teams should apply for their own job postings to experience the process firsthand.

 When recruiting, I routinely apply for my own job openings so I can detect any hurdles in the process.

Transparency is a good antidote to black markets. Black markets are inherently nontransparent, providing benefit to only a small subset of people. When users gain full transparency of the official processes, such as ordering a server, they might be less inclined to want to order one from the black market, which does carry some overhead and uncertainty. For example, will a black market server be supported or perhaps reallocated during the next inventory sweep? Therefore, full transparency should be embedded into an organization's systems as a main principle.

Replacing a black market with an efficient, democratic white market also *makes control less of an illusion* (Chapter 27): if users employ official, documented, and automated processes, the organization can observe actual behavior and exert governance; for example, by requiring approvals or issuing usage quotas. No such mechanisms exist for black markets.

The main hurdle to drying up black markets is that improving processes has a measurable up-front cost while the cost of the black market is usually not measured. This gap leads to *the cost of no change* (Chapter 33) being perceived as being low, which in turn reduces the incentive to change.

30

Scaling an Organization

*How to Scale an Organization? The Same
Way You Scale a System!*

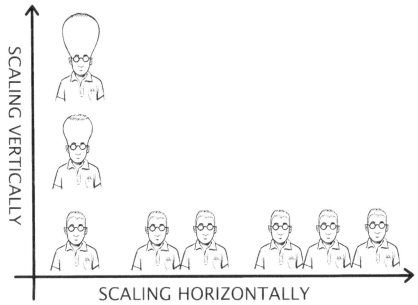

SCALING VERTICALLY

SCALING HORIZONTALLY

Horizontal scaling seems more natural

The digital world is all about scalability: millions of websites, billions of hits per month, petabytes of data, more tweets, more images uploaded. To make this work, architects have learned a ton about scaling systems: make services stateless and horizontally scalable, minimize synchronization points to maximize throughput, keep transaction scope local, avoid synchronous remote communication, use clever caching strategies, and shorten your variable names (just kidding!).

With everything around us scaling to never-before-seen throughput, the limiting element in all of this is bound to be us, the human users, and the organizations we work in. You might wonder, then, whether IT architects, who know so much about scalability, can apply their expertise to scaling and optimizing throughput in organizations. I might have become an architect astronaut[1] suffering from oxygen deprivation due to exceedingly high levels of abstraction, but I can't help but feel that many of the scalability and performance approaches known to experienced IT architects can just as well be applied to scaling organizations. If a *coffee shop* (Chapter 17) can teach us about maximizing a system's throughput, maybe our knowledge of IT systems design can help improve an organization's performance?

Component Design—Personal Productivity

Increasing throughput starts with the individual. Some folks are simply 10 times more productive than others. For me it's hit or miss: when I am "in the zone," I can be incredibly productive but lose traction just as quickly when I am being frequently interrupted or annoyed by something. So, I won't bestow on you any great personal advice, but instead refer you to the many resources like GTD (Getting Things Done),[2] which advises you to minimize your inventory of open tasks (making the Lean folks happy) and to break down large tasks into smaller ones that are immediately actionable. For example, "I really ought to replace that old clunker" turns into "visit three dealerships this weekend." Incoming stuff is categorized and either immediately processed or parked until it's actionable, thus reducing the number of concurrent threads. The suggestions are very sound, but as always it takes a bit of trust and lots of discipline to succeed at implementing them.

Avoid Sync Points—Meetings Don't Scale

Let's assume people individually do their best to be productive and have high throughput, meaning we have efficient and effective system components. Now we need to look at the integration architecture, which defines the interaction between components; in other words, people. One of the most common interaction points (short of email, more on that later) surely is the *meeting*. The name

---

1 Joel Spolsky, "Don't Let Architecture Astronauts Scare You," April 21, 2001, Joel on Software (blog), *https://oreil.ly/MafCn*.

2 Wikipedia, *"Getting Things Done," https://oreil.ly/PRfdu*.

alone gives some of us goose bumps because it suggests that people get together to "meet" one another, but doesn't define any specific agenda, objective, or outcome.

Meetings are synchronization points—a well-known throughput killer.

From a systems design perspective, meetings have another troublesome property: they require multiple humans to be (mostly) in the same place at the same time. In software architecture, we call this a *synchronization point*, widely known as one of the biggest throughput killers. The word "synchronous" derives from Greek and essentially means things happening at the same time. In distributed systems for things to happen at the same time, some components must wait for others, which is quite obviously not the way to maximize throughput.

The longer the wait for the synchronization point, the more dramatic the negative impact on performance becomes. In some organizations finding a meeting time slot among senior people can take a month or longer. Such resource contention on people's time significantly slows down decision making and project progress (and hurts *economies of speed*; see Chapter 35). The effect is analog to locking database updates: if many processes are trying to update the same table record, throughput suffers enormously as most processes just wait for others to complete, eventually ending up in the dreaded *deadlock*. Administrative teams in large organizations acting as *transaction monitor* underlines the overhead caused by using meetings as the primary interaction model. Worse yet, full schedules cause people to start blocking time "just in case," a form of *pessimistic resource allocation*, which has exactly the opposite of the intended effect on the *system behavior* (Chapter 10).

Getting together can be useful for brainstorming, critical discussions, or decisions, but the worst kind of meetings must be status meetings. If someone wants to know where a project stands, why would they want to wait for the next status meeting that takes place in a week or two? To top it off, many status meetings I attended had someone read text off a document that wasn't distributed ahead of the meeting lest someone read through it and escape the meeting.

Interrupts Interrupt—Phone Calls

When you can't wait for the next meeting, you tend to call the person. I know well as I log half a dozen incoming calls a day, which I routinely don't answer (they typically lead to an email starting with the phrase "I was unable to reach you by phone," whose purpose I never quite understood). Phone calls have short wait times when compared to meetings, but are still synchronous and thus require all resources to be available at the same time. How many times have you played "phone tag" where you were unable to answer a call just to experience the reverse when you call back? I am not sure there's an analog to this in system communication (I should know; after all, I am documenting conversation patterns),[3] but it's difficult to imagine this as effective communication.

Phone calls are "interrupts" (they are blockable by muting your ringer), and in an open environment, they not only interrupt you but also your coworkers. That's one reason that Google Japan's engineering desks were by default not equipped with phones—you had to specifically request one, which was looked upon as a little old fashioned. The damage ringing phones can do in open office spaces was already illustrated in Tom DeMarco and Tim Lister's classic *Peopleware*.[4] The "tissue trick" won't work anymore with digital phones, but luckily virtually all of them have a volume setting. My pet peeve related to phones is people busting into my office while I am talking on the speaker phone, so I'd like to build a mini project to illuminate an "on air" sign while I am on the phone.

Piling on Instead of Backing off

Retrying an unsuccessful operation is a typical conversation pattern. It's also a dangerous operation because it can escalate a small disturbance in a system into an onslaught of retries, which brings everything to a grinding halt. That's why *Exponential Backoff* [5] is a well-known pattern and forms the basis of many low-level networking protocols, such as Carrier Sense, Multiple Access with Collision Detection (CSMA/CD), which is a core element of the Ethernet protocol.

Ironically, humans tend to not back off if a phone call fails, but have a tendency to pile on: if you don't pick up, they tend to call you at ever shorter

---

3 Hohpe, "Conversation Patterns," Enterprise Integration Patterns, *https://oreil.ly/qHzFw*.

4 Tom DeMarco and Timothy Lister, *Peopleware: Productive Projects and Teams*, 3rd ed. (Upper Saddle River, NJ: Addison-Wesley, 2013).

5 Wikipedia, "Exponential Backoff," *https://oreil.ly/A4QbL*.

intervals to signal that it's urgent. Ultimately, they will back off, but only after burdening the system with overly aggressive retries. Such behavior contributes to uneven resource utilization. It seems that either everyone seems to be calling you or it's extremely quiet. Asynchronous communication with queues in contrast can perform *traffic shaping*—spikes are absorbed by the queue, allowing the "service" to process requests at the optimal rate without becoming overloaded. That's why I prefer to receive an email starting with "I was unable to reach you by phone": I converted a synchronous operation into an asynchronous one.

Asynchronous Communication—Email, Chat, and More

In corporate environments, email tends to draw almost as much ire as meetings. It has one big advantage, though: it's *asynchronous*. Instead of being interrupted, you can process your email whenever you have a few minutes to spare. Getting a response might take slightly longer, but it's a classic "throughput over latency" architecture, best described by Clemens Vaster's analogy of building wider bridges, not faster cars, to solve the perennial congestion on the two-lane floating bridge that's part of Washington State Route 520 between Seattle and Redmond.

Email also has drawbacks, the main one being people flooding everyone's inbox because the perceived cost of sending mail is zero. Unfortunately, the cost of reading an email isn't. You must therefore have a good inbox filter if you want to survive. Also, mail isn't collectively searchable—each person has their own record of history. I guess you could call that an *eventually consistent* architecture of sorts and just live with it, but it still seems horribly inefficient. I wonder how many copies of that same 10 MB PowerPoint presentation plus all its prior versions are stored on a typical Exchange server.

Integrating chat with email can overcome some of these limitations: if you don't get a reply or the reply indicates that a real-time discussion is needed, the "reply by chat" button turns the conversation into quasi-synchronous mode: it still allows the receiver to answer at will (so it's asynchronous) but allows for much quicker iterations than mail. Products like Slack, which favor a chat/channel paradigm, also enable asynchronous communication without email. Systems architects would liken this approach to *tuple spaces*, which, based on a *blackboard* architectural style, are well suited for scalable, distributed systems thanks to loose coupling and avoiding duplication.

Asking Doesn't Scale—Build a Cache!

Much of corporate communication consists of asking questions, often via synchronous communication. This doesn't scale because the same questions are asked again and again. Architects would surely introduce a cache into their system to offload the source component, especially when they receive repeated requests for basic information, such as a photo of a new team member. In such cases, I simply type the person's name into Google and reply with a hyperlink to an online picture, asking Google instead of another person.

Search scales, but only if the answers are available in a searchable medium. Therefore, if you receive a question, reply so that everyone can see (and search) the answer; for example, on an internal forum—that's how you load the cache. Taking the time to explain something in a short document or forum post scales: 1,000 people can search for and read what you have to share. 1,000 one-on-one meetings to explain the same story would take half of your annual work time.

One cache killer that I have experienced is the use of different templates, which aim for efficiency but hurt data reuse. For example, when I answer requests for my resume with a link to my home page or LinkedIn, I observe a human transcribing the data found online into a prescribed Word template. Some things are majorly wrong in the digital universe.

Poorly Set Domain Boundaries—Excessive Alignment

Even though some communication styles might scale better than others, all will ultimately collapse under heavy traffic because humans can handle only so much throughput, even in chat or asynchronous communication. The goal therefore mustn't only be to tune communication but also to reduce it. Large corporations suffer from a lot of unnecessary communication, caused, for example, by the need "to align." I often jest that "aligning" is what I do when my car doesn't run straight or wears the tires unevenly. Why I need to do it at work all the time puzzled me, especially as "alignment" invariably triggers a meeting with no clear objective.

In corp speak, to align means to coordinate on an issue and come to some sort of common understanding or agreement. A common understanding is an integral part of productive teamwork, but the act of "aligning" can start to take on a life of its own. My suspicion is that it's a sign of misalignment (pun intended) between the project and organizational structures: the people who are critical to a project's success or are vital decision makers aren't part of the project, requiring frequent "steering" and "alignment" meetings. The system design analog for this problem is setting domain boundaries poorly, drawing on Eric Evans's Domain-Driven Design[6] concept of a Bounded Context.[7] Slicing a distributed system across poorly set domain boundaries is almost guaranteed to increase latency and burden both the system and its developers, who must grapple with increased complexity. Sam Newman would surely agree.[8]

Self-Service Is Better Service

Self-service generally has poor connotations: if the price were the same, would you rather eat at McDonald's or in a white-tablecloth restaurant with waiter service? If you are a food chain looking to optimize throughput, though, would you rather be McDonald's or the quaint Italian place with five tables? Self-service scales.

Requesting a service or ordering a product by making a phone call or emailing spreadsheet attachments for someone to manually enter data doesn't scale, even if you lower the labor cost with near- or offshoring. To scale, *automate everything* (Chapter 13): make all functions and processes available online on the intranet, ideally both as web interfaces and as (access protected) service APIs so that users can layer new services or custom user interfaces on top; for example, to combine popular functions.

Staying Human

Does scaling organizations like computer systems mean that the digital world shuns personal interaction, turning us into faceless email and workflow drones that must maximize throughput? I don't think so. I very much value personal interaction for brainstorming, negotiation, solution finding, bonding, or just having a good time. That's what we should maximize face-to-face time for. Having someone read slides aloud or calling me the third time to ask the same question could be achieved many times faster by optimizing communication patterns. Am I being impatient? Possibly, but in a world in which everything moves faster and faster, patience might not be the best strategy. High-throughput systems don't reward patience.

---

6 Eric Evans, "About Domain Language," Domain Language (website), *https://oreil.ly/m71x1*.

7 Martin Fowler, "Bounded Context," MartinFowler.com, *https://oreil.ly/AtY88*.

8 Sam Newman, *Building Microservices: Designing Fine-Grained Systems* (O'Reilly, 2015).

31

Slow Chaos Is Not Order

Going Fast? Bring Discipline!

Agile or just fast? The next turn will tell.

We all have our pet peeves or hot buttons, things that we've come across often enough that, despite their insignificance, really annoy us. In private life, these issues tend to revolve around things like toothpaste tubes: cap off versus cap on, or squeezed from the bottom versus from the middle. Such differences have been known to put numerous marriages and live-in relationships in danger (hint: a second tube runs about $1.99).

In the corporate IT world, pet peeves tend to be related to things more technical in nature. Mine is people using the word *agile* without having understood its meaning, almost two decades after the Agile Manifesto (*http://agilemani festo.org*) was authored. Surely you have overheard conversations like the following:

- What's your next major deliverable? Dunno—we are *Agile*!
- What's your project plan? Because we are *Agile*, we are so fast that we couldn't keep the plan up to date!
- Could I see your documentation? Don't need it—we are *Agile*!
- Could you tell me about your architecture? Nope—*Agile* projects don't need this!

And when one dares to ask how the teams know that they are Agile, you're sure to hear the following response:

- We are guaranteed to be *Agile* because we're officially certified!

Such ignorance is topped only by statements that Agile methods aren't suited for your company or department because they are too chaotic for such a structured environment. Ironically, the opposite is usually the case: corporate environments often lack the discipline to implement Agile processes.

Fast Versus Agile

My first annoyance about the widespread abuse of the word *agile* is repeatedly having to remind people that the method is called "Agile," not "fast," and for a good reason. Agile methods are about hitting the right target through frequent recalibration and embracing change rather than trying to predict the environment and eliminating uncertainty. Firing from afar at a moving target is fast, but not Agile: you will likely miss. Agile methods allow course corrections along the way, more like a guided missile (though I am not fond of the weapons analogy). Agile quickly gets you where you need to be. Running in the wrong direction faster isn't a method, but foolishness.

Speed and Discipline

When observing something that moves fast, it's easy to feel a sense of chaos: too many things are happening at the same time for someone to judge how it all really fits together. A good example is a Formula 1 pit stop: *screech, whir, whir, roar,* and the car has four new tires in under four seconds (refueling is no longer allowed in F1 racing). Watching this process happening at such high speeds leaves one feeling slightly dizzy and that it's some sort of miracle or in fact a bit chaotic. If you watch the procedure a few times, ideally in slow motion, you can appreciate that few teams are more disciplined than a pit stop crew: every move-ment is precisely choreographed and trained hundreds of times. After all, at F1 speed a second longer in the pit means lagging almost 100 meters behind.

Moving fast in the IT world likewise requires discipline. Automated tests are your safety belt—how else would you be able to deploy code into production at a moment's notice, e.g., in case of a serious problem? The most *valuable* time for an online retailer to deploy code is right in the middle of the holiday season, when customer traffic is at its peak. That's when a critical fix or a new feature can have the biggest positive impact on the bottom line. Ironically, that's exactly the time when most corporate IT shops impose a "frozen zone," during which they forbid the deployment of code changes. Making a code push in peak traffic takes confidence. Having iron discipline and lots of practice can make you more confi-dent and fast. Fear will slow you down. Confidence without discipline will make you crash and burn.

Fast and Good

Agile development overcomes the perception that things are either fast or of high quality by adding a *new dimension* (Chapter 40). This admittedly makes it difficult to really grasp the concept without seeing it in action. I often claim that "Agile cannot be taught, it can only be shown," meaning that you should learn Agile methods by working on an Agile team, and not from a textbook.

I describe the attributes required for fast software development and deploy-ment as follows:

Velocity

Development *velocity* assures that you can make code changes swiftly. If the code base is fraught with technical debt, such as duplication, you will lose speed right there.

Confidence

Once you made a code change, you must have the *confidence* in your code's correctness, e.g., through code reviews, rigorous automated tests, and small, incremental releases. If you lack confidence, you will hesitate, and you can't be fast.

Repeatable

Deployment must be *repeatable*, usually by being 100% automated. All your creativity should go into writing great features for your users, not into making each deployment work. Once you decide to deploy, you must depend on the deployment working exactly as it did the last 100 times.

Elastic

Your runtime must be *elastic* because once your users like what you built, you must be able to handle the traffic.

Feedback

You need *feedback* from monitoring to make sure you can spot production issues early and to learn what your users need. If you don't know in which direction to head, moving faster is no help.

Secure

And last but not least, you need to *secure* your runtime environment against accidental and malicious attacks, especially when deploying new features frequently, which may contain, or rely on libraries that contain, security exploits.

In unison, these qualities make for a disciplined but fast-moving and agile development process. People who haven't seen such a process live often cannot quite believe how liberating it is to work with confidence. Even with the 15-year-old build system for my Enterprise Integration Patterns website (*https://oreil.ly/hV3NG*) I don't hesitate for a second to delete all build artifacts to rebuild and redeploy them from scratch.

Slow-Moving Chaos

If high speed requires high discipline (or ends up in certain disaster), is it true then that slow speed allows sloppiness? While not logically equivalent, the reality shows that this is usually the case. Once you look under the cover of traditional processes, you realize that there's a lot of messiness, rework, and uncontrolled *black markets* (Chapter 29). For example, US auto plants in the 1980s apparently dedicated up to one-quarter of the floor space to rework.[1] No wonder Japanese car companies came in and ate their lunch with a disciplined, zero-defect approach,

---

1 John Roberts, *The Modern Firm: Organizational Design for Performance and Growth* (Oxford: Oxford University Press, 2007).

which acknowledged that stopping a production line to debug a problem is more effective than churning out faulty cars. These manufacturing companies were disrupted 30 years ago much in the same way digital companies are disrupting slow and chaotic service businesses now. Hopefully, you can learn something from their mistakes!

Alarmingly, you can find the same level of messiness in corporate IT: why would it take two weeks to provision a virtualized server? For one, because most of this time is *spent in queues* (Chapter 35), and second, because of "thorough testing." Hold on, why would you need to test a virtual server that should be provisioned in a 100% automated and repeatable fashion? And why would it take two weeks? Usually because the process being followed isn't actually 100% automated and repeatable: a little duct tape is added here, a little optimization is done over there, a little script is edited, and someone forgot to mount the storage volumes. Oops. That's one reason to *never send a human to do a machine's job* (Chapter 13).

Once you look under the veil of "proven processes," you quickly discover chaos, defined as a state of confusion or disorder. It's just so slow moving that you have to look a few times to recognize it. A good way to test for chaos is to request precise documentation of the aforementioned proven processes: most of the time it doesn't exist, is outdated, or is not meant to be shared. Yeah, right...

ITIL to the Rescue?

If you challenge IT operations about slow chaos, you will likely receive a stare of disbelief and a reference to ITIL,[2] a proprietary but widely adopted set of practices for IT service management. ITIL provides common vocabulary and structure, which can be of huge value when supplying services or interfacing with service providers. ITIL is also a bit daunting, consisting of five volumes of some 500 pages each.

When an IT organization refers to ITIL, I am generally suspicious whether there's a gap between perception and reality; i.e., does the organization really follow ITIL, or is this label used to shield further investigation into the slow chaos? A few quick tests give valuable hints: I ask a sysadmin which ITIL process they primarily follow. Or I ask an IT manager to show me the strategic analysis of the customer portfolio described in section 4.1.5.4 of the volume on service strategy.

---

2 "ITIL—IT service management," Axelos (website), *https://oreil.ly/PN_Mj.*

Most of the time we find that the ITIL ideal and the ITIL reality differ dramatically.

 I prominently displayed a set of ITIL manuals in my office to thwart anyone's temptation of hand-waving their way through a conversation.

ITIL itself is a very useful collection of service management practices. However, just like placing a math book under your pillow didn't get you an "A" grade in school, simply referencing ITIL doesn't repel slow chaos.

Objectives Require Discipline

Many organizations are managed by objectives and grant teams autonomy in achieving these objectives. While this in general is a sound approach, it can fail spectacularly in organizations that lack discipline, because teams may use any means to achieve the objective, compromising on base values such as quality. If reaching objectives by any means is rewarded, result-oriented objectives can actually cause a lack of discipline.

 A provider's large datacenter migration project had been set a clear goal of migrating a certain number of applications into a new datacenter location (a quite sensible objective). Alas, the provider had difficulties reliably provisioning servers in the new datacenter, causing many migration issues. To drive out this issue first, I suggested creating an automated test that repeatedly placed orders for servers in a variety of configurations and validated that all servers were delivered to spec. We would then start application migration once reliable provisioning was proven. The project manager exclaimed that if they did that, they'd never migrate a single application in 10 years! The team preferred to migrate applications regardless of their underlying problems, just so that they could achieve the project objective.

Setting output-oriented objectives therefore requires an agreed-upon discipline as a baseline for achieving those objectives. This is why the *Prussian ideal of Auftragstaktik* (Chapter 27) depended on active discipline: increasing an organization's discipline allows more far-reaching and meaningful objectives to be set.

The Way Out

You may be asking yourself: why does no one clean up the slow chaos? Many traditional but successful organizations simply have too much *money* (Chapter 38) to really notice or bother with it. They must first realize that the world has changed from pursuing economies of scale to pursuing *economies of speed* (Chapter 35). Speed is a great forcing function for automation and discipline. For most situations besides dynamic scaling, it's OK if provisioning a server takes a day. But if it takes more than 10 minutes, you know there'll be the temptation to perform a piece of it manually. And that's the dangerous beginning of slow-moving chaos. Instead, let *software eat the world* (Chapter 14) and *don't send humans to do a machine's job* (Chapter 13). You'll be fast and disciplined.

32

Governance Through Inception

I Am from Headquarters, I Am Here to Help You

Corporate governance circa 1984

Corporate IT tends to have its own vocabulary. A top contender for the most frequently used phrase must be *to align*, which translates vaguely into the activity of holding a meeting with no particular objective beyond mulling over a topic and coming to some sort of agreement short of an official approval. Large IT organizations tend to *get slowed down* (Chapter 30) by doing this a lot. After *alignment*, *governance* likely comes in second.

Living in Perfect Harmony

Governance generally describes the act of harmonizing and standardizing things across the organization by means of rules, guidelines, and standards. IT harmonization done well increases purchasing power through economies of scale, reduces downtime thanks to less operational complexity, and boosts IT security by eliminating unnecessary diversity.

While pursuing harmonization is a rather worthwhile goal, governance can also do harm; for example, by converging on a lowest common denominator, which in the end doesn't meet the business's need. Also, many enterprises standardize on an all-encompassing solution that ends up being too expensive for many use cases. Lastly, if the wrong things are standardized, it can stifle creativity.

Harmonization can reduce cost and complexity, increase uptime, and strengthen cybersecurity. But, if done in the abstract, it can also stifle innovation, lead to a lowest-common-denominator solution, or propose overengineered and overpriced universal solutions.

One common cause of suboptimal standards is that those setting the standards don't have the necessary skill set and the full context of a situation. Worse yet, these teams often lack meaningful feedback on the effect of the standards they set. Things may look orderly from the top—e.g., everyone uses the same type of laptop—but developers lack administrative access and main memory, while frequent travelers must lug around a desktop-equivalent monster laptop.

In many large IT organizations, top decision makers don't use the very tools they standardize. For example, *they rarely use the standard workplace or HR tools* (Chapter 29), because they're entitled to special solutions or they have admins who do this work for them. They hence can lack both the situational context and a critical feedback cycle.

Exerting governance in an existing organization or one that grew by acquisition involves migrating from the "wrong" system implementation to the "standard." Such migrations bring cost and risk without an apparent benefit for the local entity, making enforcement difficult. The enemy of governance is the "shadow IT," which describes local development outside the reaches of central governance.

The Value of Standards

Standardization has enormous value, as epitomized by what happened during a devastating 1904 fire in Baltimore, Maryland. When much of downtown Baltimore was ablaze, firemen from surrounding cities rushed to help with their fire engines. Sadly, many of these firefighters and much of their equipment ended up standing idle because the fire hose connections of other cities' departments wouldn't fit Baltimore's fire hydrants. The National Fire Protection Association was quick to learn from this disaster and in 1905 established a standard for fire hose connections, still known as the "Baltimore Standard."

Corporate governance typically starts by defining a set of standards that are to be adhered to. A standards organization will define and administer these standards for many types of products that are being used. For example, they may decree that software *ABC* shall be used as the internet browser and vendor product *XYZ* for databases. But if we look at the real world, the most successful standards have been of a different nature.

The standards with the biggest economic impact have been *compatibility* or *interface* standards: specifications that allow interchangeability of parts. Fire hoses and hydrants are a great example, as is HTTP. In an IT environment, interface standards translate to standardizing interfaces rather than products; for example, standardizing on HTTP or a specific minimum version of HTML, as opposed to setting Internet Explorer as the browser.

The most successful IT standards over the past half-century have been TCP/IP and HTTP—these brought us universal connectivity and the internet. However, neither is a product standard, but both are interface standards. Also, both are *open* standards.

Interface Standards

Interface standards bring flexibility and *network effects*: when many elements can interconnect, the benefit to all participants increases. The internet, originally based on the HTML and HTTP standards for content and connectivity, is the perfect example. Thanks to these standards, any browser could connect to any web server regardless of the implementation technology used. Such effects also highlight again how *lines are more interesting than boxes* (Chapter 23).

Enterprises must therefore articulate their main driver behind setting standards: standardizing vendor products aims to reduce cost and complexity through economies of scale, while compatibility or connectivity standards boost flexibility and innovation. Both are useful, but call for different types of standards.

Not all interface standards look like interfaces. For example, when standardizing inside an enterprise, elements, or "boxes," can act as connecting elements. Monitoring and version control systems are great examples: while they are components, their purpose is to connect many applications so that one can gain a unified view across software development or operational status, respectively. That's why in my view it's more beneficial to standardize the version control system than standardize the integrated development environment (IDE) that developers use: the former is a connecting element, while the latter is a node. Storing all sources in a single repository allows easy reuse or shared code ownership, something that shared IDEs can't do.

It's more beneficial to standardize connecting elements, such as monitoring or source control, than endpoints such as laptops or IDEs. Google took this to the extreme by storing (almost) all of its source code in a single version control system.

Mapping Standards

However, setting standards, even for interfaces, isn't quite as simple. For example, sizing all fire hose connections the same turns out to not be such a good idea. For a standard to be useful, it needs to be based on a *common worldview and vocabulary* (Chapter 16) that specifies the standard's scope. For example, IT standards for databases, application servers, or integration run the risk of being meaningless without a distinction of the types of databases or servers under consideration.

The Baltimore fire hydrant standard distinguishes two kinds of standards, one for pumper connections and one for fire hose connections. Pumper connections feed water from the hydrant to a pump truck and have a large diameter. Hose connections feed an individual fire hose and are smaller in diameter.

For example, if an organization wants to standardize database products, you'd need to first define whether you standardize relational databases separately from NoSQL databases and, if so, whether you want to distinguish between document and graph databases (Chapter 16). Only then should you look at products: before you visit a car dealer you should know whether you want a minivan or a two-seater sports car. Or visit Porsche—they seem to be making everything these days.

For storage, you need to distinguish a SAN from NAS and differentiate backup storage from direct-attached storage (DAS). And you may be looking into HDFS and converged/so-called "hyperconverged" storage (a storage virtualization layer over local disks).

Governance by Decree

Enforcing standards can be a bit like herding cats, even when the economic value is blatantly obvious. For example, almost one hundred years after the Baltimore standard, fighting large fires such as the Oakland Hills Fire of 1991 is still impeded by cities not following the standard.[1] Often, the deviation from the standard is a historical artifact or purposely driven by vendors to gain lock-in.

In many organizations, a diagnostic "police" will visit different entities to ascertain their standard compliance, which gives rise to the joke about the biggest lie in a corporate environment: "I am from headquarters; I am here to help you." Cybersecurity can be a useful vehicle to drive standardization: nonstandard or outdated versions of software generally carry a higher risk of vulnerability than well-maintained, harmonized environments.

A specific challenge is posed by users who *also* use a standard, in addition to their own solution. They thus will correctly proclaim "yes, we do drive BMW cars," in line with a corporate standard that they do so, despite the parking lot being full of Mercedes, Rolls-Royces, and Yugos. In another phenomenon, users employ a standard, but for the wrong purpose. For example, they may use the standard BMW as a meeting room for four people, and don't actually drive it (they prefer Mercedes for that). Sounds absurd? I have seen many similarly absurd examples in corporate IT!

Governance Through Infrastructure

Interestingly, in my seven years at Google no one ever mentioned the word *governance* (or *SOA* or *big data*, for that matter). Knowing that Google not only has a fantastic service architecture and world-leading big data analytics, you might guess then that it also has strong governance. In fact, Google has an extremely

---

1 Momar Seck and David Evans, "Major U.S. Cities Using National Standard Fire Hydrants, One Century After the Great Baltimore Fire," NISTIR 7158, National Institute of Standards and Technology.

strong governance in places where it matters most; for example, runtime infrastructure. Employees were free to write code in Emacs, vi, Notepad, IntelliJ, Eclipse, or any other editor, but there was basically only one way to deploy software to the production infrastructure, on one kind of OS (in the old days, you could choose between 32 or 64 bit), on one kind of hardware.

While occasionally painful, this strictness worked because most software developers would put up with pretty much anything to have their software run on a Google-scale infrastructure: it was, and likely still is, a decade ahead of what most other companies were using. The governance didn't need to take the form of a decree because the system was vastly superior to anything else, rendering not following it a guaranteed waste of time. If the corporate car is a Ferrari or has a flux capacitor for time travel,[2] people won't be running to the VW dealer. In Google's case, the flux capacitor was the amazing "Borg" deployment and machine management system, which has been publicly described in a Google research paper.[3] For Google the system's economies of scale worked so well that in the end it became reasonable to have everyone drive a Ferrari while enjoying the fast pace.

RUNTIME GOVERNANCE

Netflix exerts governance over application design and architecture by running their infamous *Chaos Monkey* (*https://oreil.ly/Xgm7_*) against deployed software to verify that the software is resilient. Noncompliant software will be pummeled in production by automated compliance testers. Hardly any organization that brags about its corporate governance group would have the guts to do the same.

Inception

In large IT organizations the motivation is generally a little less pronounced and the infrastructure a little less advanced. If you've been to the movies in recent years you must have come across *Inception*, an ingenious Christopher Nolan flick depicting corporate criminals who steal trade secrets from victims' subconscious minds. The title derives from the plot, in which the corporate team usually operates in "read only" mode to extract secrets from the victim's memory, but that for their big coup they must actively implant an idea into a victim's mind to cause

---

2 A reference to the '80s movie *Back to the Future*.

3 A. Verma et al., "Large-Scale Cluster Management at Google with Borg."

him to take a particular action—a process referred to "inception." In the movie the tricky part is to make the victim truly believe it was his idea.

If we could perform inception, corporate governance would be much easier: IT units would independently come to the conclusion to use the same software. This isn't quite as absurd as it sounds because there's one magic ingredient in today's IT world that makes it possible: change. With change comes the need to update systems (still have Lotus Notes somewhere?) and the opportunity to set new standards without any additional migration costs. You "simply" have to agree on which incarnation of the new piece of technology you want to employ, for example for a software-defined network, a big data cluster, or an on-premise platform-as-a-service. That you have to do by inception.

Inception in corporate IT works only if the governing body is ahead of the rest of the world, so they can set the direction before the widespread need arises. Acting as an educator, they supply new ideas to their audience and can inject, or incept, ideas, such as demand for a specific product or standard. In a sense, that's what marketing has been doing for centuries: creating demand for the product that manufacturing happened to have built.

In times of change, the "new" will ultimately replace the "old" and through constant inception the landscape becomes more standardized. The key requirement is that "central" needs to innovate faster than the business units so that when a division requests a big data analytics cluster, corporate IT already has clear guidance and a reference implementation. Doing so requires foresight and funding, but beats chasing business units for noncompliance and facing migration costs.

The Emperor's New Clothes

Traditional IT governance can also cause an awkward scenario best described as the "emperor's new clothes": a central team develops a product that exists primarily in slide decks, so-called *vaporware*. When such a product is decreed as a standard, which is essentially meaningless, customers may happily adopt it because it's an easy way to earn a "brownie point," or even funding, for standard compliance without the need for much actual implementation. In the end everyone appears happy, except the shareholders: it's a giant and senseless waste of energy.

Governance Through Necessity

In an interesting book about refugee camps in the Western Sahara,[4] I learned that almost everyone in these camps who owns a car has the same older car models, either a Land Rover all-terrain vehicle or an early 1990s Mercedes sedan. Together, these models make up more than 90% of all local cars, with 85% of sedans being Mercedes—a corporate governor's dream! Why? Residents chose an inexpensive and very reliable car that could withstand the rough terrain and heat. The standardization came through simple necessity, however: buying another model of car would mean not being able to take advantage of the existing skill set and the pool of available spare parts. In an environment of economic constraints, these are major considerations. Corporate IT has the same forces, especially regarding IT skill set availability for new technologies. The observed diversity in corporate environments is therefore a *rich company problem* (Chapter 38): the scarcity of skills or resources just isn't strong enough to drive joint decision making—they can easily be solved with more money. You could also argue that the refugee camps had the advantage of a so-called greenfield installation, even though that term seems awfully inappropriate for people being displaced in the desert.

---

4 Manuel Herz, *From Camp to City: Refugee Camps of the Western Sahara* (Lars Muller, 2012).

PART V

Transformation

When setting up modern technology in a large IT organization, you'll invariably find that there's an impedance mismatch. Using elastic billing from a cloud provider won't work well if you have to make an annual budget forecast anyway. And being able to provision infrastructure with an API call becomes a lot less exciting if there's a two-month approval process attached to it. Therefore, the last and final leg on your architect journey is being able to change the way organizations work.

Change Is Risky

Bringing change into large organizations is rewarding but challenging, requiring you to utilize everything you've learned so far: you must first use your architectural thinking to understand how complex organizations work and which "levers" you may have. Superb communication skills help you garner support, while leadership skills are needed to effect a lasting change. Last, your IT architect skills are needed to plan and implement the technical changes necessary for the organization to work in a different way. As an architect you are best qualified to understand how technical and organizational changes depend on each other so that you can solve the Gordian knot of interdependencies.

Citing *The Matrix* one more time (after all, Neo is quite a change agent in a tough environment!), the exchange between the Architect and the Oracle draws the apt context:

> *The Architect:* You played a very dangerous game.

> *The Oracle:* Change always is.

Interestingly, in *The Matrix*, the Architect is the main entity trying to prevent change. You should identify yourself with Neo, instead, making sure to have an Oracle to back you up.

Not All Change Is Transformation

Not every kind of change deserves to be called "transformation." You change the layout of the furniture in your living room, but you *transform* (or maybe convert) your house into a club, retail store, or place of worship. The word *trans-form* has its origin in Latin with a literal meaning of "to change shape or structure." When we speak of IT transformation, we therefore imply not an incremental evolution, but a fundamental restructuring of the technology landscape, the organizational setup, and the culture. Basically, expect to have to turn the house upside down, cut it into pieces, and put it back together in a new shape.

Bursting the Boiler

A prevalent risk in corporate transformation agendas is upper management recognizing the need for change and subsequently applying pressure to the organization to become faster, more agile, more customer centric, etc. However, the organization, and especially middle management, is often not ready to transform and attempts to achieve the targets set by upper management within the old way of working. This can put enormous strain on the organization and is unlikely to meet the ambitions. I compare this to a steam engine that is surpassed by a fast electric train. In an attempt to speed up, the steam-engine operator throws more coals onto the fire to increase the boiler pressure. While it may initially speed up the steam engine, soon the boiler will burst. You can't compete with an electric train by putting more pressure on the boiler. Instead, you need to devise a new engine that can keep up. That's what architects do.

Why Me?

As an architect, you might think: "Why me? Isn't this where the high-paid consultants come in?" They can certainly help, but you can't just inject change from the outside with a slide deck. Lasting change must come from the inside through role models, rapid feedback cycles, celebrated achievements, and much more. To effect lasting change in an organization you'll need to understand the following:

Chapter 33, No Pain, No Change!
Organizations are unlikely to change if there's no pain.

Chapter 34, Leading Change
You must show a better way of doing things.

Chapter 35, Economies of Speed
Organizations need to think in economies of speed instead of economies of scale.

Chapter 36, The Infinite Loop
Running in circles is an essential part of digital organizations.

Chapter 37, You Can't Fake IT
You must be digital on the inside to be digital on the outside.

Chapter 38, Money Can't Buy Love
There is no SKU for transformation.[1]

Chapter 39, Who Likes Standing in Line?
You can speed up organizations by waiting less instead of working more.

Chapter 40, Thinking in Four Dimensions
To transform, organizations need to think in new dimensions.

---

1 SKU = Stock Keeping Unit, used for order and inventory management.

33

No Pain, No Change!

And Watching Late-Night TV Does Not Help...

Go, go, gooooo!

A colleague of mine once attended a "digital showcase" event in his company, which highlighted many innovative projects and external hackathons the company had organized. Upon returning to his desk, though, he found himself in the same old corporate IT world where he is forced to clock time, cannot get a server in less than three weeks, and isn't allowed to install software on his laptop. He was wondering whether he was caught in some twisted incarnation of two-speed IT, but that made little sense; after all, his project was part of the fast-moving "digital" speed.

Stages of Transformation

I had a different answer: transformation is a difficult and time-consuming process that doesn't happen overnight. People just don't wake up one day and behave completely differently, no matter how many TED Talks they listened to the day before. (A talk I once attended illustrated how difficult it is to change which part of the body you dry first with your towel after taking a shower in the morning. I guess the speaker was right—I never changed that.)

To illustrate the stages a person or an organization tends to go through when transforming their habits, I drew up the example of someone changing from eating junk food to leading a healthy lifestyle. With no scientific evidence, I quickly came up with 10 stages:

1. You eat junk food. Because it's tasty.

2. You realize eating junk food is bad for you. But you keep eating it. Because it is tasty.

3. You start watching late-night TV weight-loss programs. While eating junk food. Because it is so tasty.

4. You order a miracle exercise machine from the late-night TV program. Because it looked so easy.

5. You use the machine a few times. You realize that it's hard work. Worse yet, no visible results were achieved during the two weeks you used it. Out of frustration you eat more junk food.

6. You force yourself to exercise even though it's hard work and the results are meager. You're still eating some junk food, though.

7. You force yourself to eat healthier, but find it not tasty.

8. You actually start liking vegetables and other healthy food.

9. You become addicted to exercise. Your motivation changed from losing weight to doing what you truly like.

10. Friends ask you for advice on how you did it. You have become a source of inspiration to others.

Change happens incrementally, and it will take a lot of time plus dedication.

Digital Transformation Stages

Drawing the analogy between my colleague's situation and my freshly created framework, I concluded that they must be somewhere between stage 3 and 4 on their transformation journey. What he attended was the digital equivalent of watching late-night miracle solutions. Maybe the company even invested in or acquired one of the nifty startups, which are young, hip, and use DevOps. But upon returning to his desk, he experienced that the organization was still eating lots of junk food.

I suggest that the transformation scale from 1 to 10 isn't linear: the critical steps occur from stage 1 to 2 (awareness, not to be underestimated!), 5 to 6 (overcoming disillusionment) and from 7 to 8 (wanting instead of forcing yourself). I would therefore give his company a lot of credit for starting the journey, but warn them that disillusionment is likely to lie ahead.

Wishful Thinking Sells Snake Oil

It can be amazing how gullible smart individuals and organizations become when they are presented with miracle claims for a better life. As soon as people or organizations have entered stage 3, whole industries that are built on selling "snake oil" eagerly await them, overweight individuals and slow-paced corporate IT departments alike: late-night weight-loss commercials and shiny demos showing business people building cloud solutions in no time. As Russell Ackoff once pointedly put it, in "A Lifetime of Systems Thinking":[1]

> Managers are incurably susceptible to panacea peddlers. They are rooted in the belief that there are simple, if not simple-minded, solutions to even the most complex of problems.

When you are looking for a quick change, it's difficult to resist, especially if you don't have your own *world map* (Chapter 16).

Digital natives have it easy because, as the name suggests, they were born on the upper levels of the digital transformation scale and never had to make it through this painful change process. Others feel the pain and tend to search for an easy way out. The problem is that this approach will never get you beyond stage 5, where real change hasn't happened yet.

Tuning the Engine

Not everyone who buys snake oil is a complete fool, though. Many organizations adopt worthwhile practices but don't understand that these practices don't work outside of a specific context. For example, sending a few hundred managers to become Scrum Master certified doesn't make you agile. You need to change the way people think and work and establish new values. Holding a standup meeting

---

1 Russell Ackoff, "A Lifetime of Systems Thinking," The Systems Thinker (website), *https://oreil.ly/DP_Ea.*

every day that resembles a status call where people report 73% progress also doesn't transform your organization. It's not that standup meetings are a bad idea, rather the opposite, but they are about much more than standing up (*https:// oreil.ly/Le5-n*).[2] Real transformation has to go far beyond scratching the surface and change the system.

Systems theory (Chapter 10) teaches us that to change the observed behavior of a system, you must change the system itself. Everything else is wishful thinking. It's like wanting to improve the emissions of a car by blocking the exhaust pipe. If you want a cleaner running car, there's no other way than going all the way back to the engine and tuning it or transforming it into an electric car. When you want to change the behavior of a company, you need to go to its engine—the people and the way they are organized. This is burdensome, but the only truly effective way.

Help Along the Way

Some enterprise IT vendors do resemble the folks selling overpriced workout machines on late-night TV: their products work, but not quite as advertised, and they are in fact overpriced. A good walk in the park every day likely produces the same results for free. You just need to be smart enough to know that and disciplined enough to stick to it.

Many enterprise IT vendors provide genuine innovation to their customers, but at a price. Enterprise vendors range from "old school" to "selling an imitation of the new world to old enterprises" and "truly new world." The further left on this scale your organization is, the more you will pay. My goal, therefore, is to build sufficient internal skill to use products as far to the right on that spectrum as possible. As I once stated in a slightly exaggerated way: "Corporate IT tends to pay for its stupidity. If you are stupid, you better be rich!" An organization that doesn't yet have the required skill pays "tuition," a concept well-known in German as *Lehrgeld*. If spending the money helps them do better next time, it's a good investment. As always, I make sure to *document such decisions* (Chapter 8).

The *consultants and enterprise vendors that surround traditional enterprises* (Chapter 38) have a limited incentive to fully transform their clients into becoming digital: digital companies tend to shun consultants and largely employ open-source technology, often developed by themselves. Because externals are set to

---

2 Jason Yip, "It's Not Just Standing Up: Patterns for Daily Standup Meetings," MartinFowler.com, Feb. 21, 2016, *https://oreil.ly/Le5-n*.

profit from the transformation path itself, they are useful in helping an enterprise start the transformation, as this brings the willingness to invest money. However, they aren't quite as keen to catapult their customers into a state where their advice or products are no longer needed. This love-hate relationship is likely to affect the role an architect plays in the transformation effort: you can't achieve it without external help, but you have to be aware that it's a *co-opetition* rather than true collaboration.

The Pain of Not Changing

The biggest risk during the transformation journey is suffering a relapse after having bought "snake oil" just to realize that it doesn't achieve the promised results, or at least not as quickly as anticipated. This risk is particularly high at stages 4 or 5 of my model.

The inevitable pain of changing makes the lure of the easy path, that is, not changing or giving up halfway, a clear-and-present danger. The long-term effects of not changing are easily put aside because that pain isn't happening yet. Plus, you already accepted the current state, even if it clearly isn't optimal. The certainty of knowing the current state proves to be a major force against change, which carries a large amount of uncertainty—who knows whether all the projected benefits will actually materialize? It could be getting worse for all we know. This is one of the many ways we are biased and thus *poor decision makers* (Chapter 6).

IT organizations, especially operations teams, tend to *equate change to risk* (Chapter 26). The insight that change was needed often comes much later, when the cost of not having changed becomes blatantly and painfully apparent. Sadly, at that time the list of available options tends to be much shorter, or empty. This is true for individuals ("I wish I had started a healthier life when I was young") as well as organizations ("We wish we had cleaned up our IT before we became disrupted"). When people reflect on their lives, they are much more likely to regret *not* having done things as opposed to the things they did. The logical conclusion is simple: do more things and keep doing those that work well.

Getting Over the Hump

A linear chain of events has one tricky property: the probability of making it through all steps computes as the product of the individual transition probabilities between each step and the next. Let's say you are a quite determined person and have a 70% chance of making it from one step to the next, even though the machine you ordered from late-night TV didn't work quite as advertised. If you compound this probability across the 9 steps needed to go from stage 1 to stage 10, you arrive at a 4% probability, 1 in 25, of making it to the goal. If you assume a fifty-fifty chance at each step, which might be more realistic (just look on eBay for barely used exercise machines), you end up with $1/2^9$ = 0.2% or 1 in 512 (!). "Against All Odds" comes to mind, even though it's probably not Phil Collins's best song.

The biggest enemy of change is complacency: if things aren't so bad, the motivation to change is low. Organizations can artificially increase the pain of not changing, e.g., by creating fear or conjuring a (fake) crisis before the real crisis occurs. Such a strategy can work but is risky. It cannot be applied many times, as people will start ignoring the repeated "fire drill." Still, conjuring a crisis beats undergoing a real crisis. Many organizations only really start to change when they have a "near-death" experience. The problem is that near-death often results in actual death.

34

Leading Change

The Island of Sanity in the Sea of Desperation

Don't get voted off the island!

Demonstrating positive results from a different way of doing things in a small team can help overcome complacency and the fear of uncertainty, and thus is a good way to start a transformation. We shouldn't forget, though, that the "trailblazers" on such teams have a doubly tough job: they need to overcome the pain of change and do so in an environment that's still at stage 1 of the transformation journey. This is comparable to eating healthy when everyone around you at the table is having tasty cake and the restaurant has nothing healthy on the menu at all.

To succeed, you need a firm belief and perseverance. The corporate IT equivalent of trying to eat healthy at the cake party is trying to be Agile when it takes four weeks to get a new server or when contemporary development tools and hardware aren't allowed because they violate corporate security standards. You've got to be willing to swim upstream to effect change.

A Tractor Passing the Race Car

One particular danger of leading change with a different approach is that the existing, slow approaches are often more suitable for the current environment. This is a form of *systems resisting change* (Chapter 10) and can result in your fancy new software/hardware/development approach being pummeled by the old, existing ways. I compare this to building a full-fledged race car, just to find out that in your corporate environment each car has to pull three tons of baggage in the form of rules and regulations. And instead of a nice, paved racetrack, you find yourself in a foot-deep sea of process mud. You will find out that the old corporate tractor slowly but steadily passes your shiny new Formula 1 car, which is busily throwing up mud while shredding its rear tires. In such a scenario, it becomes difficult to argue that you devised a better way of doing things.

It's therefore critical to change processes and culture along with introducing new technology. A race car in a tractor pulling contest will be laughable at best. You need to build a proper road before it makes sense to commission a race car. You also need to employ your *communication skills* (Part III) to secure management support when setbacks happen.

Setting Course

To motivate people for change, you can either dangle the digital carrot, painting pictures of a happy, digital life on the far horizon, or wield the digital stick, warning of impending doom through disruption. In the end, you'll likely need a little bit of both, but the carrot is generally the more noble approach. For the carrot to work, you need to paint a tangible picture of the alternate future and set visible, measurable targets based on the company strategy. For example, if the corporate strategy is based on increasing *speed* to reduce time-to-market, a tangible and visible goal would be to cut the release cycle for your division's software products or services in half (or more) every year. If the goal is *resilience*, you set *a goal of halving average recovery times* (Chapter 12) for outages. Some goals can even be enforced through automation.

 Digital companies may enforce a goal to improve resilience by deploying a *Chaos Monkey* (Chapter 32) that randomly disables components.

Setting goals can be a tricky affair, as the organization might meet the goals without completing the intended change. For example, setting a reduction in number of outages as a goal surfaces two major issues. First, it incentivizes hiding outages and, second, it'll make teams invest in more up-front testing, slowing down the organization. Lastly, it's not necessarily the number of outages that negatively affect the business, but the total observed downtime.

Venturing Off the Mainland

You cannot expect everyone to instantly join you on your journey, though, simply because you're telling stories about the magic land awaiting them in the far distance. You will surely find some explorers or adventurers-at-heart who are willing to get on the boat just based on your vision or charisma. Some may not even believe your promises, but find sailing to unknown shores more appealing than just sitting around. These folks are your early adopters and can become powerful multipliers for your mission. Find them, connect them in a community, and take them along.

Others will wait to see whether your ship actually floats. Be kind to them and pick them up for the journey once they are ready. These folks may actually be more committed as they overcame an initial hurdle or fear. Yet others will want to see you return with your ship loaded with gold. That's also fine—some have to see to believe. So you need to be patient and recruit for your transformation journey in waves.

Burning the Ships

Even after folks have joined you on the transformation journey, the chance of a relapse is high: on your journey you will encounter storms, pirates, sharks, sandbanks, icebergs, and other adverse conditions. Captains of a digital transformation have to be skilled sailors, but also strong leaders. A tough approach is to "burn the ships," derived from the story that upon arriving on a new shore the captain would burn the ships so no one could propose to retreat and go back home. I am not sure whether this approach really increases the odds of success. You want a team that's committed and believes in success, as opposed to one that has doubts but no ship on which to return.

Offshore Platforms

Some companies' change programs sail far off the mainland to overcome the constraints imposed by the old world. Copying what they observe in successful so-called "digital" companies, teams move into colorful buildings with open seating plans and baristas, use Apple laptops full of open source stickers, and wear shorts or hoodies. Such units, resembling offshore drilling platforms far from the mainland—run under fancy labels like "innovation center," "digital hub," or "digital factory"—can be a lot of fun, but suffer from several major issues:

1. These new islands often don't have a meaningful bridge back to the mainland, meaning they largely operate in isolation. They therefore don't act as a transformation vehicle for the main island. My cynical advice for such a setup is: "if you want to show that smart people in an ideal environment can create valuable things, you could have just bought Facebook stock."

2. Such islands often don't have economic pressure because they are well-funded by the mothership. They thus end up being "digital trust fund" playgrounds that don't deliver concrete business value. Those setups could be handy for press releases and corporate tours, but not for working in rapid-value delivery cycles.

3. And last, copying digital leaders' working environments isn't going to make you "digital." This fallacy, known as the *cargo cult*,[1] ignores the mechanisms behind the visual facade. A barista stand doesn't magically accelerate your release cycles: you can't copy-paste culture.

You can't copy-paste culture. So, just building a new island in a different ocean isn't going to help with an organization's transformation. You need to strike a balance between sufficiently reducing constraints but still being relevant to the mainland. How to find the right balance? The best approach I found is to keep iterating (Chapter 36).

The Island of Sanity

Still, the temptation to create a better working environment for at least a subset of the organization can be strong. I followed this approach, which I refer to as building an "island of sanity in the sea of desperation," myself in the year 2000. Back then, just before the internet bubble burst, our somewhat traditional consulting company vied for talent with internet startups like WebVan and Pets.com (a plastic bag and a sock puppet decorate my private internet bubble archive). I

---

1 Wikipedia, "Cargo Cult," *https://oreil.ly/GpesJ.*

therefore helped create an environment that would be attractive for such candidates and was successful in recruiting a stellar team of top-notch technologists.

Sooner or later, though, your island will become too small for the people on it, causing them to feel constrained in their career options. If the island has drifted far from the mainland because the mainland hasn't changed much at all, reintegration will be very difficult, increasing the risk that people leave the company altogether. That's what happened to most of my team in 2001. Second, people will wonder why they have to live on a small and remote island when other companies feature the same, desirable (corporate) lifestyle on their extensive mainland. Wouldn't that seem much easier? Or, as a friend once asked, or, rather, challenged me in a very pointed way: "Why don't you just quit and let them die?" While transformation is hard work, you also gotta know when you're trying too hard.

Skunkworks That Works

People working in a separate location can however create significant innovations and transform the mothership, though. The best-known example perhaps is the IBM PC, which was developed in Boca Raton, Florida, far away from IBM's New York headquarters. The development bypassed many corporate rules, for example, by mostly using parts from outside manufacturers, by building an open system, or by selling through retail stores. It's hard to imagine where IBM (and the rest of the computer industry) would be if they hadn't created the PC.

IBM was certainly not a company used to moving quickly, with insiders claiming that it "would take at least nine months to ship an empty box." But the prototype for the IBM PC was assembled in one month and the computer was launched only one year later, which required not only development, but also manufacturing to be set up. Several factors likely contributed to the team's success:

- This skunkworks was tasked with launching a real, sustainable product on the market. It wasn't a playground.

- The team streamlined many processes but didn't circumvent all corporate guidance. For example, its products passed the standard IBM quality assurance tests and thus gained acceptance on the mainland. The team didn't deliver a toy but a successful commercial product.

- Lastly, teams back on the mainland probably didn't see this project as a threat. They were simply convinced that it was impossible for IBM to make a computer for less than $15,000 and were happy to be proven wrong.

These factors led to the IBM PC becoming a positive example of an ambitious project team questioning existing assumptions while being led by existing management. A more recent example of how large-scale transformation can work is Microsoft under CEO Satya Nadella, who opted not to sail off the mainland but rather led the transformation by "rediscovering the soul of Microsoft."[2]

Leaving Your Island Will Get Your Feet Wet

You also need to be cautious that most *systems* (Chapter 10) operate on a local optimum. While that local optimum might be extremely far removed from the much more agile and fast way digital organizations work, it's usually still better than the "surrounding" operating modes that you end up with when you make a small change to the system.

For example, an organization may only be able to push code into production every six months, which is a practical joke in the digital world. However, it has managed to establish processes that make this cadence workable. If you change the release cycle to three months, you will make people's lives worse and may hurt the product quality and even the company's reputation. Hence, you should first introduce automated build and deployment tools to form the basis for faster releases. Sadly, doing so also makes the operations staff's lives worse because they are already very busy with production support, and now in addition they must attend training and learn new tools. They will also make mistakes while doing so.

In your view, the organization might live on a tiny molehill while you know of a high mountain of gold somewhere else. However, between the molehill and the mountain is a muddy swamp. Because you won't be able to leap straight to the mountain of gold, you first have to get folks off the molehill, convincing them to keep moving after their feet get wet and muddy. That's why you must communicate a clear vision and prepare them for tougher times ahead before the new optimum can be reached.

---

2 Satya Nadella, *Hit Refresh: The Quest to Rediscover Microsoft's Soul and Imagine a Better Future for Everyone* (New York: HarperBusiness, 2017).

The Country of the Blind

One shouldn't underestimate the resistance to change and innovation in large and successful enterprises that have "done things this way" for a long time. H. G. Wells's short story "The Country of the Blind" comes to mind: an explorer falls down a steep slope and discovers a village in a valley that is completely separated from the rest of the world. Unbeknownst to the explorer, a genetic disease has rendered all of the villagers unable to see. Upon realizing this peculiarity, the explorer feels that because "the one-eyed man is king" in this town he can teach and rule them. However, his ability to see proves to be of little advantage in a place designed for blind people, without windows or lights. After struggling to take advantage of his gift, the explorer is to have his eyes removed by the village doctor to cure his strange obsessions.

Oddly, two versions of this story exist, each with a different ending: in the original version, the explorer escapes the village after struggling back up the slope. The revised story has him observe that a rockslide is about to destroy the village and he's the only one able to escape, along with his blind girlfriend. In either case, it's not a happy ending for the villagers. Be careful not to fall into the "in the land of the blind, the one-eyed man is king" trap. Complex organizational systems settle into specific patterns over time and actively resist change. If you want to change their behavior, you have to change the system.

35

Economies of Speed

Death by Efficiency Is Slow and Painful

Economies of scale versus economies of speed

Large companies looking to speed up are used to optimizing the way they work: they can make production a few percent more efficient, negotiate a slightly higher discount from vendors, and reduce budget by printing in black and white. Sadly, though, their digital competitors don't move 10% faster, but 10 times faster, leaving traditional IT departments somewhat puzzled by how this is even possible.

30,000 Times Faster

A quick example showing how a 10-times speed-up can still be a quite conservative figure comes from setting up a version control system. A large IT organization looking to define a standard for source control invested six months of community work to conclude that the company should be *using Git* (Chapter 25). However, it was considered too difficult to migrate other projects off Subversion, so both products were recommended. The preparation cycle for the global architecture steering board meeting took another month, bringing the total elapsed time to seven months or roughly 210 days.

 Some tasks that would take traditional organizations months of preparation and approvals, digital companies can accomplish in a few minutes.

A modern IT organization or startup would have spent a few minutes deciding on the product and have accounts set up, a private repository created, and the first commit made in about 10 minutes. The speed-up factor between the two examples comes to 210 days * (24 hours/day) * (60 minutes/hour) / 10 minutes ≈ 30,000!

If that number alone doesn't scare you, keep in mind that one organization published a paper (without selecting or implementing a product such as Bit-Bucket, GitHub, or GitLab) and is merrily dragging along its legacy. Its "decision" is thus about as meaningful as prescribing that men should wear black shoes, but brown is also allowed for historical reasons. Meanwhile, the other organization is already committing code in a live repository.

Admittedly, large organizations have more parties to align across, existing source repositories, and many other factors that will make it difficult to set up a shared service in 10 minutes. However, if you augment the timeline to include vendor selection, license negotiation, internal alignment, paperwork, and setting up the running service, the ratio could well end up in the hundreds of thousands. Should these organizations be scared? Yes!

Old Economies of Scale

How can modern organizations act at orders of magnitude faster than traditional ones? Traditional organizations pursue economies of scale, meaning they are looking to benefit from their size. Size can indeed be an advantage, as can be seen in cities: density and scale provide short transportation and communication paths, diverse labor supply, better education, and more cultural offerings. Cities grow because the socioeconomic factors scale in a superlinear fashion (a city of double the size offers more than double the socioeconomic benefits), while increases in infrastructure costs are sublinear (you don't need twice as many roads for a city twice the size). But density and size also bring pollution, risk of epidemics, and congestion problems, which ultimately limit the size of cities. Still, cities grow larger and live longer than corporate organizations. One reason lies in the fact that organizations suffer more severely from the overhead introduced by processes and control structures that are required or perceived to be required to keep a large organization in check. Geoffrey West, past president of the Santa Fe Institute, summarized this dynamic in his fascinating video conversation "Why Cities Keep Growing, Corporations and People Always Die, and Life Gets Faster."[1]

In corporations, economies of scale are generally driven by the desire for efficiency: resources such as machines and people must be used as efficiently as possible, avoiding downtimes due to idling and retooling. This efficiency is often pursued by using large batch sizes: making 10,000 of the same widget in one production run costs less than making 10 different batches of 1,000 each. The bigger you are, the larger batches you can make, and the more efficient you become. This view is overly simplistic, though, as it ignores the cost of storing intermediate products, for example. Worse yet, it doesn't consider revenue lost by not being able to serve an urgent customer order because you are in the midst of a large production run: such an organization values *resource efficiency* over *customer efficiency.*

The manufacturing business realized this about half a century ago, resulting in most things being manufactured in small batches or in one continuous batch of highly customized products. Think about today's cars: the number of options you can order is mind boggling, causing the traditional "batch" thinking to completely fall apart. Cars are essentially batches of one. With all the thinking about "Lean" and "Just-in-Time" manufacturing, it's especially astonishing that the IT industry is often still chasing efficiency instead of speed.

A software vendor once stated that, "Obviously the license cost per unit goes down if you buy more licenses." To me, this isn't obvious at all as there's no distribution cost per unit of software, aside from that very salesperson sitting across the table from me. Whether 10,000 customers download one license or one customer buys 10,000 licenses should be the same, as long as the software vendor *doesn't send humans to do a machine's job* (Chapter 13). Cloud computing finally broke the old model.

---

1 Geoffrey West, "Why Cities Keep Growing, Corporations and People Always Die, and Life Gets Faster," Edge, May 23, 2011, *https://oreil.ly/UAh5C.*

It looks like enterprise software sales and enterprise procurement both have some transformations ahead of themselves. In their defense, though, you have to admit that their behavior is determined by enterprise customers still stuck in the old thought pattern: supersize it to get a better deal!

In the digital world, the limiting factor for an organization's size becomes its ability to change. While in static environments being big is an advantage thanks to economies of scale, in times of rapid change *economies of speed* win out and allow startups and digital-native companies to disrupt much larger companies. Or as Jack Welch famously stated: "If the rate of change on the outside exceeds the rate of change on the inside, the end is near."

Behold the Flow!

The quest for efficiency focuses on the individual production steps, looking to optimize their utilization. What's completely missing is the awareness of the production flow, i.e., the flow of a piece of work through a series of production steps. Translated into organizations, individual task optimization results in every department requiring lengthy forms to be filled out before work can begin: I have been told that some organizations require that firewall changes be requested 10 days in advance. And all too often the customer is subsequently told that some thing or another is missing from the request form and is sent back to the beginning of the line. After all, helping the customer fill out the form would be less efficient. If that reminds you of government agencies, you might get the hint that such processes aren't designed for maximum speed and agility.

Besides the inevitable frustration with such setups, they trade off *flow efficiency* for *processing efficiency*: the work stations are nicely efficient, but the customers (or products or widgets) chase from station to station, fill out a form, pick a number, and wait. And *wait* (Chapter 39). And wait some more just to find out they are in the wrong line or their need cannot be processed. This is dead time that isn't measured anywhere except in the customers' blood pressure. Come to think of it, in most of these places, the people going through the flow are not customers in the true sense given that they don't choose to visit this process, but are forced to. That's why you are bound to experience such setups at government offices, where you could at least argue that misguided efficiency is driven by the pursuit to preserve taxpayer money. You'll also commonly find it in IT departments that exert strong *governance* (Chapter 32).

Cost of Delay

For innovation and product development processes, this type of efficiency is pure poison. While digital companies do care about resource utilization (at Google, datacenter utilization was a CEO-level topic), their real driver is speed: time-to-market.

Traditional organizations often misunderstand or underestimate the value of speed. In a joint business-IT workshop, a business owner once described his product as carrying substantial revenue opportunities. At the same time, the product owner asked for a specific feature that required significant development effort, but which would realize value only when rolled out in another country. Deferring that feature would speed up the initial launch, thus harvesting the portrayed revenue opportunities sooner.

Flow-based thinking calls this concept the *cost of delay* (see the excellent book *The Principles of Product Development Flow*[2]), which must be added to the cost of development. Launching a promising product later means that you lose the opportunity to gain revenue during the time of delay. For products with large revenue upside, the cost of delay can be higher than the cost of development, but it's often ignored. On top of avoiding the cost of delay, deferring a feature and launching sooner also allows you to learn from the initial launch and adjust your requirements accordingly. The initial launch may be an utter failure, causing the product to never be launched in the second country. By deferring this feature you avoided wasting time building something that would have never been used. Gathering more information allows you to *make a better decision* (Chapter 6).

A great example of a non-high-tech company that embraced economies of speed is the fashion brand Zara, part of the Inditex fashion empire. When the pursuit of efficiency drove most fashion retailers to outsource production to low-cost suppliers in Asia, Zara implemented a vertically integrated model and manufactured three-quarters of its clothing in Europe, which allowed it to bring new designs into stores in a matter of weeks as opposed to the industry average of three to six months. In the fast-moving fashion retail industry, speed is such a significant advantage that this strategy propelled Inditex's founder to be one of the 10 richest people on the planet. However, the world of fashion is also one of constant change and even "fast fashion" retailers face stiff competition from

---

2 Donald G. Reinertsen, *The Principles of Product Development Flow: Second Generation Lean Product Development* (Redondo Beach, CA: Celeritas Publishing, 2009).

online retailers such as boohoo, which works in small batch sizes coupled with extremely short product cycles.

The Value and Cost of Predictability

Why do intelligent people ignore basic economic arguments such as calculating the cost of delay? Because they are working in a system that favors predictability over speed. Adding a feature later or, worse yet, deciding later whether to add it or not may require going through lengthy budget approval processes. Those processes exist because the people who control the budget value predictability over agility. Predictability makes their lives easier because they plan the budget for the next 12 to 24 months, and sometimes for good reasons: they don't want to disappoint shareholders with runaway costs that unexpectedly reduce the company profit. As these teams manage cost, not opportunity, they don't benefit from an early product launch.

Optimizing for predictability ignores the cost of delay.

Chasing predictability causes another well-known phenomenon: *sandbagging*. Project and budget plans sandbag by overestimating timelines or cost in order to more easily achieve their target. Keep in mind that estimates aren't single numbers but probability distributions: a project may have a 50% chance of being done in four weeks' time. If "you are lucky and all goes well," it may be done in three weeks, but with only a 20% likelihood. Sandbaggers pick a number far off on the other end of the probability spectrum and would estimate eight weeks for the project, giving them a greater than 95% chance of meeting the target. Even worse, if the project happens to be done in four weeks, the sandbaggers idle for another four weeks before release to avoid having their time or budget estimates cut the next time. If a deliverable depends on a series of activities, sandbagging compounds and can extend the time to delivery enormously.

The Value and Cost of Avoiding Duplication

On the list of inefficiencies, *duplication* of work must be high up: what could be more inefficient than doing the same thing twice? That's sound reasoning, but you must also consider that avoiding duplication doesn't come for free: you need to actively de-duplicate, i.e., detect duplicates and merge them.

The primary cost involved in de-duplication is coordination: to avoid duplication you first need to detect it. In a large codebase this can be done efficiently through code search. In a large organization, it can require many "alignment" meetings—synchronization points—high up in the hierarchy, *which we know not to scale* (Chapter 30) in both computer systems and organizations.

 A story on duplication, attributed to Jeff Bezos, CEO of Amazon: When a manager pointed out that efforts might be duplicated, the senior executive walked to the board and wrote "2 > 0."

Evolving a widely reused resource also requires coordination because changes must be compatible with all existing systems or users. Such coordination can slow down innovation. On the flip side, modern development tools, such as automated testing, can reduce the traditional dangers of duplication. Some digital companies have even begun to explicitly favor duplication because their business environment rewards economies of speed.

How to Make the Switch?

Changing from efficiency-based thinking to speed-based thinking can be difficult for organizations: after all, it's less efficient! In most people's minds being less efficient translates into wasting money. On top of that, people being idle is more visible than the damage done by missed market opportunities.

Usually, this change in attitude happens only when IT is seen as driving business opportunity instead of being a cost center. While corporate IT is stuck in a cycle of cutting cost and increasing efficiency, economies of scale will prevail, which gives the digital giants an ever-bigger lead over traditional companies that dream of becoming digital but cannot shed their old habits.

36

The Infinite Loop

Sometimes Running in Circles Can Be Productive

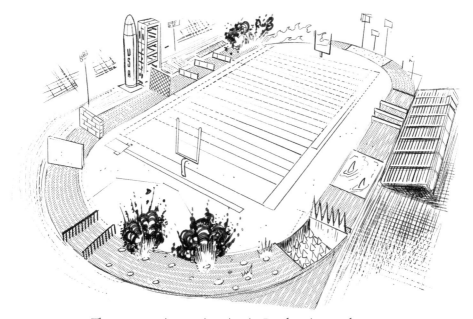

The corporate innovation circuit. Best lap time: unknown

In programming, an infinite loop is rarely a good thing (unless you are Apple, Inc., and your address is 1 Infinite Loop in Cupertino, California). But even Apple HQ appears to be moving off the infinite loop, which is a noteworthy feat in and of itself. In poorly run organizations (not Apple!) employees often make cynical remarks about how they run in circles and when the desired results aren't achieved, management tells them to run faster. You surely don't want to be part of that infinite loop!

Build-Measure-Learn

There's one loop, though, that's a key element of most digital companies: the *continuous learning loop*. Because digital companies know well that *control is an illusion* (Chapter 27), they are addicted to rapid feedback. Eric Ries eternalized this concept in his book *The Lean Startup*[1] as the *Build-Measure-Learn* cycle: a company builds a minimum viable product and launches it into production to measure user adoption and behavior. Based on the insights from live product usage, the company learns and refines the product. Jeff Sussna aptly describes the "learning" part of the cycle as "operate to learn"—the goal of operations isn't to maintain the status quo but to deliver critical insights into making a better product.

Digital RPMs

The critical KPI for most digital companies is how much they can learn per dollar or time-unit spent, i.e., how many revolutions through the Build-Measure-Learn cycle they can make. The digital world has thus changed the nature of the game completely and it would be foolish at best (fatal at worst) to ignore this change.

Taking book authoring as an example: publishing *Enterprise Integration Patterns* took a year of writing, followed by some six months of editing and three months of production. While we had a feeling that the book might be a success, it wasn't until another year later that we could measure the success in actual copies sold. So, making one-half revolution from Build to Measure took about four years! Completing the cycle, i.e., publishing a second edition, would have taken another 6 to 12 months. In comparison, I wrote the original version of this book as an ebook that was published while it was still a work in progress. The book sold several hundred copies before it was even done, and I received reader feedback by email and Twitter almost in real time as I was writing.

The same is true for many other industries: digital technology has made customer feedback immediate. This is a huge opportunity, but also a huge challenge as customers have learned to expect rapid changes based on their feedback. If I don't post an update to my book in two or three weeks, people may worry that I might have given up on writing. Luckily, I find instant feedback (comments as

---

1 Eric Ries, *The Lean Startup: How Today's Entrepreneurs Use Continuous Innovation to Create Radically Successful Businesses* (New York: Crown Business, 2011).

well as purchases) hugely motivating, so I have been far more productive in writing this book than ever before.

Adopting learning as an organization's key metric is good news for another reason. While many tasks are taken over by machines, learning how to build a product that excites users remains firmly in the hands of humans.

Old-World Hurdles

Unfortunately, traditional companies aren't built for rapid feedback cycles. They often *still separate "run" from "change"* (Chapter 12) and assume a project is done by the time it reaches production. Launching a product is about the 120-degree mark in the innovation wheel of fortune, so making one-third of a single revolution counts for nothing if your competition is on its one-hundredth refinement.

What keeps traditional organizations from completing rapid learning cycles? Their structuring as a layered hierarchy: in a fairly static, slow-moving world, organizing into layers has distinct advantages; it allows a small group of people to steer a large organization without having to be involved in all details. Information that travels up is aggregated and translated for easy consumption by upper management. Such a setup works very well in large organizations, but has one fundamental disadvantage: it's horribly slow to react to changes in the environment or to insights at the working level. It takes too much time for information to travel all the way up to make a decision because each "layer" in the organization brings communication overhead and requires a translation. Even if *architects can ride the elevator* (Chapter 1), it still takes time for decisions to trickle back down through a web of budgeting and steering processes. Once again, we aren't talking about a difference of 10% but of factors in the hundreds or thousands: traditional organizations often run feedback cycles to the tune of 18 months while digital companies can do it in days or weeks.

Layered organizations benefit from separation of concerns. However, it becomes a liability in *Economies of Speed*.

In times when nearly every organization wants to become more "digital" and the technical platforms are readily available as open source or cloud services, building a fast-learning organization is a critical success factor.

Looping in Externals

With every revolution, the organization not only learns what features are most useful for the users, but the project team also learns how to build enticing user experiences, how to speed up development cycles, or how to scale the system to meet increasing demand. This learning cycle is critical for the organization's digital transformation because it enables in-house innovation and rapid iterations.

 Digital transformation begins with changing HR and recruiting practices.

Inversely, if corporate IT depends heavily on the work of external providers, which is rather common, the ones benefiting from this learning are the external consultants. Organizations should therefore place their internal staff inside the learning cycle and use external support mainly to coach or teach them. Taking this logic a step further, digital transformation begins with transforming HR and recruiting practices to hire qualified staff and to educate existing employees so that they can become part of the learning cycle.

Pivoting the Layer Cake

To speed up the feedback engine you need to turn the organizational layer cake on its side by forming teams that carry full responsibility from product concept to technical implementation, operations, and refinement. Often such an approach carries the label of "tribes," "feature teams," or "DevOps," which is associated with a "you build it, you run it" attitude. Doing so not only provides a direct feedback loop to the developers about the quality of their product (pagers going off in the middle of the night are a very immediate form of feedback), but it also *scales the organization* (Chapter 30) by removing unnecessary synchronization points: all relevant decisions can be made within the project team.

Running in independent teams that focus on rapid feedback has one other fundamental advantage: it brings the customer back into the picture. In the traditional pyramid of layered command-and-control, the customer is nowhere to be found—at best somewhere interacting with the lowest layer of the organization, far from where decisions are made and strategies are set. In contrast, "vertical" teams draw feedback and their energy directly from the customer.

The main challenge in assembling such teams is to get a complete range of skill sets into a compact team, ideally not exceeding the size of a "two-pizza team"; that is, one that can be fed by two large pizzas. This requires qualified staff, a willingness to collaborate across skill sets, and a low-friction environment. The Spotify team concepts[2] of chapters and guilds are likely the most useful resource in this context.

Maintaining Cohesion

If all control rests in the vertically integrated team, what ensures that these teams are still part of one company and for example use common branding and common infrastructure? It's OK to have some pie crust on the vertical layer cake: for example, one at the top for branding and overall strategy and one at the bottom for common infrastructure that *never sends a human to do a machine's job* (Chapter 13).

Once you have perfected the rapid Build-Measure-Learn feedback cycle, you may wonder how many revolutions you will need to make. In digital companies the feedback engine stops spinning only when the product is dead. That's why, for once, it's good to be part of an infinite loop.

---

2 Henrik Kniberg, "Spotify Engineering Culture (Part 1)."

37

You Can't Fake IT

To Be Digital on the Outside, You First
Need to Be Digital on the Inside

Who can spot the dinosaur programmer?

Rapid feedback cycles (Chapter 36) help digital companies understand customer demand and improve the product or service offered. Naturally, this feedback loop works best when the product or service has direct exposure to the end customer or consumer. Corporate IT, in contrast, is relatively far removed from the end customer because it supplies IT services to the business, which in turn is in contact with the customer. Does this imply that corporate IT shouldn't be the focal point for digital transformation as it's too far removed from digital customers? Many digital transformation initiatives that are driven "from the top" appear to support this notion: they have special teams engage with customers in focus groups before handing down the specs to IT for implementation.

Laying the Foundation

But just like you cannot build a fancy new house on an old, fragile foundation, you cannot be digital on the outside without transforming the IT engine room: IT must deliver those capabilities to the business that are needed to become Agile and to compete in the digital marketplace. If it takes eight weeks to procure a virtual server based on an email request, the business cannot scale up with demand, unless it stockpiles a huge number of idling servers, which would be the exact opposite of what cloud computing promises. Worse yet, if these servers are set up with an old version of the OS, modern applications may not run on them. On top of all this, necessary manual network changes are guaranteed to break things or slow them down.

Feedback Cycles

Rapidly deploying servers can be achieved with private cloud technologies, but that alone doesn't make IT "digital." For corporate IT to credibly offer services to businesses competing in a digital world, it must itself be ready to compete in the digital world of IT service providers, not only from a cost and quality perspective, but also from an engagement model point of view: corporate IT must become customer centric and learn from customers using its products in an *infinite loop* (Chapter 36).

If the servers that are provisioned aren't the ones the customer needs, provisioning them faster accomplishes nothing. Moreover, the customer may not want to order servers at all, but prefers to deploy applications on a so-called "serverless" architecture. To understand these trends, IT must engage with their internal customers—the business units—in a rapid feedback loop, just as the business units do with their end customers.

Delivering on Your Promises

Engaging with customers is helpful only if you can deliver on their demands. In the case of IT delivering services to its customers, the business units, it must have the capability and the attitude to deliver digital services rapidly at high quality. An MIT study[1] showed that those companies that aligned business and IT without first improving their IT delivery capability actually spent *more* money on IT but suffered from below-average revenue growth. You can't fake being digital.

Customer Centricity

Customer centricity is a common phrase incorporated into many a company's motto or "value statement." What company wouldn't want to be customer centric after all? Even institutions whose customers are decreed by law, such as the Internal Revenue Service, have exhibited a good dose of customer awareness in recent years. For many organizations, though, it's difficult to move beyond the simple slogan and truly become customer centric because it requires fundamental changes to the organizational culture and setup: hierarchical organizations are CEO centered, not customer centered. Operational teams following ITIL processes are process centered, not customer centered. IT run as a cost center is likely cost centered as opposed to customer centered. Running a customer-centric business on top of a process- or CEO-centric IT is bound to generate enormous friction.

Cocreating IT Services

To support a business in digital transformation, it's no longer enough for IT to develop and push commodity services to their customers, the business units, via *governance* (Chapter 32). IT must start to behave like a digital business, generating "pull" demand instead of pushing product. This can be done well by developing products jointly with customers, which goes under the fancy moniker of "cocreation." While many internal customers will welcome the change in mindset and the opportunity to influence a service being built, others may not want to engage unless you present a firm price and service-level agreement. Being digital works only if your customers are digital.

---

1 David Shpilberg et al., "Avoiding the Alignment Trap in IT," *MIT Sloan Management Review*, October 1, 2007, *https://oreil.ly/nK9ph*.

Eat Your Own Dog Food

Some IT departments are relatively far from the end customer, so they wonder how they can get feedback cycles started. They tend to ignore a large, readily available pool of customers that's very close by: their own employees. Employees are friendly and motivated customers that are usually eager to try out new stuff. Ironically, the common name for this clever practice is *dogfooding*, assuming people will eat their own dog food. I'd side with an old friend here who determined that it's unfair that his dog eats dog food while he's having a tasty dinner. So he decided to share his meal with his dog instead—the vet confirmed the dog is perfectly healthy doing this.

Google is famous for *dogfooding* its products, meaning its employees get to try alpha or beta versions of new products. While the name doesn't make it sound too appealing, Google's "food" includes pretty exciting products, some of which never reach the eyes of the consumer.

Dogfooding is effective because it enables an extremely rapid feedback and learning cycle in a safe and controlled environment. I start all my IT services by offering them first as an internal beta release. Once we better understand customer expectations and work out the kinks, we offer them to external customers.

Google took things a step further and merged employee and customer accounts into a single user-management system, making customers and employees appear identical to most applications, differentiated only by their domain name (google.com) and their access from the corporate network. Merging the previously disparate systems was rather painful, but the effect was hugely liberating as employees were treated as customers.

In contrast, traditional organizations can look at employees and customers very differently, as illustrated by this example:

> *At a large financial services company, employees weren't supposed to use Android phones. Without even debating the technical merit, I couldn't help but wonder how this company can then support customers using Android devices, which make up some 80% of the market. If Android isn't considered secure enough for the company's financial services employees, how can it be considered secure enough for its customers?*

Rather than trying to control the user base, it'd be more helpful to understand and address potential weaknesses, for example through two-factor authentication, mobile device management, fraud monitoring, or disallowing old versions of the OS, both for customers and employees.

Digital Mindset

Besides starting to use their own products and learning to iterate, one of the biggest hurdles in making corporate IT more digital can be the employees' mindset. When employees use previous-generation BlackBerry phones and internal processes are handled by emailing spreadsheets based on rules documented in a slide deck, it's difficult to believe that an organization can act digitally. While it's a touchy subject, the age distribution in traditional IT can be an additional challenge: the average age in corporate IT is often in the 40s or early 50s, far removed from the digital natives being courted as the new digital customer segment. Bringing younger employees into the mix can help companies become digital as it brings some of your target customer segment in-house.

The good news is that change can happen gradually, starting with small steps. When employees start using LinkedIn to pull photos or resumes instead of emailing resume templates, it's a step toward becoming digital. Checking Google Maps to find convenient hotels instead of the clunky travel portal is another. Building small internal applications to automate approval processes is a small but very important step: it gets people into a "maker mindset" that motivates them to tackle problems by building solutions, not by referring to outdated rule books. The digital feedback cycle can work only if people can build solutions. This may be the biggest hurdle for corporate IT departments, because they are *too afraid of code* (Chapter 11). Code is what software innovation is made of, so if you want to be digital, you'd better learn to code!

Opportunities for making small steps toward becoming digital are plentiful. I tend to look for little problems to solve or small things to speed up and automate.

At Google, getting a USB charger cable was a matter of 2.5 minutes: 1 minute to walk to the nearest Tech Stop, 30 seconds to swipe your badge and scan the cable at the self-checkout, and 1 minute to walk back to your desk. To do this in corporate IT, I had to mail someone, who mailed someone, who asked me the type of phone I use and then entered an order, which I had to approve. Elapsed time: about 2 weeks. Speed factor: 14 days × 24 hours/day × 60 minutes/hour / 2.5 minutes = 8064, in the same league as setting up a *source code repository* (Chapter 35).

Fixing this would make a great miniproject. You don't see a positive business case? That's probably because your company isn't yet set up to develop solutions rapidly. A digital company could likely build this solution in an afternoon, including database and web user interface, and host it in its private cloud basically for free. If you never start building small, rapid solutions, your IT will be paralyzed and likely unable to act in a digital environment.

The Stack Fallacy

As much of corporate IT is focused on infrastructure and operations, becoming *software minded* (Chapter 14) requires a huge shift. For example, my idea to build an *on air sign* (Chapter 30) that illuminates when my IP desk phone is off the hook never materialized because the team rolling out the devices didn't code or deal with software APIs.

The challenge an organization faces when "moving up the stack," e.g., from infrastructure to application software platform or from software platform to end-user application is well-known and has aptly been labeled the *stack fallacy*.[2] Even successful companies underestimate the challenge and are subject to the fallacy: VMware missed the shift from virtualization software to Docker containers for many years, Cisco has been spending billions in acquisitions to get closer to application delivery, and even mighty Google failed to move from utility software like search and mail to an engaging social network, a market dominated by Facebook.

For most of corporate IT, this means an uphill climb from a focus on operating infrastructure to engaging users with rapidly evolving applications and services. Though challenging, it is doable: internal IT doesn't need to compete in the open market, giving it the chance to change in small increments.

---

2 Anshu Sharma, "Why Big Companies Keep Failing: The Stack Fallacy," TechCrunch, Jan. 18, 2016, *https://oreil.ly/OYCi-*.

38

Money Can't Buy Love

Or a Culture Change

I need that feature by Tuesday

After transitioning from a Silicon Valley company to a traditional business, my new coworkers frequently reminded me that we're a large corporation, implying that what works for Google wouldn't apply here. My routine retort was that by applying the standard measure of market capitalization, I joined a corporation 10 times smaller. More interesting, my coworkers also pointed out that Google can do pretty much whatever it wants thanks to all the money it has. My view, in contrast, was that many successful traditional businesses suffer from exactly this problem of having too much money.

Innovator's Dilemma

How can organizations have too much money? After all, their goal is to maximize profits and shareholder returns. To do so, companies use stringent budgeting processes that control spending. For example, proposed projects are assessed by their expected rate of return against a benchmark typically set by existing investments, sometimes called internal rate of return (IRR).

Such processes can hurt innovation, though, when new ideas must compete with existing, highly profitable "cash cows." Most innovative products can't match established products' performance or profitability during early stages. Traditional budgeting processes may therefore reject new and promising ideas, a phenomenon that Christensen coined the *Innovator's Dilemma.*[1] However, when these new innovations later surpass sustaining technologies, they threaten organizations that didn't invest early on and that now lag behind.

Rich companies tend to have a high IRR and are therefore especially likely to reject new ideas. Also, they perceive the risk of no change as low—after all, things are going great. This dampens their *appetite for change* (Chapter 33) and increases the danger of disruption.

Beware of the HiPPO

Despite its downsides, companies making investment decisions based on expected return at least use a consistent decision metric. Many rich companies have a different decision process: that of the *highest paid person's opinion*, or HiPPO. This approach isn't just highly subjective but also susceptible to shiny, HiPPO-targeted vendor demos, which peddle incremental "enterprise" solutions as opposed to real innovation. Because those decision makers are far removed from actual technology and software delivery, they don't realize how fast new solutions can be built on a shoestring budget.

To make matters worse, internal "salespeople" exploit management's limited understanding to push their own pet projects, often at a cost orders of magnitude higher than what digital companies would spend. I have seen someone make it to board level with the idea of exposing functionality as an API, at a cost of many million Euros. It's easy to sell people in the stone age a wheel.

---

1 Clayton M. Christensen, *The Innovator's Dilemma: When New Technologies Cause Great Firms to Fail*, reprint ed. (New York: HarperBusiness, 2011).

Overhead and Tolerated Inefficiency

Many established companies with a profitable business model carry significant overhead: fancy corporate offices, old labor contracts with overly generous retirement provisions, overemployment for roles that are no longer needed, an army of administrative staff for executives, company cars, drivers, car washes, private dining rooms, coffee and cake being served in boardrooms—the list is long. This overhead cost is generally distributed across all cost centers, placing an enormous financial burden on small and innovative teams working on disruptive technologies.

 My small team of architects was loaded with enormous overhead cost ranging from office space and cafeteria subsidies to workplace charges (computers, phones), which I couldn't influence. In comparison, free meals offered by digital companies are a trivial expense.

Overhead costs also result from inefficiencies that are tolerated in wealthy organizations because there's little pressure to remove them. Examples are manifold: labor-intensive manual processes (I have seen people manually preparing spreadsheets from SAP data every month), lengthy meetings with 20 executives, half of whom have little to contribute, ordering processes with long paper trails, people printing reams of paper as handouts for meetings on digital strategy. All these line items add up and make it difficult for large companies to compete in new segments where margins aren't yet rich enough to support such overhead.

Hollowed-Out IT

A particularly dangerous pitfall for wealthy organizations looking to transform is the belief that any required skill can be bought at will. Years ago, many companies considered IT a commodity: a necessity, but not one that created a competitive advantage. That's why they didn't perceive any risk in keeping IT skills outside of the company. Instead, they valued the flexibility in ramping external IT staff up and down as needed just as they would with administrative or cleaning staff. They perceived this model as *more efficient* (Chapter 35).

In the late 1990s, the telecom business was very profitable thanks to a fast-growing broadband internet market. These companies outsourced virtually all technical work to external contractors and system integrators (where I was employed). Solid profits allowed them to digest the high consulting fees, high administrative overhead for contract management, and more than occasional project cost overruns.

However, outsourcing software delivery has severe drawbacks in the digital age: first, it prevents the organization from effectively participating in the *Build-Measure-Learn cycle* (Chapter 36) because externals typically work on a prenegotiated scope of work and therefore have little incentive to keep iterating on products or to shorten release cycles. Second, the organization won't be able to develop a deep understanding of new technologies and their potential, thus stifling innovation. Worse yet, in many cases knowledge of a company's existing system landscape rests with external contractors, rendering the organization unable to make rational decisions based on the status quo. If you don't know your starting point, it's difficult to get on the road to change.

Outsourcing IT has severe drawbacks in the digital age because it excludes the organization from the critical innovation cycle.

These companies' IT departments degenerated into mere budget administration structures with hardly any technology skill. The main skill needed was securing budget and spending it. Those companies couldn't attract much real IT talent because qualified candidates realized that their skills weren't valued. Nevertheless, all was perceived as working well while the money flowed freely.

Excessive Dependencies

But then everything changed: hardly any industry was overrun by internet companies as spectacularly as telecommunications. Telecoms used to "own" communication but completely failed to see the potential of the smartphone and digital consumer services. Telecoms used to generate billions of dollars in profits from short message service (SMS) products, a market that dropped significantly in just a few years thanks to WhatsApp, Facebook Messenger, and others.

Existing IT contracts focused on *improving efficiency* (Chapter 35) in backend processing, such as billing; no internal skill was available to design and deliver new services to customers; and existing organizational structures and processes squashed any innovation that was trying to happen. Eventually, telecoms were left with providing "dumb data pipes" in a downward price spiral while digital companies enjoyed almost-trillion-dollar valuations and rich profit margins. Experienced software architects know that too many external dependencies get you in trouble. The same is true for organizations.

Paying More May Get You Less

Other factors surely played a role in telecoms missing the "digital boat," but believing that technology skills can be acquired as needed is particularly dangerous. Just like you cannot buy friends, a company cannot buy motivated employees. Candidates with highly marketable skill sets, such as cloud architecture or machine learning, are attracted to teams with strong, like-minded people. This presents traditional companies with a chicken-and-egg problem.

Many companies try to overcome this hurdle by paying higher salaries. However, compensation is often not the main motivator for top candidates; they are looking for an employer where they can learn from their peers and have the freedom to implement projects rapidly. That's why it's difficult for companies to "buy" skilled employees.

Worse yet, trying to attract talent by offering higher salaries can backfire because it will attract "mercenary" developers who work for the money alone. My experience is that people who come for money leave for more money. It won't attract passionate developers who want to be part of a high-performing team to change the world. I compare this pitfall to the unpopular kid handing out candy at school: the kid won't make friends, but will be surrounded by children who are willing to pretend to be a friend in exchange for candy.

My experience is that people who come for money leave for more money.

Changing Culture from Within

Top consultants can surely help you implement new and exciting technology projects, but they won't significantly change the organization's culture; the cultural change must come from within. Roberts[2] classifies the describing

---

2 John Roberts, *The Modern Firm: Organizational Design for Performance and Growth* (Oxford, England: Oxford University Press, 2007).

characteristics of an organization as PARC–people, architecture (structures), routines (processes), and culture. Restructurings and process reengineering can change the organization's architecture and routines, but cultural changes must be instilled by the company leadership. This takes time, lots of energy, and sometimes a leadership change: "to do change management, sometimes you need to change management."

Because digital transformation requires changing both technology and culture, I opted to drive a large-scale IT transformation from the inside. It's the hard, but only sustainable way.

39

Who Likes Standing in Line?

Good Things Don't Come to Those Who Wait

100% utilization

When in university, we often wonder whether and how what we learn will help us in our future careers and lives. While I am still waiting for the Ackerman function to accelerate my professional advancement (our first semester in computer science blessed us with a lecture on computability), the class on queuing theory was actually helpful: not only can you talk to the people in front of you in the supermarket checkout line about M/M/1 systems and the benefits of *single queue, multiple servers* systems (which most supermarkets don't use), but it also gives you an important foundation to reason about *economies of speed* (Chapter 35).

Looking Between the Activities

When looking to speed things up in enterprises, most people look at how work is done: are all machines and people utilized, and are they working efficiently? Ironically, when looking for speed, you mustn't look at the activities, but *between* them. By looking at activities you may find inefficient activity, but between the activities is where you find *inactivity*, things sitting around and waiting to be worked on.

Inactivity can have a much more detrimental effect on speed than inefficient activity. If a machine is working well and almost 100% utilized but a widget must wait three months to be processed by that machine, you may have replicated the public healthcare system, which is guided by efficiency but certainly not speed. Many statistics show that wait times in typical IT processes, such as ordering a server, make up more than 90% of the total elapsed time. Instead of working more, we should wait less!

A Little Bit of Queuing Theory

When you look between activities, you are bound to find *queues*, just like the lines at your local department of motor vehicles or city office. To better understand how they work and what they do to a system, let's indulge in a bit of queuing theory. My university textbook on queuing theory, Kleinrock's *Queuing Systems*,[1] appears to be out of print, but is available used. But don't worry, you don't need to digest 400 pages of queuing theory to understand enterprise transformation.

My university professor reminded us that if we remember only one thing from his class, it should be *Little's Result*. This equation states that in a stable system, the total processing time T, which includes wait time, is equal to N, the number of items in the system (the ones in the queue plus the ones being processed) divided by the processing rate λ; in short $T = N/\lambda$. This makes intuitive sense: the longer the queue, the longer it takes for new items to be processed. If you are processing two items per second and there are 10 items on average in the systems, a newly arriving item will spend five seconds in the system. You might correctly deduce that most of those five seconds are spent in the queue, not

---

1 Leonard Kleinrock, *Queueing Systems. Volume 1: Theory* (New York: Wiley-Interscience, 1975).

actually processing the item. The noteworthy aspect of Little's result is that the relationship holds for most arrival and departure distributions.

To build a bridge between speed and efficiency, let's look at the relationship between utilization and wait time. The system is utilized whenever an item is being processed, meaning one or more items are in the system. If you sum up the probability that a given number of items are in the system, for instance, 0 items (the system is idle), 1 (one item being processed), 2 (one item being processed plus one in the queue), etc., you find that the average number of items in the system is equal to $\rho / (1 - \rho)$, where ρ designates the *utilization rate*, or the fraction of time the server is busy (we make the assumption that arrivals are independent, which is described as a *memoryless* system). From the equation you can quickly gather that high levels of utilization (ρ moving closer to 100%) lead to extreme queue sizes and therefore wait times. Increasing utilization from 60% to 80% almost triples the average queue length: $0.6/(1 - 0.6) = 1.5$ versus $0.8/(1 - 0.8) = 4$. Driving up utilization will drive away your customers because they get tired of standing in line!

Finding Queues

Queuing theory proves that driving up utilization increases processing times: if you live in a world in which speed counts, you have to stop chasing task efficiency. Instead, you need to look at your queues. Sometimes these queues are visible like the lines at government offices where you take a number and wonder whether you'll be served before closing time. In corporate IT the queues are generally less visible—that's why so little attention is paid to them. By looking a little harder, though, you can find them almost everywhere:

Busy calendars
> When everyone's calendar is 90% "utilized," important decisions queue for people to meet and discuss them. I waited for meetings with senior executives for multiple months.

Steering meetings
> Such regular meetings tend to occur once every month or quarter. Topics will be queued up for them, again holding up decisions or project progress.

Email

Inboxes fill up with items that would take you a mere three minutes to take care of, but that you don't get to for several days because you are highly "utilized" in meetings all day. Stuff often rots in my inbox queue for weeks.

Software releases

Code that is written and tested but waiting for a release is sitting in a queue, sometimes for six months.

Workflow

Many processes ranging from getting an invoice paid to requesting a raise for employees, have excessive wait times built in. For example, ordering a book takes large companies multiple weeks, as opposed to having it delivered the next day from Amazon.

To get a feeling for the damage done by queues, consider that ordering a server often takes four weeks or more. The infrastructure team won't actually bend metal to build a brand-new server just for you: most servers are provisioned as VMs these days (thanks to *software eating the world*—Chapter 14). If you reasonably assume that there are four hours of actual work in setting up a server consisting of assigning an IP address, loading an operating system image, and doing some nonautomated installations and configurations, the time spent in the queue makes up 99.4% of the total time! That's why we should look at the queues. Reducing the four hours of effort to two won't make any difference unless you reduce the wait times.

Cutting the Line

Standing in line is hardly productive, but occasionally entertaining. When waiting in line at the San Francisco Marina post office I observed the highly utilized and actually quite friendly postal workers. To give myself a bit of utilization I stepped over to grab Priority Mail envelopes for my next urgent mailing (back then I didn't know what cool things (*https://oreil.ly/RlScH/*) the Graffiti Research Lab guys made from postal supplies). When returning to my spot in the line, the guy behind me complained and after a brief argument he claimed, "You are out of line." I think the irony of his statement escaped him as I was the only one who was amused.

Digital companies understand the danger of queues quite well. The infamously tasty and free Google cafés have signs posted stating that "Cutting the line is encouraged." Google doesn't like to bear the opportunity cost of 20 people politely waiting behind a person who transports salad leaves to their plate one by one.

Making Queues Visible

"You can't manage what you can't measure," goes the old saying, apparently falsely attributed to W. Edwards Deming. In the case of queues, making them visible can be a major step toward managing them. For example, metrics extracted from the ticketing system can show the time spent in each step or the ratio of effort over elapsed time (you will be shocked!). Showing that most time is simply spent waiting could also help the organization think in *new dimensions* (Chapter 40); for example, to realize that more elapsed time doesn't equate to higher quality.

For critical business processes such as insurance claims handling, queue metrics are often managed under the umbrella of business activity monitoring (BAM). Corporate IT should use BAM to measure its own business, such as provisioning software and hardware, and reduce lag times. Slow IT these days means slow business.

Why are *single queue, multiple server* systems more efficient and why don't more supermarkets use them? Lining customers up in a single queue reduces the chances that a server (i.e., cashier) is idling due to an uneven distribution of customers across the queues. It also allows smooth increases or reduction in the number of cashiers without everyone running to the newly opened lane or being ticked off at a lane closing. Most important, it eliminates the frustration that the other line is always moving faster! However, a single queue requires a bit more floor space and a single entry point for customers. You will see *single queue, multiple server* systems in many post offices and some large electronic stores like Fry's Electronics. Apparently, they understand queuing theory!

Message Queues Aren't All Bad

So how can the coauthor of a book on asynchronous message queues conclude that queues are trouble? Queues are a great tool for building high throughput and resilient systems. They buffer load spikes to allow resources to work at optimum rates. Just imagine each person who wants to check out of the supermarket just piling their items onto the checkout counter the moment they reach it.

Hardly a useful scenario. Many businesses, such as Starbucks, *use queues* (Chapter 17) to optimize throughput.

Queues become troublesome when they get long due to excessive utilization rates. High utilization and short response times don't mix. Don't blame the queue for it.

40

Thinking in Four Dimensions

More Degrees of Freedom Can Make Your Head Hurt

Stuck in two dimensions

A university class on coding theory taught us about spheres in an *n*-dimensional space. Though the math behind it made a good bit of sense (the spheres represent the "error radius" for encoding, while the space between the sphere is "waste" in the coding scheme), trying to visualize four-dimensional spheres can make your head hurt a good bit. However, thinking in more dimensions can be the key to transforming the way you think about your IT and your business.

Living Along a Line

IT architecture is a profession of trade-offs: flexibility brings complexity; decoupling increases latency; distributing components introduces communication overhead. The architect's role is often to determine the "best" spot on such a continuum, based on experience and an understanding of the system context and requirements. A system's architecture is essentially defined by the combination of trade-offs made across multiple continua.

Quality Versus Speed

When looking at development methods, one well-known trade-off is between quality and speed: if you have more time, you can achieve better quality because you have time to build things properly and to test more extensively to eliminate remaining defects. If you count how many times you have heard the argument "We would like to have a better (more reusable, scalable, standardized) architecture, but we just don't have time," you start to believe that this God-given trade-off is taught in the first lecture of "IT project management 101." The ubiquitous slogan "quick-and-dirty" further underlines this belief (Chapter 26).

The folks bringing this argument often also like to portray companies or teams that are moving fast as undisciplined "cowboys" or as building software where quality doesn't matter as much as in their "serious" business, because they cannot distinguish fast discipline from *slow chaos* (Chapter 31). The term *banana product* is sometimes used in this context—a product that supposedly ripens in the hands of the customer. Again, speed is equated with a disregard for quality.

Ironically, the cause for the "we don't have time" argument is often self-initiated as the project teams tend to spend many months documenting and reviewing requirements or getting approval, until finally upper management puts their fist on the table and demands some progress. During all these preparation phases, the team "forgot" to talk to the architecture team until someone in budgeting catches them and sends them over for an architecture review that invariably begins with, "I'd love to do it better, but..." The consequence is a fragmented IT landscape consisting of a haphazard collection of ad hoc decisions because there was never enough time to "do it right" and no business case to fix it later. The old saying, "nothing lasts as long as the temporary solution," certainly holds in corporate IT. Most of these solutions last until the software they are built on is going out of vendor support and becomes a security risk.

More Degrees of Freedom

So what if we add a dimension to the seemingly linear trade-off between quality and speed? Luckily, we are moving only from one to two dimensions, so our head shouldn't hurt as much as with the n-dimensional spheres. We'd simply have to plot speed and quality on two separate axes of a coordinate system instead of on a single line, as illustrated in Figure 40-1. Now we can portray the trade-off between the two parameters as a curve whose shape depicts how much speed we have to give up to achieve how much better quality.

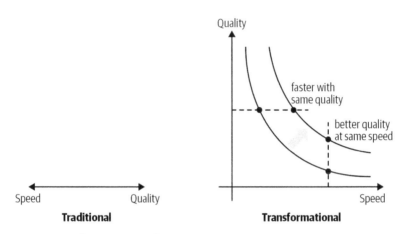

Figure 40-1. Moving from one to two dimensions

For simplicity's sake, you could assume that the relationship is linear, depicted by a straight line. This probably isn't quite true, though: as we aim to approach zero defects the time we need to spend in testing probably goes up a lot, and as we know, testing can prove only the presence of defects but not their absence. Developing software for life- and safety-critical systems or things that are shot into space are probably positioned on this end of the spectrum, and rightly so. That they rarely achieve zero defects can be seen by the example of the Mars Climate Orbiter, which disintegrated due to a unit error between metric and US measures. At the other end of the continuum, in the "now or never zone," you may simply reach the limits of how fast you can go. You'd need to slow down a good bit and spend at least some time on proper design and testing to improve quality. So, the relationship likely looks more like a concave curve that asymptotically approaches the extremes at the two axes.

The trade-off between time (speed) and quality still holds in this two-dimensional view, but you can reason much more rationally about the relationship between the two. This is a classic example of how *even a simple model can sharpen your thinking* (Chapter 6).

Changing the Rules of the Game

When you move into the two-dimensional space, you can ask a much more profound question: "Can we shift the curve?" And: "If so, what would it take to shift it?" Shifting the curve to the upper right would give you better quality at the same speed or faster speed without sacrificing quality. Changing the shape or position of the curve means we no longer need to move along a fixed continuum between speed and quality. Heresy? Or a doorstep to a hidden world of productivity?

Because digital companies see speed and quality as two dimensions, they can think about how to shift the curve.

Probably both, but that's exactly what digital companies have achieved: they have shifted the curve significantly to achieve never-before-seen speeds in IT delivery while maintaining feature quality and system stability. How do they do it? A big factor is following processes that are *optimized for speed* (Chapter 35), as opposed to *optimizing for resource utilization under the guises of efficiency* (Chapter 39).

Digital companies can shift the curve because:

- They understand that software runs fast and predictably, so they *never send a human to do a machine's job* (Chapter 13).

- They optimize end-to-end instead of optimizing locally.

- They turn as many problems as possible into software problems so they can automate them and hence move faster and often more predictably.

- If something does go wrong, they can react quickly, often with the users barely noticing. This is possible because everything is automated and they use *version control* (Chapter 14).

- They build resilient systems, ones that can absorb disturbance and self-heal, instead of trying to predict and eliminate all failure scenarios.

None of these techniques are rocket science. However, they require an organization to change the way it thinks. And that's not easy to do.

Inverting the Curve

If adding a new dimension doesn't make folks' head hurt enough, tell them that modern software delivery can even invert the curve: faster software often means better software! Much delay in software delivery is caused by manual tasks: long wait times for servers or environments to be set up by hand, manual regressing testing, and so on.

Removing this friction, usually by automating things, not only speeds up software development but also increases quality because *manual tasks are often the biggest source of errors* (Chapter 13). As a result, you can use speed as a lever to *increase* quality. For example, you can demand shorter provisioning times for servers in order to increase the level of automation and reduce defects due to human error.

What Quality?

When speaking about speed and quality, we should take a moment to consider what quality really means. Most traditional IT folks would define it as the software's conformance to specification and possibly adherence to a schedule. System uptime and reliability are surely also part of quality. These facets of quality have the essence of *predictability*: we got what we asked or wished for at the time we were promised it. But how do we know whether we asked for the right thing? Probably someone asked the users, so the requirements reflect what they wanted the system to do. But do they know what they really want, especially if you are building a system the users have never seen before? One of Kent Beck's great sayings is, "I want to build a system the users *wish* they asked for."

The traditional definition of quality is a *proxy metric*: we presuppose to know what the customers want, or at least that they know what they want. What if this

> *The traditional definition of quality is a proxy metric.*

proxy isn't a very reliable indicator? Companies living in the digital world don't pretend to know exactly what their customers want because they are building brand-new solutions. Instead of asking their customers what they want, they observe *customer behavior* (Chapter 36). Based on the observed behavior they quickly adjust and improve their product, often trying out new things using A/B testing. You could argue that this results in a product of much higher quality, one that the customers wish they could have asked for. So, not only can you shift the curve of how much quality you can get for how much speed, you can also change what quality you are aiming for. Maybe this is yet another dimension?

Losing a Dimension

What happens when a person who is used to working in a world with more degrees of freedom enters a world with fewer, such as an IT organization still holding the belief that quality and speed are opposites? This can lead to a lot of surprises and some headaches, almost like moving from our three-dimensional world to the Planiverse.[1] The best way out is *reverse engineering the organization's beliefs* (Chapter 26) and then *leading change* (Chapter 34).

---

1 Wikipedia, "*The Planiverse*," *https://oreil.ly/RncTp*.

PART VI

Epilogue:
Architecting IT Transformation

This book's main purpose is to encourage IT architects to take an active role in transforming traditional IT organizations that must compete with digital disruptors. "Why are technical architects supposed to take on this enormous task?" you may ask, and rightly so: many managers or IT leaders may have strong communication and leadership abilities that are needed to change organizations. However, today's digital revolution isn't just any organizational restructuring, but one that is driven by IT innovation: mobile devices, cloud computing, data analytics, wireless networking, and the Internet of Things, to name a few. Leading an organization into the digital future therefore necessitates a thorough understanding of the underlying technologies along with their application for competitive advantage.

Game On

Due to network effects, many digital business models follow a winner-takes-all dynamic: Google owns search, Facebook owns social, Amazon owns fulfillment and cloud, Netflix and Amazon jointly own content. Apple and Google's Android own mobile. Google tried to get into social and floundered. Microsoft struggles in search and essentially withdrew from mobile. Amazon also struggled in mobile just like Google repeatedly dabbled in fulfillment without seeing a lot of traction. In cloud computing even almighty Google is at best a runner-up with Amazon holding on to a significant lead.

Following this battle of the titans from the sidelines of a traditional organization resembles watching world-class athletes compete from the bleachers while eating popcorn: these organizations sport evaluations close to a trillion dollars (Netflix being the "baby" with roughly $150 billion market capitalization in

2020), have access to the world's top IT talent, and are run by extremely talented and skilled management teams. How would one even hope to compete?

There are several effects that play into the hands of incumbent companies. First, the digital world is one of constant evolution, and every round brings new opportunities. Uber disrupted the taxi industry by realizing that taxis aren't the only cars on the road and that taxi drivers aren't the only ones who can give others a ride. However, automotive manufacturers may have an ace up their sleeve in the next round when they launch self-driving cars. Second, traditional enterprises can utilize existing assets. For example, Fast Retailing, Uniqlo's parent company, rather than emulate an online business model, uses the physical store as its key asset and is hugely successful at it. Target, a major US retailer, sees huge uplift in ecommerce sales with its curbside pick-up model—you just drive up and your order is loaded into your car. The digital world is one of many opportunities, for those companies that can question existing assumptions and turn IT into a major innovation driver.

Transforming from the Bottom Up

It's hard to imagine that instigating a digital transformation purely from the top down can be successful. Non-tech-savvy management can at best limp along based on input from external consultants or trade journals. That's not going to cut it, though: competition in the digital world is fierce, and customer expectations are increasing every day. When we hear of a successful startup company that went public or was acquired for a huge sum of money, we usually forget the dozens or even hundreds of startups in the same space that didn't make it despite a great idea and a bunch of smart people working extremely hard on it. Architects, who are rooted in technology but can ride the elevator to the penthouse, are needed to make such a transformation successful.

Transforming from the Inside Out

Watching vendor demos and purchasing a few new products aren't going to make an organization competitive against digital behemoths. As the overall direction of the digital revolution has become fairly clear and technology has been democratized to the point where every individual with a credit card can procure servers and big data analytics engines within minutes, the main competitive asset for an organization is its ability to learn fast. External consultants and vendors can give a boost, but they cannot substitute for an organization's *ability to learn* (Chapter 36). Architects are therefore needed to drive or at least support the transformation from within the organization.

From Ivory Tower Resident to Corporate Savior

If you aren't yet convinced that transforming the organization is part of your job as an architect, you may not have much of a choice: recent technology advances can be successfully implemented only if the organizational structure, processes, and often the culture also change. For example, DevOps-style development is enabled through the advent of automation technologies but relies on breaking down *change* and *run* silos. Cloud computing can reduce time-to-market and IT cost dramatically, but only if the organization and its processes empower developers to actually provision servers and make necessary network changes. Lastly, being successful with data analytics requires the organization to stop making decisions based on management slide sets, but on hard data. All these are major organizational transformations.

In times of digital disruption, the job of the IT architect has surely become more challenging: keeping pace with ever-faster technology evolution, but also being well versed in organizational engineering, understanding corporate strategy, and communicating to upper management are now part of being an architect. But the architect's job has also become more meaningful and rewarding for those who take up the challenge.

Technology evolution has become inseparable from organizational evolution. Correspondingly, the job of the architect has broadened from designing new IT systems to also designing a matching organization and culture.

In a prior job, I often jested that I was the chief organizational engineer disguised as the chief architect.

The new world doesn't reward architects who draw diagrams while sitting in the ivory tower. It has a lot in store, though, for hands-on innovation drivers and change agents. I hope this book encourages you to take the challenge and equips you with useful guidance, some clever slogans, and a little wisdom along your journey.

41

All I Have to Offer Is the Truth

Giving Folks the Red Pill

It's so much more comfortable up here

Embarking on a transformation journey can be quite a dramatic, sometimes even traumatic, undertaking for many people working for traditional enterprises. Digital companies are run, or at least perceived to be run, by highly educated, 20-something digital natives who aren't distracted by family or social life and require little to no sleep. Their employers have hardly any legacy to deal with and billions in the bank, despite offering most services to consumers for free. For IT staff who have been working in the same, traditional enterprise, following the same processes for decades, this is likely to cause a mix of fear, denial, and resentment.

Getting these folks on board for a transformation agenda is thus a delicate affair: if you are too gentle, people may not see a need to change. If you are too direct, people may panic or resent you.

Nothing But the Truth

Wringing a final reference from the movie *The Matrix*, when Morpheus asks Neo to choose between the red pill, which will eject him into reality, and the blue pill, which will keep him inside the illusion of the Matrix, he doesn't describe what "reality" looks like. Morpheus merely states:

> *Remember: all I'm offering is the truth. Nothing more.*

If he had told Neo that the truth translates into living in the confines of a bare-bones hovercraft ship patrolling sewers in the middle of a war against the machines who perpetually hunt the ship to chop it up with their powerful laser beams, he may have taken the blue pill. But Neo had already understood that there's something wrong with the current state, the Matrix illusion, and felt a strong desire to change the system. And while you also sense that something's not quite right with the existing system, most of your corporate peers will be quite content with their current environment and position. Sadly it's not enough if you take the pill yourself, so you need to push them a little bit to come along for the ride.

Just like in the movie *The Matrix*, though, the new digital reality that awaits the red-pill-taking folks may not be exactly what they expected.

 In a meeting, a fellow architect once proudly proclaimed that for transformation to succeed the architect's life needs to be made easier. He was bound to be disappointed.

Aiming to make one's life easier is unlikely to lead into the digital future but will rather end in disappointment. Technological advances and new ways of working make IT more interesting and valuable to the business, but they don't make it easier: new technologies must be learned, and the environment generally becomes more complex, all while the pace speeds up. Digital transformation isn't a matter of convenience, but of corporate survival.

Digital Paradise?

Looking from the outside, working at digital companies appears to largely consist of free lunches, massages, and riding Segways. While digital companies do court their employees with an unheard-of list of perks, they are also hugely competitive internally and externally. They firmly embrace a culture of constant change and speed to remain competitive and drive innovation. This means that employees rarely get to rest on the laurels of their work but need to keep pushing on. Engineers don't join digital companies to relax but to push the envelope, innovate, and change the world.

The rewards match the challenge, though—not just financially, but most important, in enabling engineers to really make a difference and accomplish things they wouldn't be able to accomplish on their own. More than a decade ago at Google, you could scale an application you wrote to 100,000 servers and run analytics against petabytes of logs in a second or two. Most traditional companies still dream of these capabilities a decade later. Such are the rewards of the digital IT life. These examples also show traditional companies why they should be scared.

Don't Try This at Home

When looking to transform, traditional companies often identify practices employed by digital disruptors and try to import them into their traditional way of working. While it's important to understand how your competitors think and work, adopting their practices requires careful consideration. Digital companies are known to do things like storing all their source code in a single repository, not having any architects, or letting employees work on whatever they like. When admiring these techniques, traditional companies must realize that they are watching world-class superstars pulling off amazing stunts. Yes, there are people who walk a tightrope between skyscrapers or jump off a tower to glide into the rooftop pool of a nearby building. This doesn't mean you should try the same at home.

When adopting "digital" practices, an organization must understand the interdependencies between these practices. A single code repository requires a world-class build system that can scale to thousands of machines and execute incremental build and test cycles. Sticking all your code into a single repository without having such a system in place, and a team to maintain it, is like jumping off a building without a parachute. It's unlikely you'll be landing softly in the nearby rooftop pool.

Abandon Ship

For most organizations, sailing to the digital future is a matter of survival. Imagine that you are an officer on the *Titanic* ocean liner and were just informed that the ship will be slowly but surely sinking. Most of the passengers are completely unaware of the severity of the situation and are comfortably sipping champagne on the upper decks. If you walk up to the passengers and individually inform them:

> *Sir, excuse me if you wouldn't mind. Could you be so kind as to consider relocating to the main deck so we may transfer you to a safer vessel? After you finish your drink, obviously. Please kindly excuse the terrible inconvenience. Your well-being is our primary concern.*

You may not get much of a response, maybe just a doubtful stare. People may order another champagne and then have a peek at the vessel you are suggesting, the lifeboat, just to conclude that it appears much less safe and convenient than staying on the world's most modern and unsinkable ocean liner.

On the other hand, if you speak to the passengers as follows:

> *This ship is sinking! Most of you will drown in the icy ocean because there aren't enough lifeboats.*

you will cause widespread panic and a rush for the lifeboats that's likely to leave many passengers dead or injured before the ship even takes on water.

Motivating corporate IT staff to start changing the way they work, and to leave behind the comfort of their current position is not dissimilar. They are also unlikely to realize their ship is sinking. Where on the spectrum of communication methods you should land depends on each organization and individual. I tend to start gentle and "ratchet up" the rhetoric when I observe perpetual inaction.

Looks Are Deceiving

Just as it seems unlikely that a simple block of ice can sink a modern (at the time) marvel of engineering, small, digital companies may not appear threatening to a traditional enterprise. Many startups are run by relatively inexperienced, sometimes even naive, people who believe they can revolutionize an industry while sitting on a beanbag because their office space hasn't been fully set up yet.

They are often understaffed and need to secure multiple rounds of external funding before turning profitable, if ever.

However, just like 90% of an iceberg's volume lies under water, digital companies' enormous strength is hidden: it lies in their ability to learn much faster, often orders of magnitude faster than traditional organizations. Dismissing or trivializing startups' initial attempts to enter an established market could therefore be a fatal mistake. "They don't understand our business" is a common observation from traditional businesses. However, what took a business 50 years to learn may take a disruptor only one year or less because it is set up for *economies of speed* (Chapter 35) and has amazing technology at its disposal.

Digital disruptors also don't have to *unlearn* bad habits. Learning new things is difficult, but unlearning existing processes, thought patterns, and assumptions is disproportionately more difficult. Unlearning and abandoning what made them successful in the past is one of the biggest transformation *hurdles for traditional companies* (Chapter 26).

Some traditional businesses may feel safe from disruption because their industry is regulated. To demonstrate how thin a safety net regulation provides, I routinely remind business leaders that if the *digitals* have managed to put electric and self-driving cars on the road and rockets into space, they are surely capable of obtaining a banking or insurance license. For example, they could simply acquire a licensed company. The fintechs Lemonade (insurance) and N26 (banking) are vivid examples of successful challengers in a regulated industry.

Digital companies are not out to replicate existing business models. Rather, they choose weak spots that are highly inefficient or cause unhappy customers.

Lastly, digital disruptors don't tend to attack from the front. They tend to choose weak spots in existing business models that are highly inefficient, but not significant enough for large, traditional enterprises to pay attention to. Airbnb didn't build a better hotel, and fintech companies aren't interested in rebuilding a complete bank or insurance company. Rather, they attack the distribution channels, where inefficiency, high commissions, and unhappy customers allow new business models to scale rapidly with minimum capital investment. Some researchers claim that had the *Titanic* hit the iceberg head on, it might not have sunk. Instead, it was taken down because the iceberg tore open a large portion of the relatively weak side of the hull. That's where the digitals hit.

Distress Signals

While transformation can be a scary endeavor, you aren't the only architect who is accepting the challenge. Just like ships in distress, it's good to call for help when things look dire. You shouldn't be shy about sending a digital SOS—no one has a proven recipe for transformation, so exchanging experiences and anecdotes with your peers is highly beneficial. You may even opt to share your experiences in a book. I'll be one of your first readers.

Index

A

abstractions, levels of, 89

ACID transactions, 135

Agile methods, 77, 255-261

alignment
    defined, 12
    excessive, 252

amber organizations, 85

analysis paralysis, 70

anarchy, 230

Application Delivery Controller (ADC), 130

architect elevator, 7-13

architectural decisions, 65-68

architecture
    benefits of automation, 103-108, 253
    benefits of including built-in options, 69-78
    benefits of layers, 234
    defined, 59, 64
    evolutionary architecture, 77
    gaining insights from the real world into, 135-140
    identifying, 63-68
    multispeed, 27
    programming versus configuration, 87-94
    skills needed to create sound, 62
    value of, 60

architecture analysis, 200

architecture diagrams, 172-180, 194

architecture reviews, 54, 63

architecture sketches, 197-201

architecture without architects, 18

assumptions
    overcoming, 222
    uncovering, 54, 216-221

asynchronous communication, 251

asynchronous processing model, 136

Auftragstaktik, 229

automation
    benefits to architecture, 103-108
    configuration changes, 24, 106
    versus humans, 108, 253
    levels of, 155
    repeatability and resilience gained by, 104
    scaling through, 253
    self-service portals, 105
    tacit versus explicit knowledge, 107
    understanding current system state, 107

autonomy, 230-232

About the Author

Gregor Hohpe helps business and technology leaders transform not only their technology platform, but also their organization. Riding the Architect Elevator from the engine room to the penthouse, he assures that corporate strategy lines up with the technical implementation and vice versa.

He has served as Smart Nation Fellow to the Singapore government, as technical director in Google Cloud's Office of the CTO, and as chief architect at Allianz SE, where he oversaw the architecture of a global data center consolidation and deployed the first private cloud software delivery platform. Having worked for both digital native companies and traditional enterprise IT allows him to reveal the many misconceptions that these organizations have about each other in the form of pointed anecdotes harvested from the daily grind of IT transformation.

Gregor is known as coauthor of the seminal book *Enterprise Integration Patterns* (Addison-Wesley), which is widely cited as the reference vocabulary for asynchronous messaging solutions. His articles have been featured in numerous publications, including *Best Software Writing* (Apress), selected and introduced by Joel Spolsky, and *97 Things Every Software Architect Should Know* (O'Reilly), by Richard Monson-Haefel.

Colophon

The cover photo, *Modern Elevator*, is by Auris. The cover font is Guardian Sans. The text font is Scala Pro; the heading font is Benton Sans; and the code font is Dalton Maag's Ubuntu Mono.

O'REILLY®

There's much more
where this came from.

Experience books, videos, live online training courses, and more from O'Reilly and our 200+ partners—all in one place.

Learn more at oreilly.com/online-learning

Milton Keynes UK
Ingram Content Group UK Ltd.
UKHW011039260824
447358UK00002B/9